# INFORMATION LITERACY INSTRUCTION HANDBOOK

edited by

*Christopher N. Cox*

*Elizabeth Blakesley Lindsay*

Association of College and Research Libraries
*A division of the American Library Association*
*Chicago 2008*

The paper used in this publication meets the minimum requirements of American National Standard for Information Sciences–Permanence of Paper for Printed Library Materials, ANSI Z39.48-1992. ∞

Library of Congress Cataloging-in-Publication Data

Information literacy instruction handbook / edited by Christopher N. Cox, Elizabeth Blakesley Lindsay.
    p. cm.
Includes bibliographical references.
    ISBN 978-0-8389-0963-8 (pbk. : alk. paper)  1. Information literacy--Study and teach-ing. 2.  Library orientation.  I. Cox, Christopher N. II. Lindsay, Elizabeth Blakesley.

   ZA3075.I536 2008
   028.7071--dc22
             2008003557

Printed in the United States of America.

12  11  10  09  08   5  4  3  2  1

This book is dedicated to:

two Immersion faculty who changed my teaching life forever: Deb Gilchrist, for her beaming smile and her dedication to the assessment of teaching, and Joan Kaplowitz, who showed me there was more than one way to teach and who is also a darn good dancer! ~CNC

to Sherrill Weaver, Mary Popp and Emily Okada—in 1996 in Bloomington, they saw something in me that I did not know was there. Without their encouragement and mentoring, I would not have become an instruction librarian. ~EBL

# TABLE OF CONTENTS

# INTRODUCTION

Christopher N. Cox and Elizabeth Blakesley Lindsay

Over a decade ago, what was then called the Bibliographic Instruction Section of ACRL published two handbooks, *Sourcebook for Bibliographic Instruction* and *Learning to Teach*. These handbooks were invaluable to many instruction librarians, with one providing theoretical underpinnings and the other offering concrete examples of what works in the classroom. In 2005, the Instruction Section decided to update and expand those earlier works with this new handbook. This work provides a historical overview of information literacy, looks to the future, and surveys all aspects of our work in information literacy instruction.

We sought a wide range of contributors for this volume, and we feel confident that we have brought together a strong array of instruction librarians. One of the most important lessons is that there is no one correct way to teach, and these essays represent that spirit in their variety of style and voice.

Craig Gibson lays the groundwork for the rest of the book with a chapter on the history of information literacy. The chapter shares the evolution of the term and of the movement, and fixes its place in the larger framework of higher education. It is crucial to know where we have been as we find new ways to move forward.

Joan Kaplowitz provides an overview of learning theories and the importance of addressing different learning styles in our teaching. Learning theories such as behaviorism, cognition and humanism, and learning styles such as physiological, cognitive and affective are detailed, supplemented by examples and teaching applications. Whether this is new material or a refresher, being cognizant of the variety of theories and styles enriches our instructional efforts.

Good teaching is central to the success of any information literacy program. A selection of shorter chapters are brought together here to illustrate various teaching methods. Trudi Jacobson shares ways of motivating students to be actively engaged in the library classroom or online. Carla List Handley explores teaching as performance. The chapter explains how aspects of acting and dramatic presentation (role playing, movement and body language) can be applied to improve teaching. Alexis Smith Macklin explains how problem-based learning can be used to engage students, integrate theory and practice, and develop research skills through the solution to real world problems. In the chapter's final section, Susan Barnes Whyte offers her thoughts on the importance of finding yourself as a teacher and developing your own teaching style

In the next chapter, Hannelore B. Rader shares her thoughts on collaboration. The chapter discusses collaboration opportunities in virtual education, with faculty, both in terms of liaison work, and team-teaching and curriculum reform. Rader combines sound advice with pertinent examples of collaboration at her own and at other institutions.

Barbara Fister and Thomas Eland contributed essays on one of the central debates in our field: is IL best taught integrated into the curriculum or as a stand-alone topic? Fister discusses the benefits of tailoring IL instruction to various classes across the curriculum at the time they need research instruction, while Eland describes a successful program which offers IL as its own subject in the curriculum.

Mary C. MacDonald explores the importance of good management for any IL program, regardless of one's job title. She focuses on good communication techniques, planning, motivation, and creative thinking as keys to solid program management and coordination. These tools should help new and seasoned managers improve their programs.

Karen Williams presents insights on leadership, which will help librarians at all levels improve their advocacy skills and personal contributions to their program, regardless of their job title. Leadership and management can be done by the same person, but leadership needs to happen at all levels. Williams' chapter will inspire all of us to be better leaders in our programs and on our campuses.

Lynn D. Lampert covers the important issue of academic integrity and the role of the IL librarian in promoting ethical use of information. While plagiarism is certainly a key issue, this chapter looks broadly at all aspects of academic integrity and offers concrete ideas of how IL instruction designed with ACRL Standard 5 in mind can help students become good stewards and users of all types of information.

Debra Gilchrist and Anne Zald provide a solid overview of assessment. With this background, librarians can design an assessment program that fits their situation, or enhance the one they already have. Gilchrist and Zald offer concrete examples of making assessment programs work effectively and efficiently, blending theory with proven practice.

Lori S. Mestre reminds us of the importance of understanding diverse patrons and offers approaches for better serving diverse clientele. Diversity in this case includes not only racial or ethnic diversity, but also the diversity we see in working with students from different generations, socioeconomic backgrounds, and life experiences.

Finally, Lisa Janicke Hinchliffe looks to the future of IL, exploring trends she sees such as the fragmenting of the standards, changes in source content, the institutional assessment movement, and the administrative priority given to information literacy.

We hope this volume proves useful for new and seasoned librarians who create, deliver, assess and improve information literacy programs.

# CHAPTER 1

# *The History of Information Literacy*

Craig Gibson

## The Higher Education Backdrop

One of the most striking features of the higher education system in the United States is the paradox of successive waves of reform, coupled with the essential conservatism and traditional structures and values of the academy. Reform movements arise in almost every generation, driven by societal, economic, demographic, and technological changes, but many features of higher education endure despite all attempts of reformers to change the culture of the academy. Examples of persistent features of higher education that affect student learning include segmented, abbreviated blocks of time for class; the credit hour as unit of curricular organization and value; the faculty member as authority (the famous "transmission" model) and the student as passive recipient of knowledge; the balkanization of the academy by institution type (through Carnegie classifications); the organization of colleges and universities by academic department or discipline (despite widespread emphasis on interdisciplinary research); the affiliation of faculty with their disciplinary peers at other institutions, rather than affiliation with other faculty, in other disciplines, at their own institutions; and the lack of institution-wide assessment programs and accountability measures to examine what is added to students' educational experiences as a result of their time at a given institution. These persistent features loom large in any survey of the higher education landscape in America, despite many reform experiments: with active learning and learning communities in some academic programs or departments; with interdisciplinary initiatives such as writing across the curriculum or technology skills infused into the curriculum; with assessment measures; with linked courses, coordinated curricula, and interdisciplinary programs; and numerous other reforms. Fundamentally, the academy valorizes expertise in disciplinary silos, creates structures to transmit that expertise and acculturate that expertise into selected students, notably through "the major" and most comprehensively, through graduate training and education; and graduates students who are often not equipped to think beyond the confines of specialized training, to collaborate in the workplace or other professional venues, and to become independent problem-solvers either professionally or personally.

These structures, traits, and values are so interwoven into many colleges and universities that we need to recall the variety of reform movements at work in the past thirty years that have introduced a richer texture to the fabric of college and university life and to higher education institutions as learning environments. These ever-thickening threads are slowly changing the academy—sometimes almost imperceptibly, sometimes more rapidly, but change is occurring. One of the most significant threads, the information literacy movement, is notable because it is very much still a discernible element of the fabric but is gradually becoming part of the overall design of the tapestry.

## Definitions and the Conceptual Landscape

Perhaps there is no greater definitional conundrum in the current higher education environment than the swirling, diverging, and converging debates and discussions about a cluster of terms centered on information, technology, critical thinking, lifelong learning, resource-based learning, and skills needed in the 21$^{st}$ century. Add to this welter of terms such variations as digital literacy, e-literacy, information fluency, and a related set of pedagogies focused on evidence-based learning, problem-based learning, inquiry-based learning, and discovery learning, and we step out of a riddling state into a genuine definitional quagmire.

The lineage of certain key terms here needs some clarification not in order to define precisely each of their meanings—there is much overlap and conceptual allegiance among them—but to show something of the terrain in which we now live. In our efforts to help students become more adept in finding their way in a confusing information and technology landscape, we need to map out that terrain with some conceptual markers that show the boundaries and primary features so that all the stakeholders in the academy can participate in informed discussions about the pathways through that terrain, pathways in which students should be guided through developing their own "compass." Students need a set of abilities that they can employ independently in finding their way through this part-wilderness, partly charted territory of ever-shifting views and uncertain horizons. More important, they need this compass to point them toward appropriate information resources and technologies as they seek to succeed academically and flourish in their work and personal lives after graduation.

The foundational problem for all stakeholders in higher education is a learning one—how to address the habits and predilections of today's "NetGen" students, with their expectations for instant access to full text information resources and wireless networks that never fails. In this environment, students effortlessly conduct cost-benefit analyses of how much time and attention to expend on research, writing, and other endeavors—especially undergraduates, who are not acculturated to the academy—and settle in a great many cases for less than optimal information. Sometimes they use Google or Yahoo; sometimes they find a few articles from one popular database; and sometimes they simply rely on a friend's advice about the best information resources to locate. "Satisficing" is the best term to describe this behavior; while certainly not a new one, it has greatly increased in the exploding Web environment since 1995.

The educational response to this behavior has emerged in two parallel and partially merging streams of thought from the library and educational technology communities. First is the long-standing conviction among many librarians that a coherent, planned, program-level set of research skills and learning outcomes should be identified and integrated into the curriculum—certainly for undergraduates, and when appropriate, for graduate and professional students as well. This is the *information literacy model*—a programmatic, curriculum-integrated, and pervasive and sustained placement of information and research skills throughout the curriculum. Using alliances with faculty who employ various forms of active learning—evidence-based learning, inquiry and discovery learning, problem-based learning—and who emphasize authentic assessment and critical thinking, information literacy practitioners in the library community understand that it is best thought of as everyone's business—certainly not the exclusive domain of librarians. The information literacy model, as reform movement, intends to develop information- and research-adept students over time through carefully sequenced assignments and experiences, using both library and community information resources in the context of questions and issues embedded in modes of inquiry and that are central to academic disciplines. Information literacy, when carefully planned, offers the potential to engage students in research questions and investigations that make them want to become better—at developing their minds, in becoming vital members of a learning community, and at learning in general.

Information literacy builds on the previous work of the library community in the instructional movement called *bibliographic instruction* (sometimes called library instruction or library user education as well). This earlier effort focused on teaching students the tools, resources, and strategies for using a specific library's information resources to best advantage for particular assignments given by faculty. The earlier bibliographic instruction movement achieved considerable success in responding to faculty-mandated library assignments, but by its very nature it was—and is—inherently reactive, limited, place-bound, and constrained in terms of wider impact. Relying primarily on "one shot" instruction sessions given by librarians at the request of faculty, bibliographic instruction achieves the limited goal of addressing episodic or occasional learning about scholarly or other information. Such instruction often lacks "staying power," in precisely the same way that writing instruction or other skill- or ability-focused instruction would lack staying power, without sufficient student practice in such skills linked to disciplines, modes of inquiry, or linked to more compelling pedagogies that develop students' own research questions in the context of their own interests.

Bibliographic instruction continues to possess a valuable but limited role in helping sustain students' ability to cope with the confusing array of resources in the landscape before them—but it is not well-suited to the future because it focuses on formulaic, often linear, two-dimensional strategies for finding and evaluating information in a landscape where students are often wondering "Where am I?" These students need a compass, not a lifeline that they can use once, and then toss aside. Moreover, the landscape with which students (and in fact, all of us in the academy) must now contend has multiple dimensions—of surface ("the surface Web"), of depth ("the deep Web"), of temporality (with accelerated information cycles, changing paradigms of publishing such as the "open access" model, blogs with late-breaking news and research developments, disappearing and rapidly reconstituted web sites, and other phenomena), and mode or representation (graphical representations instead of textual ones, numeric files or data sets, learning objects, simulations, tutorials, and hybrids of all of these). This landscape presents many vexations (but also opportunities) for faculty, librarians, technologists, assessment specialists, and others who want to locate reference points that they can provide students to help chart their way. Reference points are essential, but a well-crafted skill set in using a "compass" holds greater promise for promoting independent information and technology use for students during their college years and after graduation.

The new "compass" for NetGen students is a bundle of abilities called "information literacy" (with the likely inclusion of a "fluency" element, to be discussed later). Information literacy has been formally discussed, debated, written about, planned for, and institutionalized for over twenty years in the library community, and despite some of the conceptual murkiness surrounding it—part of librarians' charting their own professional landscape—an increasing number of academic librarians as well as faculty have accepted that a broader, deeper engagement of the library's educational mission with students, faculty, and the curriculum is necessary. Many of them have also understood that bibliographic instruction is sometimes useful, but self-limiting and often peripheral to any true programmatic reach and development for teaching research and information skills.

## Milestones
The term "information literacy" itself was given a normative definition in 1989 by the American Library Association's Presidential Commission on Information Literacy; this definition focuses on the individual's ability to identify and shape

research questions, to access information, evaluate it, and manage it.[1] However, the lineage of the term "information literacy" can be traced, in fact, to an array of thinkers, not all of them librarians, who concerned themselves with liberal learning, critical thinking, and the life of the mind. One such notable, Cardinal Newman, in 1853 included the notion of information literacy (without using the term, of course) in his *Idea of a University,* focusing on a "process approach" to liberal learning.[2] In the U.S., in the late nineteenth century, public librarians emphasized an educational role for libraries; in the 1870s, for example, reference service and its associated teaching function gained recognition as a legitimate purpose of libraries, and in 1876, Otis Robinson declared that "a librarian should be more than a keeper of books; he should be an educator … no such librarian is fit for his place unless he holds himself responsible for the library education of his students … All that is taught in college amounts to very little, but if we can send students out self-reliant in their investigations, we have accomplished very much."[3] Here is an early articulation of the "lifelong learning" that is a hallmark of information literacy.

In the early to mid-twentieth century, several milestones were notable in the development of information literacy as a framework, without formal articulation or recognition of the term. In the 1930s, Louis Shores developed the "library-college" concept, in which students would meet *in the library* with faculty and librarians, instead of being the recipients of lectures in large classrooms. This arrangement would involve a large element of active learning, because students would be given assignments requiring them to find information and solve problems related to course content "on the spot"—the library would be their laboratory, in effect—under the joint guidance of faculty member and librarian.[4] Related to this development, in 1940 Harvie Branscombe, in his *Teaching with Books,* advocated the formation of teaching partnerships, involving faculty and librarians.[5] However, the individual who created the most notable pioneering experience with information literacy programming was Patricia Knapp. In 1956, at Monteith College at Wayne State University, she took Shores' concept of the "library-college" to a new level, with the library envisioned as hub for curriculum development and student-faculty interaction in courses. Her landmark study of this experiment is still cited,[6] and in one of her earlier articles, she asserted that

> Competence in the use of the library is one of the liberal arts. It deserves recognition and acceptance as such in the college curriculum. It is, furthermore, a complex of knowledge, skills, and attitudes not to be acquired in any one course but functionally related to many. It should, therefore, be integrated into the total curriculum. But it cannot be so integrated until the

faculty as a whole is ready to recognize the validity of its claim and implement this recognition through regularly established procedures of curriculum development.[7]

The promise of Knapp's experiment has never been totally realized—for many reasons, not the least of which is the lack of scalability of this model at many large institutions and the continuing drive to "cover content" in the curriculum rather than incorporate process learning or inquiry-based learning in academic courses.

Interestingly, the concepts behind the term "information literacy"—resource-based learning, effective research and information use, an emergent educational reform paradigm that would take elements of the Shores/Knapp model and apply them broadly—were first developed not by an American, but by the noted Australian educator Ernest Roe in 1965.[8] The first recorded use of the term "information literacy" itself was not by a librarian, for that matter: in 1974, an academic named Paul Zurkowski used the term, calling for the creation of a national information literacy program to achieve information literacy in the U.S. within ten years (sort of a Kennedyesque "moon shot" in an educational sense).[9] Zurkowski's ambitions focused on helping students and citizens manage rapidly increasing information and data in the context of technologies—a concern that anticipates our current challenge, but in the pre-Web mid-1970s, seems prophetic without quite understanding the magnitude of the difficulty.

Other milestones during the 1970s and 1980s in the earlier bibliographic instruction movement advanced the emerging information literacy agenda implicitly—by incorporating changes in learning theory, focusing on cognitive approaches rather than strictly behavioral, skills-based ones. This shift in thought was most evident in the "conceptual frameworks" movement that also incorporated the "second generation" school of thought among instruction practitioners in the library field. A firmer theoretical basis for instruction was sought by these practitioners, rather than the ad hoc, reactive approaches to instruction of the "first generation," and some landmark works reveal the richness of their thinking: *Learning the Library; Conceptual Frameworks for Bibliographic Education; Bibliographic Instruction: the Second Generation;* and *Theories of Bibliographic Education: Designs for Teaching.*[10] These works still emphasized the library itself as locus for instruction, but reflect the emerging environment of early online catalogs and databases, and contain some emphasis on critical thinking that would be developed more completely later.

The late 1970s, 1980s, and early 1990s saw a greatly increased interest in critical thinking and active learning among instruction librarians, paralleling similar interests through American higher education. Thinking by Frick , Wesley , Bodi,

Gibson, and others[11] about the centrality of critical thinking to the instruction agenda of libraries emphasized the active role of students in there own learning, in turn leading to changes in teaching practices and instructional design as an intentional process among librarians. Building on this earlier theoretical base and drawing on trends in the academy emphasizing student-centered learning, a key work in the library community that emerged from a decade of experience with active learning and critical thinking designs from this theoretical base was the ACRL Instruction Section's *Designs for Active Learning*, which offered numerous examples of classroom- (and some out-of-class)-based learning experiences for students.[12] This work was an indicator of an implicit shift in the library instruction community away from librarian-centered approaches to student-centered approaches, and reflected a shift as well into a school of thought known as constructivism, which asserts that students create their own meanings and are best guided in learning through coaching and "scaffolding" by instructors rather than being the passive recipients of information through the transmission model of lecture and occasional class discussion.

During the 1980s, educational reform in general was very much on the agenda in higher education. One report after another highlighted shortcomings in student learning and the values of the academy. Notable among these were *The Modern American College: Responding to the New Realities of Diverse Students and a Changing Society* (1981); *A Nation at Risk* (1983); and Boyer's *College: the Undergraduate Experience in America* (1987); and *Scholarship Reconsidered: Priorities of the Professoriate* (1990).[13] These reports laid the foundation for many educational reforms and experiments to improve teaching and learning practices, expanding access to education among a wider demographic; and creating a richer conception of "scholarship" as an integrated set of faculty responsibilities encompassing research, teaching, application, and service. These works, and others, started the long march of culture change in the academy that is still underway; many librarians concerned with information literacy saw in them depictions of an academic culture inimical to *learning* except for a favored few, and sought opportunities to use these reports to create conversations among a wider community about the role of libraries, information, and student learning.

The 1980s were marked by rapid change and stasis; educational reforms and continued adherence to the transmission model of teaching; and simultaneous and overlapping instructional paradigms in librarianship. In academic libraries, the older bibliographic instruction or library instruction models continued to flourish, but with increasing emphasis on the student as learner, on diverse learning styles, and active learning and critical thinking. Higher education reform itself was much afoot as a backdrop to the developments among instruction practitioners in libraries, but during this period reform movements in libraries were not well connected to the education reform movements in the wider academy.

A watershed year, 1987, saw the appointment of the ALA Presidential Committee on Information Literacy, a group of higher education and library leaders appointed by ALA President Margaret Chisholm to discuss reforms in curricula, teaching and learning practices, and educational policy. This group built upon the earlier work of an invitational symposium co-sponsored by the University of Colorado and Columbia University. The ALA Presidential Committee had earlier reports on the state of the academy very much in mind when it issued its own report advocating student-centered learning approaches in which students would employ a wide range of information skills—including knowing when information is needed, accessing, evaluating, and using it—to achieve not only access success but also personal empowerment, economic self-sufficiency, and sound citizenship.[14] The Presidential Committee also established the National Forum on Information Literacy, an umbrella group of educational, nonprofit, governmental, policy, foundation, and corporate organizations all concerned with advancing information literacy as a broad educational and societal agenda. This group has continued in existence since the 1990s and has taken the discussion of information literacy well beyond libraries and higher education, and has served to bridge the gap between American conceptions and practices of information literacy, and information literacy paradigms and practices around the world.[15]

The by-now classic definition of information literacy adopted by the American Library Association also originated during this period, based on the Delphi methodology of Christina Doyle , who collected elements of definitions of information literacy from experts in the field.[16] Her work created a "normative" conception of information literacy that is still the standard reference point for discussions of the concept. In this conception, the teaching agenda associated with information literacy is still paramount, and there is a predominant cognitive focus on attributes of hypothetical learners. This conception provided the intellectual foundation for the later *Information Literacy Competency Standards for Higher Education,* and marked a major milestone in providing a coherent framework for librarians and others to discuss a large and often diffuse educational reform agenda that, during the late 1980s and early 1990s, began to loom much larger than just a "library issue."

Since 1989 and the formal articulation and formal recognition of "Information Literacy," librarians have been very concerned with integrating this concept into their instructional practices—and they have repeatedly seen the shortcomings of using the older "bibliographic instruction/one-shot instruction session" approach to expand the reach of the model. They have understood the need to

involve faculty and work with faculty to take ownership of information literacy, and in the current Web environment, many faculty have happily obliged on
their own terms. Librarians have also understood the need to collaborate with a
range of other academic professionals—educational technologists, assessment
specialists, instructional designers—in developing more sustainable curricular
models for information literacy programming.

A decade after the ALA Presidential Committee wrote its report on information literacy to advance the information literacy agenda, it became clear to
some in the library and higher education communities that program development for the information literacy agenda within the academy at large would
need a set of "content standards" to guide practitioners. The Association of College and Research Libraries appointed a group of leaders to prepare such a set of
standards in 1999; the group included librarians, academic administrators, and
an assessment specialist. The result of their work, the *Information Literacy Competency Standards for Higher Education,* set forth five standards: recognizing the
need for information, information access, information evaluation, information
management, and the ethical, legal, and societal dimensions of information.[17]
These standards are seeing slow but increasing acceptance in academic libraries
and their institutions. The endorsement of these Standards by the former AAHE
(American Association of Higher Education) in 1999 was a notable development in increasing their visibility and importance to some members of the academy; their later endorsement by the CIC (Council on Independent Colleges) in
2004 reinforced their value as an instrument of curricular reform among a large
sector of colleges and universities. The *Information Literacy Competency Standards* are a departure for American higher education in one key respect: they are
a "national norming" criterion-based approach to information literacy program
content and assessment, in one sector of American education in which national
norms have been noticeably absent.

The second major stream of thought related to information literacy comes
from the academic and research computing community. Of more recent ori-
gin than the information literacy model, the "IT Fluency" paradigm was first
articulated in a major report written and published by the National Academy
of Sciences' National Research Council.[18] The report makes a major advance in
providing deeper intellectual foundations for technology use in a rapidly changing landscape than had previously been available to faculty and educational technologists through "computer literacy," a legacy term of the early 1980s focused
on skills related to specific computing platforms, a necessary stage of development because of the advent of personal computing. The "IT Fluency" paradigm
asserts that students and others should develop foundational knowledge of computer concepts and networks; critical thinking about uses and misuses of tech-

nology, and contemporary skills ("computer literacy") focused on productivity software. This deepened conception of technology-related abilities parallels the deepened conception of research skills and information use involved in information literacy. Just as "bibliographic instruction," with its limited and constrained impact, was a precursor to (and current subset of) "information literacy," "computer literacy," tied to specific skill development and regularly updated software and outdated computer hardware, is a precursor to (and subset of), fluency with information technology (IT Fluency).

This second stream of intellectual endeavor, combined with information literacy, offers us an opportunity to create the "ideal compass" for NetGen students—one that assists them in negotiating the confusing, multidimensional landscape, one in which their preferred mode of information-seeking is technology-mediated, but which requires agility, flexibility, astute judgment, and frequent adjustments or changes in seeking new paths. These blended set of abilities will help students locate themselves conceptually in the information landscape (the scholarly information sector; the popular news information sector, now morphing into the "blogosphere"; the welter of unverifiable data sources on the Web), as well as use technologies effectively to tap research information, manage it, evaluate it, and create it themselves. IT fluent students should be information literate; information literate students should also necessarily use technology adeptly and therefore become IT fluent.

## Contemporary Trends and Issues

Other issues have emerged that have both enriched and complicated initiatives marching under the banner of "information literacy." Among these are the assessment and accreditation; disciplinary applications of information literacy standards; student engagement and the "pedagogies of engagement"; collaboration in the academy; program development and sustainability through benchmarking; and the emergence of research practices and traditions and the associated professionalization of information literacy practitioners.

The increasing concern with assessment of information literacy is linked closely with increased emphasis on student learning outcomes and outcomes-based approaches to learning throughout the academy, as governing boards, accrediting bodies, community members, and various publics ask questions about the "value added" throughout the undergraduate experience.[19] Regional accrediting agencies, particularly the Middle States Commission and the Western Association of Schools and Colleges, have incorporated information literacy as a key learning goal in their documentation which member institutions in their geographic areas are required to use in preparing self-studies.[20] Complementing this general, institutional accreditation agenda for information literacy is one still much under development by discipline- or field-specific professional associations. Professional library membership associations such as the Music Library Association and the ACRL Science and Technology Section appointed committees and task forces to adapt the Information Literacy Competency Standards to their specific disciplines in 2005[21]; other professional associations beyond librarianship such as the American Political Science Association, made up of faculty members, are also adapting the *Standards* to the particularities of disciplinary frameworks, methods, and practices. Still another development has been widespread adoption of standardized assessment measures for Information Literacy. One example is the SAILS (Standardized Assessment of Information Literacy Skills) test developed through co-sponsorship of the Association of Research Libraries, and Kent State University Libraries, who received an IMLS grant to pilot a standardized, multiple choice test tied to the *Information Literacy Competency Standards*.[22] A second, more widespread test instrument developed by the Educational Testing Service is the ISkills Test, which unifies information literacy and information technology skills in a performance- and scenario-based instrument.[23]

Another important trend is connections between information literacy and "engagement"—a term variously defined, but often referring to the internal commitments of students to their own learning and the practices and benchmarks associated with student involvement in the campus environment. The most notable instrument development to measure student engagement, the NSSE (National Survey of Student Engagement) has been used by colleges and universities to identify strengths and weaknesses in their teaching and learning practices, according to such benchmarks as: level of academic challenge; active and collaborative learning; student interaction with faculty; enriching educational experiences; and supportive campus environments.[24] Although the NSSE instrument does not include explicit references to information literacy, it points to educational practices congruent with information literacy, and George Kuh, the originator of NSSE, has addressed those connections explicitly.[25] More generally, there is an emerging trend to align information literacy more programmatically with the "pedagogies of engagement"—such clusters of educational practices and curricular structures as learning communities, undergraduate research, service learning, and field experience.[26]

Collaboration in the academy to advance information literacy has become almost a commonplace. Librarians, faculty, administrators, instructional designers, technologists, and assessment specialists all have expertise to bring to bear on information literacy programming, because it is now generally understood that information literacy is not just a library agenda, and more important, academic professionals now see that student learning is deepened by information literacy through a pervasive, curriculum-infused, faculty-led, and outcomes-driven approach to research and information literacy abilities. The landmark work in celebrating collaboration is Ward and Raspa's *The Collaborative Imperative*[27]; others have built upon the intellectual foundation of that collection of case studies that shows the challenges and rewards of collaboration.[28] Various online continuing education opportunities are now co-sponsored by ACRL and the TLT (Teaching and Learning with Technology) Group to showcase examples of successful collaboration and to surface issues inherent in collaboration for information literacy.[29] The hard work of collaboration that moves institutions toward a shared vision for information literacy, with real programmatic depth and changes in culture, is still ahead of many colleges and universities.

As the information literacy movement has grown and matured, librarians and other academic professionals have wanted benchmarks for planning and measures of success, which would enhance program development, planning, and sustainability. The former need has been met, in part, by the ACRL "Best Practices" Initiative, a multi-year project that showcased some programs with effective practices for information literacy programming, resulting in a summit of leaders and program managers of those programs at the ALA Annual Conference in 2002, and a document summarizing "Characteristics of Best Practices of Information Literacy Programs," which identifies features of programs such as mission and goals, staff development, collaboration, curricular integration, and infrastructure issues.[30] Many in the library community have found such an inventory of best practices very useful.

Finally, emerging research with information literacy programs and practices figures importantly in higher education in general since the late 1990s. American librarians have become familiar with the research traditions created by Christine Bruce, Philip Candy, and others in Australia, using other research methodologies such as phenomenography to explore how people actually "experience" information.[31] This emerging tradition is now being explored in the United States as an alternative to the normative conception of information literacy that undergirds the *Information Literacy Competency*.[32] American librarians are becoming increasingly aware of international dimensions of information literacy and country- and culture-specific discussions of it through the research papers presented at two high-level conferences on information literacy held since 2003, the International Conference of Information Literacy Experts in Prague, and the High-Level International Colloquium on Information Literacy and Lifelong Learning in Alexandria; these conferences drew together experts from education, government, librarianship, economic development, and other sectors from many different countries to present research findings on information literacy in those sectors.[33] Cultural dimensions of information literacy are also increasingly discussed in other countries as well as in the U.S., particularly socio-cultural dimensions of learning as a framework for information literacy.[34] This research agenda expands upon the standards-based approach prevalent currently in the U.S. that sees individual empowerment as an information user as a primary goal. Cultural frameworks, norms, workplace practices and affective dimensions (the latter previously anticipated in the work of Kuhlthau[35] are all important newer areas for research and exploration as information literacy becomes a movement with wider and deeper impact.

## The Future

In the United States, there is greater coherence in 2006 in discussions of information literacy and in an emerging research agenda than ever before, but definitional debates continue in higher education and elsewhere, slowing momentum for change in some cases and enriching discussions in others. In the academy, whatever our role, librarians, technologists, faculty, administrators, and others need to transcend the Information Literacy/IT Fluency bifurcation if we are to advance comprehensive and sustained educational reform. The transformation needed calls upon greater collaboration to advance sustained programmatic development to carry the classic aims of liberal education—a broad perspective on knowledge, a sympathy with a wide range of modes of inquiry, a capacity for critical thinking, flexible reasoning, and adept problem-solving—into highly demanding workplaces where the chief constants are innovation, technological change, and fluid and uncertain information resources. In these workplaces, the chief expectations are collaborative ability, agility and adaptability, and constant learning while discarding settled ideas and assumptions—these abilities encompass "information fluent" behaviors that are constantly needed in research, communication, and collaboration. In fact, the global marketplace for today's professionals and workers, in all emerging professions, demands what former U.S. Labor Secretary, Ray Marshall, called "Thinking for a Living" in a book with the same title.[36]

The abilities needed for the future are now widely discussed in such documents as the *Greater Expectations* report published by AACU (American Association of Colleges and Universities),[37] and the *21st Century Skills Project*. The latter is a wide-ranging inventory of many "literacies," including digital literacies (basic, economic, scientific, technology, information, and visual); effective communication; high productivity; and inventive thinking. This project grew out of the *Partnership for 21st Century Skills Project*,[38] a group of business, education, and governmental leaders concerned about skills young people will need to function effectively in the workplace and as citizens in a competitive global environment. This Partnership Project is now supporting a new standard term, ICT—Information and Communication Technology Skills—which blends many of the facets of information literacy and IT fluency.

The former document, the *Greater Expectations* report, focuses specifically on the higher education community, and calls for educating a new generation of "intentional learners," those who can deal with complexity, manage information from disparate and confusing sources and employ technologies effectively, and collaborate while tolerating ambiguity. The call for "intentional" learners who are self-directed parallels librarians' and educational technologists' continuing concern about "intentionality" on the part of students and others in making astute choices among information resources, research data, technologies, as part of becoming educated. The *Greater Expectations* report and the *21st Century Skills Project* afford the library and educational technology communities a broader perspective on, and deeper engagement with, the continuing challenges of educating students in an unsettled academy, marked by demographic changes, ever-increasing expectations concerning quality of the student experience, and demands for prepackaged educational experiences that translate into readily transferable "credits" for highly mobile students. In this environment, creating liberally educated, technologically sophisticated, and information-adept students is, perhaps, *the* challenge for all academic professionals—faculty, administrators, technologists, curriculum and instructional designers, and librarians.

To bring together these two streams of educational reform—information literacy and IT Fluency—should therefore be an overarching goal for us, because of the possible programmatic synergies. Moreover, the sustained attention paid to helping students create their own "compass" within their chosen majors, as a guide to negotiating the information landscape, will send a powerful message to students, their parents, community members, and others that liberally educated graduates of the university, equipped with the best technological and research abilities, will be productive workers, professionals, leaders, and competent citizens in an uncertain world.

## Notes

1. American Library Association, "Final Report of the ALA Presidential Commission on Information Literacy" (1989). Available online from http://www.ala.org/ala/acrl/acrlpubs/whitepapers/presidential.htm. [Accessed 20 August, 2006].

2. Newman, John Henry, *The Idea of a University* (Washington, D.C.: Regnery Publishers, 1999).

3. Otis H. Robinson, "Proceedings: First Session," *American Library Journal* 1, (1876): 123-24.

4. Louis Shores, *Library-College USA: Essays on a Prototype for American Higher Education* (Tallahassee, FL: South Pass Press, 1970).

5. Bennett Harvie Branscombe, *Teaching with Books: A Study of College Libraries* (Hamden, CT: Shoe String Press, 1964).

6. Patricia B. Knapp, *The Monteith College Library Experiment* (New York: The Scarecrow

Press, 1966).

7.  Patricia B Knapp, "A Suggestive Program of College Instruction in the Use of the Library," *Library Quarterly* (July 1958): 230.

8.  Ernest Roe, "The Educational Irrelevance of Libraries," *The Australian Journal of Education* 9, no. 1 (1965): 1.

9.  Paul Zurkowski, *The Information Service Environment: Relationships and Priorities.* 1974. ED 100 391.

10.  Anne K. Beaubien, Sharon Hogan, and Mary W. George, *Learning the Library: Concepts and Methods for Effective Bibliographic Instruction* (New York: Bowker, 1982); Mary Reichel and Mary Ann Ramey, eds., *Conceptual Frameworks for Bibliographic Education* (Littleton, CO: Libraries Unlimited, 1987); Constance Mellon, ed., *Bibliographic Instruction: The Second Generation* (Littleton, CO: Libraries Unlimited, 1987); and Cerise Oberman and Katina Strauch, eds., *Theories of Bibliographic Education: Designs for Teaching* (New York: Bowker, 1982).

11.  Elizabeth Frick, "Information Structure and Bibliographic Instruction," *Journal of Academic Librarianship* 4, no.1 (1975): 12-14; Theresa Wesley, "The Reference Librarian's Critical Skill: Critical Thinking and Professional Service," *The Reference Librarian* 30 (1990): 71-81; Sonia Bodi, "Critical Thinking and Bibliographic Instruction: The Relationship," *The Journal of Academic Librarianship* 14 no. 3 (1988): 150-53; and Craig Gibson, "Alternatives to the Term Paper: An Aid to Critical Thinking," *The Reference Librarian* 24 (1989): 297-309.

12.  Gail Gradowski, Loanne Snavely, and Paula Dempsey, eds. *Designs for Active Learning* (Chicago: American Library Association, 1998).

13.  Arthur Chickering and Associates, *The Modern American College: Responding to the New Realities of Diverse Students and a Changing Society* (San Francisco: Jossey-Bass, 1981); *A Nation at Risk: the Imperative for Educational Reform: A Report to the Nation and the Secretary of Education* (Washington, D.C.: National Commission on Excellence in Education, United States Department of Education, 1983); Ernest Boyer, *College: the Undergraduate Experience in America* Carnegie Foundation for the Advancement of Teaching. (New York: Perennial Library, 1988); Ernest Boyer, *Scholarship Reconsidered: Priorities of the Professoriate* (Princeton, N.J.: Carnegie Foundation for the Advancement of Teaching, 1990).

14.  Patricia Senn Breivik, *Student Learning in the Information Age* (Phoenix: Oryx Press, 1998).

15.  Craig Gibson, "Information Literacy Develops Globally: the Role of the National Forum on Information Literacy," *Knowledge Quest* 32:4 (March/April 2004): 16-18.

16.  Christina Doyle, *Outcome Measures for Information Literacy within the National Education Goals of 1990: Final Report to the National Forum on Information Literacy* 1992. ED 351 033.

17.  *Information Literacy Competency Standards for Higher Education.* Association of College and Research Libraries, 2000; Available online from http://www.ala.org/ala/acrl/acrlstandards/informationliteracycompetency.htm [Accessed 20 August 2006].

18.  *Being Fluent with Information Technology,* U.S. National Academy of the Sciences. National Research Council. Available online from http://newton.nap.edu/html/beingfluent/notice.html [Accessed 20 August, 2006].

19.  Richard H. Hersh and John Merrow, eds. *Declining by Degrees: Higher Education at Risk* (New York: Palgrave Macmillan, 2005).

20.  Bonnie Gratch Lindauer, "Comparing the Regional Accreditation Standards: Outcomes Assessment and Other Trends," *Journal of Academic Librarianship,* 28:1/2 (January/March 2002): 14-25; and Lindauer, "Defining and Measuring the Library's Impact on Campuswide Outcomes," *College and Research Libraries,* 59:6 (November 1998): 546-570.

21.  The drafts of disciplinary standards from the Music Library Association and the ACRL Sci-

ence and Technology Section were reviewed by an ACRL task force composed of Lori Goetsch, Bonnie Lindauer, Susan Whyte, and Craig Gibson, in summer 2005.

22. "Project SAILS: Standardized Assessment of Information Literacy Skills," *ARL Bimonthly Report*, 230/31 (October/November 2003). Available online from http://www.arl.org/news-ltr/230/sails.html [Accessed 20 August 2006].

23. See information on the ICT Literacy Assessment instrument on the Educational and Testing Service web site at http://www.ets.org.

24. *National Survey of Student Engagement—Our Origins and Potential.* Available online from http://nsse.iub.edu/html/origins.cfm [Accessed 20 August 2006].

25. George D. Kuh and Robert Gonyea, "The Role of the Academic Library in Promoting Student Engagement in Learning," *College and Research Libraries* 64, no. 4 (July 2003): 256-82.

26. Craig Gibson, ed., *Student Engagement and Information Literacy* (Chicago: ACRL, 2006).

27. Richard Raspa and Dane Ward, eds., *The Collaborative Imperative: Librarians and Faculty Working Together in the Information Universe*, Association of College and Research Libraries (Chicago: ALA, 2000).

28. Jane Scales, Greg Matthews, and Corey Johnson, "Compliance, Cooperation, Collaboration, and Information Literacy," *Journal of Academic Librarianship* 31, no.3 (May 2005): 229-235.

29. For examples see http://www.ala.org/ala/acrl/acrlproftools/elearning.htm.

30. "Characteristics of Programs of Information Literacy that Illustrate Best Practices: A Guideline." Available online from http://www.ala.org/ala/acrl/acrlstandards/characteristics.htm [Accessed 20 August 2006].

31. Christine Bruce, *The Seven Faces of Information Literacy* (Blackwood, South Australia: Auslib Press, 1997); Christine Bruce and Philip Candy, eds., *Information Literacy Around the World: Advances in Research and Practice* (Australia: Charles Sturt Center for Information Studies, 2000).

32. Clarence Maybee, "Undergraduate Perceptions of Information Use: The Basis for Creating User-Centered Student Information Literacy Instruction," *Journal of Academic Librarianship* 32, no. 1 (2006): 79-85.

33. "The 2003 International Conference of Information Literacy Experts," Available online from http://www.infolit.org/2003.html [Accessed 20 August 2006]; and "The 2005 High-Level International Colloquium on Information Literacy and Lifelong Learning." Available online from http://www.infolit.org/2005.html [Accessed 20 August 2006].

34. Ann Lloyd, "No Man (or Woman) is an Island: Information Literacy, Affordances, and Communities of Practice," *Australian Library Journal* 54, no.3 (August 2005): 230-37; Craig Gibson, "Introduction," *Student Engagement and Information Literacy*, Association of College and Research Libraries (Chicago: ALA, 2006).

35. Carol Collier Kuhlthau, *Seeking Meaning: A Process Approach to Library and Information Services* (Westport, CT: Libraries Unlimited, 2004).

36. Ray Marshall and Marc Tucker, *Thinking for a Living: Education and the Wealth of Nations* (New York, Basic Books, 1992).

37. *Greater Expectations: A New Vision for Learning as a Nation Goes to College* (Washington, D.C: American Association of Colleges and Universities, 2002). Available online from http://www.greaterexpectations.org [Accessed 20 August 2006].

38. *Partnership for 21st Century Skills, Learning for the 21st Century: A Report and Mile Guide for 21st Century Skills* (Washington, D.C.: Partnership for 21st Century Skills, 2003). Available online from http://www.21stcenturyskills.org [Accessed 20 August 2006].

# CHAPTER 2

# The Psychology of Learning: Connecting Theory to Practice

Joan Kaplowitz

Whether you know it or not, you are all experts in the psychology of learning. Learning happens all the time. Every time we encounter something new we have had a learning experience. And every time we show a friend, family member or colleague how to do something new, we become a teacher. Furthermore, through these teaching and learning experiences, we all discover the most effective ways for us to learn, and the most successful ways for us to teach others. We may not know why these techniques work. But like art—we know it when we see it.

The aim of this chapter is to reveal the theories behind these practices in order to help you better understand why certain things work in certain situations. Once you become more familiar with these theories, you may develop new insights into the learning process, and consequently will discover how to select appropriately from the multitude of techniques that are supported by these various theories.

It is not the aim of this chapter to turn you all into mini-psychologists or even mini-experts in the field of learning. What this chapter can do, however, is introduce you to a way of viewing learning theories that can help you make sense of this vast body of information, and will hopefully assist you in your instructional endeavors. The chapter will be divided into two parts. The first part deals with learning theories and points out how the teacher can bring these theories into the instructional process. The second part examines the realm of learning styles and will look at differences in how people learn.

## Psychology of Learning: Schools of Thought

A brief examination of the literature into the psychology of learning will uncover massive amounts of books, articles, research papers and opinions about how learning happens. This overwhelming amount of information can be confusing, contradictory, and therefore less than helpful to the fledging instructor trying to make some practical use of it all. However, a look at the historical underpinnings of the various theories can offer some assistance and I believe leads to the development of a useful conceptual framework. Theories, upon closer scrutiny, seem to fall into three major categories or schools of thought—DOING, THINK-ING, and FEELING. If we look at the theories this way, we not only have a way to organize them, but we can see what each category of theories has to contribute to the instructional endeavor.[1]

## Doing—The Behaviorist Model

The oldest of the theories fall into the DOING school of thought. This school is generally referred to as Behaviorism and is associated with researchers such as Pavlov, Watson, and Skinner. Behaviorism was an attempt to create a more scientific approach for the study of behavior. Influenced by the rise of the scientific method in the late 1800s, Behaviorists wished to study behavior through observable, scientific experimentation and to move the field away from the philosophical introspective analysis that had been the previous norm. The basic idea behind Behaviorism is that everything is learned through a process of trial and error and that those responses or behaviors that receive positive reinforcement are the ones that will be repeated in the future—in other words, learned. Setting measurable observable objectives and developing standardized ways to measure learning are all based in the Behaviorist approach.[2]

Since much of human learning goes beyond the "pressing a bar to receive food" level of complexity, the Behaviorists developed applications based on animal learning models, which could be extrapolated to the human arena. One such idea is that of shaping behavior. Complex skills are broken up into component parts through a process called task analysis. Each part or approximation of the desired behavior is reinforced until the entire skill is learned. At first, very rough approximations are rewarded. But as learning progresses, the standard is raised so that more complex levels of the behavior are required to receive the reward. Improvement as well as perfection is recognized in this approach. Furthermore, mastery must be demonstrated at each stage before the learner is allowed to progress to the next stage.[3] The notion of chunking a topic into easily digestible segments and teaching each in sequence is a direct application of this shaping idea and is used not only in the classroom, but in computer-based instruction as well.

A major component of this school of thought is that the learner must be actively engaged in the process. This harkens back to the idea of doing. Learners do not learn by watching. They learn by interacting with the material itself. Furthermore, Behaviorists measure learning through observable changes in behavior. So the learner must perform in order to prove they have learned the material at hand.[4] The notion of having our students engage in hands-on activities and other active learning exercises during instruction is based on this Behaviorist idea. Moreover, the notion of assessing learning through observable behavior is also directly tied to this school of thought.

Behaviorism also contributes the concepts of immediate feedback, modeling and the idea that people learn best if allowed to move at their own pace.[5] We again see implications for instruction in these ideas. Learners do best if they are told as close as possible to their actions if they have performed correctly. In-class exercises allow the teacher to point out errors and praise accomplishments on the spot. Online tutorials often include feedback mechanisms that allow the learner to monitor his or her progress. Even the act of smiling and nodding in response to students' comments is a form of immediate feedback. And we all know how that type of student-teacher interaction can improve the atmosphere in the classroom and encourage more active participation on the part of the students. Correcting and returning homework in a timely manner is also important in this scenario.

Modeling is another important notion in this approach as there are times when it might be too dangerous to allow for the trial and error approach to learning. For example, you would not want someone to just go out and try to drive a car or learn which of several chemicals would explode when combined. On the surface, modeling does not seem to fit into the ideas underlying Behaviorism. Learning occurs not by doing, but by watching someone else perform. However, Skinner and other Behaviorists use the notion of vicarious reinforcement to account for this type of learning. We watch others bask in the warmth of praise and we wish to be praised as well. This idea is the fundamental principle that lies behind the entire advertising industry.[6] Modeling is, of course, what we do when we demonstrate resources to our learners either in a classroom setting or in some sort of virtual training scenario. Our learners want to emulate our successes and are motivated to do so by watching us succeed.

Finally, we see how the notion that individuals learn at their own pace and in their own way has had a great influence on the study of learning styles which we will address later in this chapter. Although Behaviorism is just one of the three approaches we will examine in this chapter, we can see how much it has influenced educational thinking over the years. Chunking of learning, checking for mastery at each stage of learning, offering immediate feedback and reinforcement for learning, providing opportunities for active involvement or participation in the learning experience, and modeling or demonstrating complex skills and strategies are all examples of Behaviorist principles at work in the modern educational enterprise.[7]

### Thinking—The Cognitive Model

The second set of theories deal with thinking. Just as Behaviorism was a product of its time and a reaction to theories that preceded it, these "thinking" theories were an attempt to move psychology in a different direction. These theorists, who are broadly termed Cognitive Psychologists, criticized Behaviorism as being too narrow in focus. They postulated that learning occurs beyond the narrow focus of trial and error and observable behavior. The Cognitive Psychologists point to concepts such as insight, also referred to as the "aha" phenomenon, as an example of learning taking place without practice. Here the learner solves a problem without practice by thinking about and determining a pattern or relationship between the aspects of the problem to develop the solution. This school, which grew out of research on perception, is interested in how the learner imposes order on his or her environment by determining how elements, ideas, concepts and topics relate to each other. In much the same way that we perceive movement when a sequence of lights turn on and off in neon signs, or view a rapid sequence of still images as moving pictures (often referred to as the Phi Phenomenon), we are motivated to impose order on our experiences even if at first glance none seems to exist.[8]

Wolfgang Kohler's famous experiments in which monkeys are placed in a room containing a bunch of bananas hanging just out of reach from the ceiling is often cited as an example of this Cognitive approach and a clear example of the "aha" phenomenon. The only other objects in the room are some cardboard boxes. The monkeys are observed to sit quietly looking around the room for a period of time. At the end of this "contemplation," monkeys pile the boxes underneath the bananas in order to provide a way to reach them. No trial and error, successive approximations, shaping or reinforcement of behaviors takes place in this situation. The monkeys "solve" the problem by observing and thinking. The solution is arrived at by what appears to be a sudden perception of the relationship between the boxes and the bananas.[9]

Learners (in this case the banana-deprived monkeys) view new situations in terms of patterns. If the patterns are consistent with their worldview, the patterns are accepted and serve to reinforce the accepted worldview. If, however, situations or experiences are at odds with an individual's internal mental models, a tension or ambiguity results. People (and apparently monkeys) have a strong desire to reduce this tension and so must reexamine or reconstruct their worldview in order to incorporate this new piece of information. If successful, a revised worldview is developed, and the new information becomes part of the learners' mental model.[10] In the case of the hungry monkeys, the cardboard boxes were reexamined to create a new function, that of a ladder to reach the bananas. In much the same way, learners will reconsider input in new and creative ways in order to solve problems presented to them.

Within the overall Cognitive or thinking viewpoint, are two subsets of research. Both deal with how knowledge is acquired and how information is perceived, organized and stored. However one, which is most notably associated with the works of Jean Piaget, is based primarily on stages of development or maturation. The other, called Constructivism, explores the idea that learners actively construct new worldviews through their interactions and experiences. Both deal with changes in behavior. However, the strict Piagetian developmental model postulates that children move from concrete to abstract thinking in a precise chronological order. Constructivists counter that learning is more dependent upon the types of opportunities or experiences offered the student than on the learners' maturational stage of development. Learning is viewed as a process in which learners construct understanding rather than merely take in ideas and memorize them.[11] The Constructivist model depends quite a bit on social interactions that allow learners to test their understandings against that of others. Social construction of knowledge occurs when communities of learners collaborate to formulate ideas and test the validity of those ideas.[12]

People learn by connecting ideas to previously learned concepts. Therefore, instruction should be sequenced in order to help learners construct new cognitive frameworks that allow them to organize ideas into more complex understanding. Learning happens when currently presented material can be connected to previously learned concepts. It is up to the instructor to provide ways in which the learner can see relationships between the new and old information and to help them organize the new information as they experience.[13] Regardless of the ways in which these theorists view how learning occurs, they all agree on one fact. Learning is not merely based on trial and error experimentation. It results from the learner making changes to the way he or she views the world.

Although the Cognitive/Constructivist viewpoints are an attempt to refute Behaviorism, there are some interesting commonalities between these two schools of thought. The most striking one is that both schools view active participation as crucial to the learning process. They differ, however, on why that active participation is necessary. The Behaviorist would say that active participation increases the opportunity to "stumble" upon the correct solution through trial and error and gives the instructor the chance to shape behavior in the desired direction via positive reinforcement and immediate feedback.

The Cognitive Psychologist (especially one who supports the Constructivist model) views active participation as an opportunity for learners to discover new ways of knowing and to construct or reconstruct their mental models. No external reinforcement is necessary in this outlook. The learner is internally or intrinsically motivated to fit new knowledge into his or her world or, if that is not possible, to change his or her view of the world to accommodate it. As a result of this active engagement with the data, the learner constructs mental models that are consistent with this new information. The Piagetian or maturational model also supports active participation as it is necessary for children to experience disconnects between their current stage of development and encounters in the world in order to stimulate them to move onto the next, more complex or abstract stage of development.[14]

The second commonality between the two schools is in the arena of readiness. Behaviorists talk about mastery and not moving learners to more complex concepts until they have mastered the more basic ones. In other words, not until they have reached a state of readiness. The Cognitive Psychologist agrees. However, readiness for the latter is based on the level of complexity in the learners' mental models rather than the mastery of concepts. Whether looking at this evolution of complexity from the strict maturational position postulated by Piagetian theorists or the construction of more complex mental models resulting from interactions with the environment, theorists following the Cognitive approach would agree that trying to force learners to acquire knowledge, skills or abilities when they are not ready to do so is doomed to failure.[15]

Before we look at the ways that the Cognitive viewpoint plays out in the instructional setting, it is important to discuss one more important aspect of this school of thought—that of relevance. The Cognitive Psychologist would postulate that the more engaged learners are with their environment, the more likely they will be motivated to incorporate what they are experiencing into their worldview. Clearly, learners are more apt to work on problems that have some relevance or significance to them. The notion of authentic instruction, and problem or case-based learning can be seen as having its foundations in this concept of relevance.[16]

So what does the Cognitive approach contribute to our instructional endeavors? We have already commented on readiness and relevance as necessary components to learning from this perspective. But how do we get learners to incorporate new information into their worldview? Just as B.F. Skinner was a major influence from the Behaviorist view, Jerome S. Bruner provided major insight into how the Cognitive perspective can be applied in the classroom. Since learning happens as a result of the learner imposing order on the chaos of information he or she experiences, the role of the instructor shifts from that of leader to that of facilitator.

Bruner's work emphasizes the idea of discovery. The instructor designs learning experiences in which learners discover for themselves solutions to problems and by extension the concepts, skills or strategies needed to formulate these solutions.[17] What does this mean for our teaching? It means that the teacher steps back from center-stage and allows the learners to find their own way to solutions. The success or failure of this approach is dependent upon the teacher designing ways for learners to interact with the material in a way that will facilitate the "discovery" of the solution and to subtly guide them during the process by asking thought-provoking questions or providing illustrative examples.

In some ways it means letting go of control during the instructional interaction by allowing learners to move through the material in ways that are meaningful to them. However, in reality, the development of effective discovery experiences require that the instructor be observant and flexible in order to continually monitor learners' progress, and offer alternative approaches and gentle guidance if learners seem to be bogged down in the process. While the discovery method of teaching frequently takes more time than the traditional teacher-centric approach, it offers the advantage of allowing the learner to both discover and incorporate the learning into his or her own mental model, and thereby owning it in a real way. This ownership of new learning should result in future retrieval of this information when it is needed since the information is stored in a way that is meaningful to the learner.[18]

Sometimes what is being taught may be too complex for learners to discover by themselves. The Cognitive Psychologist, David Ausubel, developed an approach that addresses this concern. He calls them Advance Organizers and defines them as abstract, general overviews of the information to be presented in advance of the learning experience. These Advance Organizers create a framework into which the learner can fit the new information being presented. To be most effective, Advance Organizers should help the learner bridge the gap between what is known—that is, what is already a part of their worldview—and the new knowledge, skill or strategy being presented.[19] Often referred to as conceptual frameworks, these organizers offer the learner a way to structure the new material in a meaningful way. They prepare the learner for learning to take place. Frameworks such as controlled versus natural language searching, primary versus secondary sources, or popular versus scholarly sources are just a few examples of how Advance Organizers or conceptual frameworks have been used to teach information literacy.[20]

The concept of metacognition—or thinking about thinking—is also directly related to the Cognitive approach to learning. In order to really learn, learners must not only interact with the material to be learned, they must also reflect on the learning process itself. This empowers them to develop strategies for learning how to learn in addition to learning the material that is being presented. Since some of the basic tenets of becoming information literate include learning how to learn and becoming life-long learners, this idea of metacognition should really resonate with the information literacy instructor. Learners can be encouraged to think about their learning process through being asked to reflect upon their experiences. Instructors may wish to model the process in their presentations, demonstrations and discussions. They may also ask learners to develop research journals in which they discuss how they looked for and retrieved the information they needed for their projects or papers. The One-Minute paper and other Classroom Assessment Techniques or CATs, when used as a means of summarizing the learning experience, can also be viewed within this framework. They provide learners with an opportunity to reflect upon and reorganize their thinking based on the material that was presented.[21]

Cognitive instructors provide opportunities for learners to actively experiment with the material to be learned. They encourage learners to seek out their own answers to questions and/or problems. Authentic, real-life, meaningful and relevant examples are utilized in order to really engage and motivate the learner. Abstract concepts become meaningful, transferable and retained through the use of active participation with material.[22] This is truly the realm of "guide on the side" rather than "sage on the stage." The instructor acts as a facilitator who orchestrates learning experiences in order to assist the learner to discover his or her own truth. Sharing of experiences is emphasized so the Cognitive experience frequently utilizes collaborative learning and group work. Learners spend a great deal of their time communicating with each other. They formulate their own questions and look for their own ways of answering these questions. When teachers do ask questions it is to challenge the learners, arouse their curiosity and move them forward, not as a way to test retention.[23] Furthermore, learners are encouraged to think about the learning process while they are acquiring new material in order to develop conceptual frameworks of their own that can be applied in or transferred to new learning situations. The Cognitive instructional experience is both learner-centric and self-reflective.[24]

### Feeling—The Humanist Model

As in the case of the models we have already reviewed, the Humanist approach was both a product of its time and a reaction to the established models or schools of thought that preceded it. The Humanist approach to learning was greatly influenced by the free-spirited nature of the 60s. This was the era of "do your own thing," of free love, and of an emphasis on the importance of emotions rather than on cold, hard, cognitive facts. What the Humanist brought to the table in terms of learning was a recognition that we must teach to the whole person. These theorists surfaced the importance of recognizing that our learners' emotions, affective or feeling states influence their educational successes.

The Humanist Psychologist would assert that how learners feel about themselves and the material to be learned is as important to the process as what they think about it. In this regard the Humanist Psychologist has something in common with the Cognitive Psychologist in that both would agree that material should have personal meaning for the learner or it will not be learned.[25]

Furthermore, the Humanist Psychologist is concerned with what motivates the individual to learn. A major influence in this arena is Abraham Maslow, who hypothesized a hierarchy of needs that motivate behavior. This hierarchy moves from the most basic needs such as food, shelter, and sex, through higher needs exemplified by safety, love, belonging and self-esteem, to culminate at the highest need: that of self-actualization. Maslow further postulates that until the lower needs are satisfied the individual will not be motivated to address the higher ones. Since self-actualization represents the ability to maximize a person's potential, Maslow suggests that learning does not occur until the basic needs are met. While it was clear how being hungry or sick might interfere with a person's ability to learn, the idea that feelings of love, belonging and esteem have an influence on the learning process was a new and somewhat revolutionary concept.[26]

A second Humanist Psychologist whose work had a great impact on education was Albert Bandura's work on self-efficacy.[27] Self-efficacy, as described by Bandura, is a belief in the possibility for success regardless of a person's abilities or skills. Encouraging learners to believe in themselves should, in Bandura and the Humanist Psychologist's view, lead to greater levels of success. This idea led to the creation of a classroom environment in which students are given opportunities to succeed, where their efforts are respected, and in which teachers demonstrate their beliefs in the abilities of their students. This is not a classroom in which the teacher grades on a curve, thereby implying that at least some of the students are doomed to fail. Rather, this is a learning environment in which everyone is expected to do well. That belief shows in the ways in which teachers interact with their students. Students in turn reflect their teachers' beliefs, become more self-confident, and begin to believe in their own self-efficacy.[28]

A logical outgrowth of these ideas of self-actualization, self-efficacy and the importance of relevance in the educational endeavor is the movement toward more student-centered and student-directed learning environments. Learning is viewed as a shared responsibility. In this respect, the Humanist approach agrees with the Cognitive one as both cast the teacher in the role of facilitator rather than lecturer. Both the Humanist and the Cognitive teacher create experiences in which the learners can interact with the material on their own and discover, create, or construct their own meanings. Motivation is based on intrinsic rather than extrinsic rewards.[29] Learners are interacting with the material in their own way and to please themselves.[30] Furthermore, Kulhthau's work indicates that learners who accept feelings of uncertainty and anxiety as a natural part of research are more comfortable and confident as they move through the search process.[31]

However, the Humanist takes this idea a step further than the Cognitive Psychologist. In the Humanist approach, learners are given choices in how they will learn and often in how their learning will be assessed or graded. So you might see the students being offered the option of taking a test on the material, writing a paper on a topic, creating a web page or video, or making a live presentation. In addition, students may be allowed to decide how much each of their assignments may be worth and may also be invited to assess their own or their fellow learners' work. This idea of learning contracts allows students not only to take responsibility for learning, but to also feel a sense of ownership in the process. In a small way, when we offer students the option of selecting their own topics for in-class exercises or for papers and projects, we are following the Humanist approach to teaching. The Humanist approach requires quite a leap of faith on the part of the teacher. It is based on the belief that, if given the chance, students will have the ability to both take charge of their own learning and also be able to succeed in achieving their goals.[32]

One way to apply these Humanist ideas to the educational endeavor is to follow the ARCS model of instructional design developed by John Keller. ARCS, which stands for Attention, Relevance, Confidence, Satisfaction, offers a technique for structuring the instructional experience in a way that maximizes the learners' opportunities to develop self-confidence and self-efficacy.[33]

The ARCS educational experience emphasizes the capturing and sustaining of attention, incorporating relevant and diverse examples into the process, building confidence by creating opportunities for success, and creating satisfaction as the learners acquire new skills and abilities. When you start your instruction with some thought-provoking quote or an attention getting video, you are applying the Attention part of the ARCS methodology. Follow that with opportunities for learners to work on topics of their own choice and you are employing Relevance. Using a variety of examples that reflect various cultural, ethnic, gender and age differences in your learners also enhances the Relevance of the learning experience. Confidence and Satisfaction can occur through allowing learners some hands-on practice time in which they can demonstrate their newly developed skills. Using the ARCS methodology in this manner can help us incorporate much of the Humanist approach into our instructional endeavors.[34]

The Humanist approach is very much one of learner empowerment. It is an especially nurturing approach with its view that everyone can succeed if given the right support, opportunities and encouragement. The Humanist would agree with the Behaviorist that individuals should be allowed to learn at their own pace. The Humanist would also agree with the Cognitive Psychologist's Discovery method of teaching in which learners are allowed to find their own way through the material to be learned. Both Humanist and Cognitive Psychology support the idea of relevance and personal meaning as crucial to the learning process. The current instructional trends that we are beginning to see, especially in higher education, which shift the responsibility for learning from the teacher to the learner, reflects the Humanist philosophy and may mark a change in emphasis from the more Behaviorist and Cognitive approaches.[35]

For our part as instructors we must learn to let go if we wish to follow the Humanist example. We must move off of center-stage even more, and concentrate not on providing information, but on creating opportunities for the learners to take control of and responsibility for their own learning. In doing so, we will be encouraging them to develop their own strategies for learning and will be encouraging them to becoming information literate individuals who are lifelong learners.

The three theories of schools of thought discussed in the above sections have all influenced education to some degree. Certain methodologies have been more influential at various points in history than others. But none have been completely discredited or discarded by their competitors. The bottom line for us as instructors is to understand that no single approach, theory, school of thought or idea is completely right or completely wrong. Each offers ideas for us to think about and use. A variety of practices have been inspired by these diverse ideas. Some work better in certain situations or with particular types of learners than others. The trick is to be flexible. If we come to our teaching with a good grounding in these ideas and the techniques that were derived from them, we are better able to adjust our methodology as needed. We have all experienced situations in which our most carefully thought out instructional plans fail for some reason or another. Understanding why the plan is failing, and the ability to make on the spot adjustments based on sound educational principles can turn a potential disaster into a triumphant experience for both you and your learners.[36]

## Learning Styles: The Learners' Perspective

Our examination of the various schools of thought related to the psychology of learning has really concentrated on the teaching side of the instructional equation. We have examined how each school developed, what its characteristics and viewpoints were, and how those viewpoints connect to our instruction practice. Now let's turn our attention to the other side of the equation, that of the learner. While we as teachers must decide how to use our knowledge of psychological learning theory to develop our instructional experiences, we must also be familiar with the ways in which learners prefer to perceive, interact with, and respond to learning experiences.[37]

If we know how to teach, and we understand the theoretical basis behind our practice, why is it so important for us to also know how individuals differ in the ways they learn? Just as there are many different ways to teach, so too are there many different ways to learn. And if we are to effectively reach all our learners, we must know what each of them need from us in order to profit from their instructional experiences. Furthermore, since we are only human, each of us tends to teach in the ways that are most comfortable for us to learn. We sort of operate from the "if it is good for me, it must also be good for you" principle. However, in doing so we are disenfranchising a portion of our learners. So not only do we need to understand how learning styles differ, we need to become familiar with our own style so that we can move beyond it and reach out to those with styles different from our own.[38]

Just as many theorists have developed ideas about learning, so too are there numerous ideas about learning styles. How can we possibly teach to each of these styles? Fortunately, a closer examination of the multitude of styles shows that they can be categorized into three types: Physiological, Cognitive, and Affective.[39] In some ways, these three styles can be aligned with the three models or schools of thought regarding learning that was described above. Physiological learning styles deal with how learners interact with or behave in relation to the material to be learned. These styles are most aligned with the Behaviorist model. Cognitive styles are related to the Cognitive model as both the styles and the model deal with how learners perceive, think about, organize and retain the material they are attempting to learn. And finally, the Affective styles are concerned with how learners feel about the material to be learned and so are linked to the Humanist school of thought.

Keep in mind that the following is a very brief, cursory overview of the various styles that have been researched over the years. A more detailed description of these styles appears in Grassian and Kaplowitz's 2001 publication Information Literacy Instruction: Theory and Practice which is referred to frequently in the following text. The reader who would like to delve more deeply into this topic is encouraged to explore the psychological and educational literature. Good starting points are the writings of W. Ray Crozier, James Keefe, Stephen Rayner and Richard Rider, Ronald Schmeck, Ronald and Servrenia Sims, and Robert Sternberg.[40] See also two reviews of the literature that appeared in 2004 by Simon Cassidy and by Ella Desmeldt and MartinValcke.[41] Gardner's work on multiple intelligences and their relation to styles is also worth pursuing.[42]

### *Physiological Styles—How Learners Interact with the World*

Physiological styles describe how learners react to the world around them. They are related to physical aspects such as health and nutrition; environmental aspects such as light, time of day, temperature, and noise; gender differences, and brain functions. We can all relate to the difficulties that arise from trying to learn when we are hungry, cold, tired, etc., although people vary in their tolerance for these discomforts. Furthermore, people seem to have a varying ability for working under different levels of external noise. Also among these styles are different levels of mobility needs or how often a person wants to get up and move around. Allowing for breaks in our instruction, incorporating different types of activities, or giving learners the freedom to move around and stretch if they wish, can help to level the playing field for those with differing mobility needs. And then there are the times of day preferences, which lead some people to feel they learn best in the mornings, while others prefer the evenings or even nighttime. Although we may not have much control over when a class is scheduled or have the luxury of scheduling multiple classes at different times, we should still be aware of these differences and see if we can offer some alternatives to assist those learners trapped in a non-preferred situation.[43]

Discussions of gender differences and learning can become quite heated. It should be noted that these differences do not differentiate between males and females, but rather between what is termed a masculine and a feminine style. Furthermore, it is unclear if these are innate styles or if people develop them through socialization. Spatial and mathematical skills are said to be masculine, while verbal and fine motor control skills are termed feminine.[44]

Brain hemispheric preference styles (commonly referred to as right brain/left brain preferences) refer to whether the learner relies more heavily on the left hemisphere style of behavior (analytical, linear, detail-oriented) or the right hemisphere style (global, holistic, pattern-oriented). Left-brain people are thought to be more verbal while right-brained people are more visual and spatial. Varying our instructional techniques can help us reach both the left and the right-brained learners in our populations.[45] The idea of variation in teaching approaches is a theme we will return to often as we move through our examination of learning styles.

### Cognitive Styles—How Learners Think about Their World

Cognitive styles are described as information processing habits that describe how people observe, think, problem-solve, and remember. They are the preferred ways that learners perceive, organize, and retain information. Individuals do not all learn in the same way nor do they perform equally well in all types of situations. Experiences that promote learning in some may not be as helpful in promoting learning in others.[46] Although many researchers feel that these preferences seem to be consistent across different situations and throughout life, people seem to have the ability to accommodate or adjust their styles if the need arises. In other words, they can manage to learn using a non-preferred style if pressed to do so. It may take longer to absorb the material under these circumstances as the learner tries to take in material that is being presented in a way that does not fit in to how he or she thinks. Furthermore, unless the learner can figure out how to re-organize the material so that it does fit with his or her mental models, the learner may have difficulty retaining the material for very long.

Many different cognitive styles are described in the learning literature. The one most commonly referred to is perceptual modality preference or the way a person prefers to absorb information—visually through reading, aurally through hearing, and kinesthetically through doing. Remember this is only a preference and the more successful learners can adapt and make use of all three modalities as they mature. However, if given a choice, the learner would pick one modality over the other two.[47]

The common instructional design that combines lecture/demonstration, written handouts, and hands-on exercises is an attempt to appeal to the aural, visual, and kinesthetic learner. Aural learners get the most from the lecture and descriptions that accompany the demonstration. Visual learners appreciate the demos, but are even more delighted to have handouts (or Web pages) that they can read and refer to at a later time. And the kinesthetic learner enjoys the opportunity to actively interact with the material to be learned.

Other cognitive styles deal with broad, holistic or abstract approaches versus narrow, specific or concrete ones. Field Independence/Dependence is a good example of these types of styles. In this style, people differ in whether they concentrate on the whole or on the specific parts of the material. Dependents see the forest, while independents focus on the individual trees. In terms of teaching, the broad, holistic, abstract, field-dependent types would probably prefer starting with a big picture view of material while the narrow, specific, concrete, independent types probably like starting with explicit examples.[48]

Another way in which people can differ in their cognitive styles is in the speed in which they respond to input. Sometimes referred to as Conceptual Tempo or Reflective/Impulsive, this style describes how quickly people process information.[49] The impulsive type is all about speed. They want learning to move quickly and are most energized by brainstorming type activities where responses are flying fast and furious. Impulsives are more interested in moving things along sometimes at the cost of responding incorrectly to the questions being asked. Reflectives, on the other hand, need time to absorb and think before responding to questions. They are frequently the quiet ones in your classrooms who are somewhat overwhelmed by the behavior of the impulsives. It is important to remember that although the reflectives may not be as involved in quick-paced discussions, they are still engaged in the learning process. They are just not ready to make their opinions known. Allowing for times of quiet refection during instruction can assist these types of learners. Furthermore, allowing for a mechanism in which learning goes on beyond the in-person, classroom experience can also be beneficial to these types of learners. Advances in instructional technology and course-management systems allow everyone to express their opinions and exhibit their grasp of the material in their own time and in their own way.[50] Offering some options for learning and responding is a way to reach those with different approaches to learning—in this case differing cognitive styles.

### Affective Styles—How Learners Feel about Their World

Finally, we come to the body of styles referred to as Affective. These styles are concerned with feelings or the emotional aspects of learning. They focus on how we relate to and value information. Motivation and attention also fall into this category. Curiosity, perseverance, risk taking, and competition/cooperation are some examples of affective styles. How much structure a person needs in order to learn also falls into this category, as does their tolerance for frustration. Whether learners are intrinsically or extrinsically motivated to learn is related to the affective style called internal/external locus of control. The internal person feels they are responsible for the consequences of his or her actions while the external person sees circumstances beyond his or her control.[51]

Taken together, the Affective styles remind us to pay attention to the Humanistic model of learning. When we make sure our topics are relevant to our learners, when we use attention-getting examples in our demos, and when we offer various learning experiences that appeal to the competitor, the cooperative learning, the intrinsically and the extrinsically motivated individual, we are widening our appeal to the various type of affective learners. Taking a page from the Cognitive model we can offer conceptual frameworks or Advance Organizers to help those learners with high structural needs and provide opportunities for exploration and discovery to appeal to those with low structural needs.

### Measuring Learning Styles

Looking at the various learning styles from this Physiological, Cognitive and Affective perspective and connecting them to the various learning theories is one way to try and make some practical sense out of this enormous body of information. Various researchers have gone a step further and have attempted to present a more over-reaching structure to this material. Many of these researchers not only provide this structure, they go on to develop instruments for measuring and describing how an individual learns.

The most famous and widely used paradigm for learning styles comes from David Kolb.[52] Known as the Experiential Learning Model, this approach not only emphasizes how experience is translated into concepts, it also describes four different types of behaviors that are necessary to accomplish this translation. The four behaviors are described as two pairs of polar opposites or dimensions—that of concrete/abstract and active experimentation/reflective observation. The active/concrete refers to how the learner prefers to process information, while the active/reflective refers to how the learner prefers to interact with it. Kolb further postulates that people tend to prefer one or the other of aspects of each of the two dimensions. So one is either a more concrete or a more abstract learner and is also either a more active or reflective one. The net result is four possible combinations or styles known as Divergers (concrete and reflective), Convergers (abstract and active), Assimilators (abstract and reflective), and Accommodators (concrete and active). Learners can use the Kolb's Learning Styles Inventory (LSI) to discover which of these four types best describe their preferred style.

However, while this offers us fewer options to worry about, we are still left with what to do about reaching these four types when designing our instruction. Kolb helps us out by offering an instruction model that creates opportunities for each type of learner. The method consists of four stages: Concrete Experience, Reflective Observation, Abstract Conceptualization, and Active Experimentation. Let's look at each of these in turn.

CONCRETE EXPERIENCE—During this portion of the instruction, learners should be offered concrete examples and be allowed to interact with them in order to develop their own generalizations. The Discovery method and other types of hands-on experiences would fall into this category. If there is not enough time for the Discovery method or if you do not have a hands-on facility, you can accomplish concrete experience through demonstrations and examples. Demonstrating what you wish students to learn and encouraging them to formulate ideas about what they are seeing is a form of concrete experience.

REFLECTIVE OBSERVATION—Here the students are encouraged to observe their experiences and reflect upon them in order to form their own explanation of these experiences. Providing opportunities for students to gather their thoughts about these demonstrations and/or their own experiences in the form of a research journal would qualify as reflective observation. Research journals can also be seen as a way for learners to develop metacognition skills since they are encouraged to reflect upon their thinking during the research process.[53] This can also be done through in-class or virtual discussions as well as Classroom Assessment Techniques[54] such as the One-Minute Paper.

ABSTRACT CONCEPTUALIZATION—This is the theory-building stage during which learners are actively involved in testing out their ideas. Group activities can be valuable at this stage as individual learners compare their ideas and test out assumptions in order to develop their final theoretical framework. Writing research papers, using analogies during discussions, or developing models or frameworks all appeal to the abstract conceptualizer.

ACTIVE EXPERIMENTATION—At this point, learners are applying their theories to real-life situations. This is the realm of problem or case-based exercises where practical applications are tested out to see how well theories hold up. Fieldwork or laboratory experimentation also falls into this category.

Each of these stages appeals to a different type of learner and offers each of them the opportunity to interact with the material in a preferred manner. Although they have been presented in a particular order, it is not necessary to always follow that order. However, according to Kolb, the learner must go through all four stages in order for learning to be complete. The value of this approach is that somewhere during the instruction, each learner is given the opportunity to shine—that is to work within his or her preferred style.

To see how this plays out for Information Literacy, take a look at Sonia Bodi's 1990 article.[55] In this application of Kolb's Experiential Learning Method, Bodi illustrates how you can vary your instruction even in a fifty-seventy minute session. The instruction includes a lecture/demo accompanied by sample material. Students then must complete a worksheet and develop a partially annotated bibliography on a topic of their own choice following the lecture. Students are required to meet with the instructor to discuss their progress after they have had to time to reflect on their experiences. Finally, the students must write a five-page research paper based on the gathered information. Each of the four learning styles is addressed by this methodology, thereby increasing the likelihood that students will interact with the material in a way that matches their style. Note that this method expands the learning experience to beyond the actual in-person contact time. Although Bodi's scenario relies heavily on face to face experiences, the current instructional technology environment would allow for many of these interactions to occur virtually instead.[56] For example, students could discuss progress with the instructor via e-mail. Video conferencing can allow for collaborative work in real-time. Computer generated simulations can be made available for those who learn through experience. Web-casts can assist the visual learner. Worksheets could be translated into online exercises. Feedback on these exercises could be built into the online experience directly, or the exercises could be sent to the instructor for review. Technology has not only expanded our reach, but has offered us more opportunities to create experiences that appeal to different types of learners.

Although the Kolb LSI is widely used, the inventory itself is somewhat difficult to administer and score. Even if you are not planning to actual give the inventory to your students, the four style types are not that easy to understand. Words like diverger, converger, accommodator, and assimilator are not readily identified with. Furthermore Kolb's Experiential Learning Method stresses the necessity of integrating all four experiences, but some researchers question whether this model is necessary in all types of learning situations.[57]

The Learning Styles Questionnaire (LSQ) developed by Peter Honey and Alan Mumford[58] offers another, more accessible paradigm. This questionnaire differs from the Kolb in two ways. First the types of learners are called Activists, Reflectors, Theorists and Pragmatists—a far more understandable set of categories. Furthermore, as opposed to the Kolb, the learner who completes the Learning Styles Questionnaire receives not one score, but a score in each of the four styles. While one or two might stand out as having the highest score, a complete picture of the learner develops as he or she views ratings in each of the four types.

If we use the LSQ styles paradigm and wish to appeal to each of the four types of learners, we should again have a variety of experiences in our instruction. The Activists like the thrill of discovery and enjoy new experiences. They bore easily and like fast-paced instruction, with lots of opportunities to try new things. They are also very social in their approach and so like opportunities to interact with other learners. Activists are concerned with "what's next?" or "what's new?" To appeal to the Reflectors we need to offer opportunities to stand back and review experiences from different perspectives. They tend to be more cautious and do not jump to conclusions. Reflectors enjoy observing others in action and so the use of demonstrations is particularly good with this type of learner. Reflectors are interested in the "whys" and need time to think about things. Theorists enjoy developing theories, principles, models and systems. They tend to be logical, detached and analytical. Subjective or ambiguous situations can be disturbing for the Theorist who focuses on the "what" behind the situation. Finally, the Pragmatist likes to apply theory to practice. They look for new ideas and approaches that they can experiment with and apply to their particular situation. Pragmatists like to work with situations that have a clear purpose and outcome. These are the learners who ask "how can I use that in my environment?"

Whether we look at the individual learning styles, group them into Physiological, Cognitive and Affective, or work with one of the many styles inventories available such as the Kolb or the Honey-Munford, the moral of the styles story is that if our users vary in their styles for learning, we must also vary our instructional methodologies in order to reach them effectively. While it is important to understand what the various styles mean in terms of behavioral and learning preferences, it is a familiarity with a variety of instructional methodologies that allows us to provide the varied instructional experience that has the best chance of reaching all our learners. Knowing the various methods and the theories behind those methods can give us insight into the types of experiences that different types of learners will relate to. The more we know about the methods, the better we can select from them to develop a varied instructional experience that has the best chance of appealing to every one of our users. Providing varied learning opportunities within the classroom as well as in our online environment enhances the usefulness of these experiences. Combining in-person with virtual instruction broadens our reach and our effectiveness. Creating instruction that appeals to various learning styles also has another benefit. This type of instruction with its mix of methods and techniques tends to result in a more dynamic and interesting experience for both the learner and the teacher.

## Final Remarks

So how does this brief exploration of the psychology of learning, and the learning styles literature help us in our teaching? First of all, it informs us why certain teaching methods, practices, and techniques work. Second, it helps us to decide which of these various methods are suitable in different situations and for different topics. And third, it alerts us to the fact that our learners vary in the ways they prefer to learn. In applying these ideas to our instructional endeavors, we begin to realize that flexibility and variety is the key to successful teaching. We need to be willing to step outside our comfort zone and try different methods of teaching. We need to mix our methods as much as possible.

We also should encourage our learners to try new ways of learning so that they too will be more flexible in their approaches to new information in the future. Varying teaching approaches encourage learners to move beyond their preferred styles, and to become familiar with a range of different learning strategies.[59] An example of mixing methods in order to appeal to a variety of learners is the Think/Pair/Share technique. It begins with a time for quiet reflection as each individual thinks about the problem at hand. Next, learners collaborate with a partner during the pair segment to exchange and discuss their individual ideas. Finally, during the sharing segment, ideas are exchanged in a larger and more diverse environment. This also gives those more out-going learners a time to shine as they present their pairs' ideas.

We should try to design instruction that stresses inquiry through authentic problem solving, active learning and collaboration in order to encourage curiosity and creativity. Allow for thinking, talking, listening, hands-on activities, individual and group work by varying the ways in which learners are asked to interact with information. Try the Experience-Practice-Application model as the structure upon which to build this variation. Start with exploring what the learner already knows or has experienced. Build on this prior knowledge. Use techniques such as reflective writing, finding analogies, and directed question and answer sessions to get at this information. Move on to practice so that learners can build a sense of personal confidence in their newly acquired skills. And finally, make sure that the learners can transfer these skills to different situations by giving them a chance to apply what they learned to something new.[60]

Take a moment to be self-reflective about your teaching methods. Do you tend to teach in one particular way more than in any other? Do you present your material in a variety of ways or do you rely heavily on one modality (sight, sound, kinesthetic activity)? If so, try to add a little more variety in your approach. Team-teach with someone who uses different methods so that you can learn from them and to ease yourself into using techniques with which you may not feel comfortable. Whenever possible, offer options to your learners. Let them decide if they want to learn the material by reading, listening, or doing. Allow for reflection as well as active participation. Give learners who find it difficult to sit still the opportunity to move around a bit. Use technology whenever possible to assist you in offering options. Online material that learners can access whenever they like offers the possibility of practice and review at the learners' own pace. Print material or instructional web pages can also help the learner who wishes to return to the material or who prefers to absorb information through reading about it.

Examine your instructional endeavors and see if you can identify the use of Behavioral, Cognitive, and Humanist approaches in your teaching. Look for techniques that you do not generally use and try to incorporate some of them into your instruction. Start small. Try just one new thing at a time. Once you are used to that one, try something else. After a while you will begin to expand your instructional repertoire.

Be a critical observer of other people's teaching. Watch to see if you can identify methods that relate to one of the three schools. Then decide if you like that technique and would like to try it yourself. If you did not like the technique, ask yourself why not? Furthermore, ask yourself it there was some way you could modify the technique so you would want to use it.

Find a learning styles inventory that appeals to you and use it to identify your own learning preferences. Use that information to ensure that you are not focusing your methodology on teaching to your own style. Try to think of ways that you could develop approaches that would appeal to other types of learners. Start with the types that are most unlike your own. Those are the hardest for us to deal with and the ones we frequently tend to ignore. Push yourself to try something new and perhaps difficult for you. Remember teaching is not about us. It is about them—the people who depend upon us to help them develop the skills, strategies and knowledge they need to become information literate.

Most importantly of all, remember that using a limited range of techniques can disenfranchise at least some of your users. Embrace flexibility; focus on curiosity, creativity and critical thinking. Acknowledge that people learn in a variety of ways. One of the lessons that the Humanists emphasized is that everyone is capable of learning. But it is up to us as teachers to provide the best, most suitable experiences and opportunities so that our learners can benefit from them. Variety is the key to success both for us and for our learners. Styles research shows us how people vary. Learning theories and their practical applications give us the tools to vary our teaching methods and reach all of our learners.[61]

## Notes

1. Esther Grassian and Joan Kaplowitz, *Information Literacy Instruction: Theory and Practice* (New York: Neal-Schuman Publishers, 2001).

2. Grassian and Kaplowitz, *Information Literacy Instruction*; Joy H. McGregor, "How Do We Learn?" in *Learning and Libraries in an Information Age: Principles and Practice*, edited by B. K. Stripling. (Englewood Co: Libraries Unlimited, 1999): 25-53; Mark Tennant, *Psychology and Adult Learning* (London: Routledge, 2006).

3. Benjamin Samuel Bloom, George F. Madaus, and J. Thomas Hastings, *Evaluation to Improve Learning* (New York: McGraw-Hill. 1981); Stephen N. Elliott, Thomas R. Kratochwill, Joan Littlefield, and John F. Travers, *Educational Psychology: Effective Teaching, Effective Learning.* 2nd ed. (Madison, Wis.: Brown & Benchmark, 1996); Grassian and Kaplowitz, *Information Literacy Instruction*; B.F. Skinner, *The Technology of Teaching* (New York: Appleton-Century-Crofts, 1968).

4. Grassian and Kaplowitz, *Information Literacy Instruction.*

5. Grassian and Kaplowitz, *Information Literacy Instruction*; B. F. Skinner, *The Behavior of Organisms* (New York: Macmillan, 1938) ; Skinner, *About Behaviorism* (New York: Knopf, 1974).

6. Albert Bandura, *Social Foundations of Thought and Action: A Social Cognitive Theory* (Englewood Cliffs, N. J.: Prentice Hall, 1986); Elliott et al., *Educational Psychology*; Grassian and Kaplowitz, *Information Literacy Instruction.*

7. Grassian and Kaplowitz, *Information Literacy Instruction*

8. Elliott et al., *Educational Psychology*; Grassian and Kaplowitz, *Information Literacy Instruction*; Max Wertheimer, "Experimental Studies of the Perception of Movement," *Zeitschrift fur Psychologie* 61 (1912): 161-265.

9. Grassian and Kaplowitz, *Information Literacy Instruction*; Wolfgang Köhler and Ella Winter, *The Mentality of Apes* (New York, London: Harcourt Brace & Company, 1925).

10. Marcy Perkins Driscoll, *Psychology of Learning for Instruction* (Boston: Allyn and Bacon, 1994) ; Catherine Twomey Fosnot, "Media and Technology in Education—A Constructivist view," *Education Communication and Technology Journal (ECTJ)* 32 (1984): 195-205; Grassian and Kaplowitz, *Information Literacy Instruction*; Jean Piaget, *The Construction of Reality in the Child* (New York: Basic Books 1954).

11. Robert B. Barr and John Tagg, "From Teaching to Learning—A New Paradigm for Undergraduate Education," *Change* 27 (1995): 13-25; Jeffrey N. Gatten, "Student Psychosocial and Cognitive Development: Theory to Practice in Academic Libraries," *Reference Services Review* 32 (2004.): 157-163; Grassian and Kaplowitz, *Information Literacy Instruction*; Dianne Oberg, "A Community of Learning for the Information Age," in *Learning and Libraries in an Information Age: Principles and Practice*, edited by B. K. Stripling. (Englewood CO: Libraries Unlimited, 1999): 299-323.

12. Susan E. Cooperstein and Elizabeth Kocevar-Weidinger, "Beyond Active Learning: A Constructivist Approach to Learning," *Reference Services Review* 32 (2004.): 141-148; Barbara Fister, "Teaching Research as a Social Act: Collaborative Learning and the Library," *RQ* 29 (1990): 505-509; Lev S. Vygotsky and Michael Cole, *Mind in Society: The Development of Higher Psychological Processes* (Cambridge, MA: Harvard University Press, 1978).

13. Jerome Bruner, *Toward a Theory of Instruction* (Cambridge, Mass: Belknap Press of Harvard University, 1966); McGregor, "How Do We Learn?" 25-53; Georgia Sparks-Langer, *Teach-*

*ing as Decision Making* (Upper Saddle River, New Jersey: Prentice-Hall, 2000); Lev S. Vygotsky, *Thought and Language* (Cambridge: M.I.T. Press Massachusetts Institute of Technology, 1962); Mary Ellen Weimer. Focus on Learning. Transform Teaching. *Change* 35 (2003): 49-54.

14. Grassian and Kaplowitz. *Information Literacy Instruction;* Sparks-Langer, *Teaching as Decision Making.*

15. Grassian and Kaplowitz, *Information Literacy Instruction.*

16. Ibid.

17. Jerome Bruner, *The Process of Education* 2nd Ed. (New York: Random House. 1963; Driscoll, *Psychology of Learning for Instruction;* Elliott et al., *Educational Psychology;* Grassian and Kaplowitz, *Information Literacy Instruction;* Neil Postman and Charles Weingarten, *Teaching as a Subversive Activity.* (New York: Delacorte Press, 1971).

18. Philip C. Candy. "How People Learn to Learn," in *Learning to Learn Across the Life Span,* edited by R. M. Smith and et al. (San Francisco: Jossey-Bass, 1990): 30-63; Grassian and Kaplowitz, *Information Literacy Instruction.*

19. David P. Ausubel, "The Use of Advance Organizers in the Learning and Retention of Meaningful Verbal Material," *Journal of Educational Psychology* 51 (1960): 267-272; Elliott et al., *Educational Psychology;* Grassian and Kaplowitz, *Information Literacy Instruction;* John P. Rickards, "Instructional Psychology: From Behavioristic to Cognitive Orientation," *Improving Human Performance Quarterly* 7 (1978): 256-266.

20. Grassian and Kaplowitz, *Information Literacy Instruction.*

21. Thomas A. Angelo and K. Patricia Cross, *Classroom Assessment Techniques: A Handbook for College Teachers.* 2nd Ed, *The Jossey-Bass Higher and Adult Education Series* (San Francisco: Jossey-Bass Publishers, 1993); Cooperstein and Kocevar-Weidinger, "Beyond Active Learning" 141-148; Driscoll, *Psychology of Learning for Instruction;* Grassian and Kaplowitz, *Information Literacy Instruction;* Virginia Rankin, "One Route to Critical Thinking," *School Library Journal* 34 (1988): 28-31; Marilla D. Svinicki, "Practical Implications of Cognitive Theories," in *Teaching and Learning in the College Classroom,* edited by K. A. Feldman and M. B. Paulsen. (Needham, Hts. MA: Ginn Press, 1994): 69-99.

22. Cooperstein and Kocevar-Weidinger, "Beyond Active Learning," 141-148; Sandra M. Hughes and Jacqueline C. Mancall, "Developing a Collaborative Access Environment: Meeting the Resource Needs of the Learning Community," in *Learning and Libraries in an Information Age: Principles and Practice,* edited by B. K. Stripling. (Englewood CO: Libraries Unlimited, 1999): 231-259; Barbara Seels, "The Instructional Design Movement in Educational Technology," *Educational Technology* 29 (1989): 11-15; Beth S. Woodard, "Technology and the Constructivist Learning Environment: Implications for Teaching Information Literacy Skills," *Research Strategies* 19 (2003): 181-192.

23. Barr and Tagg, "From Teaching to Learning," 13-25; Oberg, "A Community of Learning for the Information Age," 299-323.

24. Grassian and Kaplowitz, *Information Literacy Instruction;* McGregor, "How Do We Learn?" 25-53.

25. Myron H. Dembo, *Applying Educational Psychology in the Classroom.* 3rd Ed. (New York: Longman, 1988); Elliott et al., *Educational Psychology;* Grassian and Kaplowitz, *Information Literacy Instruction;* Carl R. Rogers, *Freedom to Learn: A View of What Education Might Become* (Columbus, Ohio: C. E. Merrill Pub. Co. 1969); Tennant, *Psychology and Adult Learning.*

26. Driscoll, *Psychology of Learning for Instruction;* Grassian and Kaplowitz, *Information Literacy Instruction;* Abraham H. Maslow, *Motivation and Personality* (New York: Harper and Row, 1987); Tennant. *Psychology and Adult Learning.*

27. Albert Bandura, "Self-efficacy Toward a Unifying Theory of Behavioral Change," *Psycho-*

*logical Review* 84 (1977): 191-215; Candy, "How People Learn to Learn," 30-63; Driscoll, *Psychology of Learning for Instruction.*

28.  Grassian and Kaplowitz, *Information Literacy Instruction;* McGregor, "How Do We Learn?" 25-53.

29.  Fister, "Teaching Research as a Social Act," 505-509.

30.  Ronald J. Areglado, R. C. Bradley, and Pamela S. Lane, *Learning for Life: Creating Classrooms for Self-directed Learning* (Thousand Oaks, Ca.: Corwin Press, 1996); Grassian and Kaplowitz, *Information Literacy Instruction.*

31.  Carol Collier Kuhlthau, "Developing a Model of the Library Search Process: Cognitive and Affective Aspects," *RQ* 28 (1988): 232-242.

32.  Barr and Tagg, "From Teaching to Learning," 13-25; Candy, "How People Learn to Learn," 30-63; Grassian and Kaplowitz, *Information Literacy Instruction;* Weimer, "Focus on Learning," 49-54; Barry J. Zimmerman, "Self-regulated Learning and Academic Achievement: An Overview," *Educational Psychologist* 25 (1990): 3-17.

33.  Driscoll, *Psychology of Learning for Instruction;* Grassian and Kaplowitz, *Information Literacy Instruction;* John M. Keller, "Strategies for Stimulating the Motivation to Learn," *Performance and Instruction Journal* 26 (1987): 1-7.

34.  Grassian and Kaplowitz, *Information Literacy Instruction.*

35.  Barr and Tagg, "From Teaching to Learning," 13-25; Weimer, "Focus on Learning,"49-54.

36.  Grassian and Kaplowitz, *Information Literacy Instruction.*

37.  Grassian and Kaplowitz, *Information Literacy Instruction;* James W. Keefe, "Assessing Student Learning Styles: An Overview," in *Student styles and brain behavior.* (Reston, VA: NAASP, 1982): 43-53.

38.  Grassian and Kaplowitz, *Information Literacy Instruction.*

39.  Keefe, "Assessing Student Learning Styles," 43-53.

40.  W. Ray Crozier, *Individual Learners: Personality Differences in Education* (London; New York: Routledge, 1997); Keefe. "Assessing Student Learning Styles," 43-53; Keefe, *Learning Style: Theory and Practice.* (Reston, Va.: National Association of Secondary School Principals, 1987); Stephen Rayner and Richard Riding. "Toward a Categorisation of Cognitive Styles and Learning," *Educational Psychology* 17 (1997): 5-27; Ronald R. Schmeck, *Learning Strategies and Learning Styles, Perspectives on Individual Differences* (New York: Plenum Press, 1988); Ronald R. Sims and Serbrenia J. Sims, *The Importance of Learning Styles* (Westport, Conn: Greenwood Press, 1995); Robert J. Sternberg, *Thinking Styles* (Cambridge, U.K; New York, NY, USA: Cambridge University Press, 1997).

41.  Simon Cassidy, "Learning Styles: An Overview of Theories, Models, and Measures," *Educational Psychology* 24 (2004): 419-444; Ella Desmedt and Martin Valcke, "Mapping the Learning Styles "Jungle": An Overview of the Literature Based on Citation Analyses," *Educational Psychology* 24 (2004): 445-464.

42.  Howard Gardner, *Frames of Mind: the Theory of Multiple Intelligences* New York: Basic Books, 1983; Gardner, Reflections on Multiple Intelligences: Myths and Messages. *Phi Delta Kappan* 77 (1995): 200-209.

43.  Grassian and Kaplowitz, *Information Literacy Instruction;* Keefe, *Learning Style: Theory and Practice.*

44.  Grassian and Kaplowitz, *Information Literacy Instruction.*

45.  Ibid.

46.  Keefe, *Learning Style: Theory and Practice;* Sparks-Langer, *Teaching as Decision Making.*

47.  Grassian and Kaplowitz, *Information Literacy Instruction.*

48.  Ibid.

49. Ibid.

50. Dennis B. Gooler, "Changing the Way We Live in the Information Age," in *Learning to Learn across the Life Span,* edited by R. M. Smith and et al. (San Francisco: Jossey-Bass, 1990): 307-326; Richard McClintock, *Renewing the Progress Contract with Posterity: On Social Construction of Learning Communities* 1996. Available online from http://www.lt.columbia.edu/mccmintock/renew [Accessed 30 March 2006]; Thomas C. Reeves. *The Impact of Media and Technology in Schools,* 1998. Available online from http://www.athensacademy.org/instruct/media_tech/ReevesO.html [Accessed 30 March 2006]; Woodard, "Technology and the Constructivist Learning Environment," 181-192.

51. Grassian and Kaplowitz, *Information Literacy Instruction;* Keefe, *Learning Style: Theory and Practice.*

52. David A. Kolb, *Experiential Learning: Experience as the Source of Learning and Development.* (Englewood Cliffs, N.J.: Prentice-Hall, 1984).

53. McGregor, "How Do We Learn?" 25-53.

54. Angelo and Cross, *Classroom Assessment Techniques.*

55. Sonia Bodi, "Teaching Effectiveness and Bibliographic Instruction: The Relevance of Learning Styles," *College and Research Libraries* 51 (1990): 113-119.

56. Gooler, "Changing the Way We Live in the Information Age," 307-326.

57. Tennant, *Psychology and Adult Learning.*

58. Peter Honey and Alan Mumford, *Capitalizing on your Learning Style.* HRDQ 1995. Available online from http://www.hrdq.com [Accessed 30 March 2006].

59. Phil Candy, "Major Themes and Future Directions: Conference Summary and Implications," in *Learning for Life,* edited by D. Booker. (Adelaide, Australia: University of South Australia Library, 1996): 135-149; Nancy M. Dixon, "Implementation of Learning Style Information," *Lifelong Learning* 9 (1985): 16-27; Grassian and Kaplowitz, *Information Literacy Instruction;* McGregor, "How Do We Learn?" 25-53; Tennant, *Psychology and Adult Learning.*

60. Randy Burke Hensley, "Curiosity and Creativity as Attributes of Information Literacy," *Reference and User Services* 44 (2004): 31-36; Sparks-Langer, *Teaching as Decision Making.*

61. Grassian and Kaplowitz, *Information Literacy Instruction;* Karen T. Pardue. Alice E. Conway, Jan Edelstein, and et al, "Substantive Innovation in Nursing Education: The Emphasis From Concrete Coverage to Student Learning," *Nursing Education Perspectives* 25 (2005): 55-57.

# CHAPTER 3
## *Teaching*

Susan Barnes Whyte
Alexis Smith Macklin
Carla List-Handley
Trudi E. Jacobson

This section provides insights from four instruction librarians on various aspects of teaching. Susan Barnes Whyte discusses the importance of knowing oneself as a teacher. Alexis Smith Macklin provides an overview of problem-based learning, while Carla List-Handley discusses teaching as performance. Trudi E. Jacobson offers information about motivating students.

## Finding Ourselves as Teachers
*Susan Barnes Whyte*

Librarians are not trained to teach. Teaching and learning are generally not part of our graduate work. For example, learning theories, learning styles, presentation techniques, whom we may teach, whether students, faculty, or colleagues, are typically not mentioned. Yet many librarians today find themselves teaching in their first position, armed with lots of knowledge about the intricacies of database searching but with little knowledge about how to teach and who they are as teachers. This pattern is repeated in many graduate programs across this country as aspiring graduate students plumb the depths within their chosen discipline but rarely have the opportunity to learn how to teach it, or to explore how students might best learn that content, or how to work with students who very well may not be passionate about the subject.

Central to becoming a good teacher is the ability to know oneself as a teacher. Arriving at this knowledge is complex and takes time, reflection, conversation with others, and trial and error within the classroom itself. Talking about who we are or may be as teachers is hard and embarrassing and funny and not often shared. The classroom in colleges and universities is often a space inhabited only by the faculty member and his or her students. This implies a privacy that does not make for easy conversation about one of the central purposes of higher education in the United States: student learning. This privacy also implies an authority or power instantiated within this privacy, an authority that most students would not question and that most faculty would be loath to change. Who knows if their teaching works? If the students learn? This mystique preserves a nineteenth century ethos that does not work well in our transparent, open culture where the lines are obscured between private and public space for anyone under the age of thirty. Nor does it work well with often legislatively mandated evidence to demonstrate that students are learning.

To know oneself as a teacher requires knowing oneself as a student and knowing oneself on a level far beyond doing well on a test, excelling in a discipline in college, or being a good adult. To know oneself as a teacher requires thoughtful inquiry into the good teacher who touched our lives when we were students and beyond. To know oneself as a teacher requires an openness to continual learning, as Ken Bain attests in his book *What The Best College Teachers Do*.[1] Bain's research involved analyzing more than sixty faculty in universities and college, asking them and their colleagues and students what makes a good teacher. His book illuminates the characteristics of good teachers. Fundamentally, these good teachers are always learning, and their infectious enthusiasm for perpetual learning affects their students' learning.

Parker Palmer's book, *The Courage to Teach,* suggests reasonable ways to know oneself as a teacher. Importantly, Palmer reveals to all of us that talking about who we are as teachers is to open ourselves in a way that makes us vulnerable.[2] To reveal who we are in front of college students is "a daily exercise of vulnerability."[3] What if they laugh? What if they sleep? What if they walk out? What if the faculty member never brings a class back? Jane Tompkins spoke to this fear in her memoir *A Life in School*:

> Whereas for my entire teaching life I had always thought that what I was doing was helping my students to understand the material we were studying…I realized that what I had actually been concerned with was showing the students how smart I was, how knowledgeable I was, and how well prepared I was for class. I had been putting on a performance whose true goal was not to help the students learn, as I had thought, but to perform before them in such a way that they would have a good opinion of me.[4]

To focus on this fear creates a disconnection between the students and the teacher and the content. How often do we in the library fear that we will forget how to best search a particular database? In order not to forget this trick or that, we focus so intently that we tend to forget or become disconnected from the students in our classroom. Palmer's central thesis is that bad, disconnected teaching happens out of this fear of appearing not to know. Because all these bad things may happen (and, indeed they do), it's basic human nature to try to prevent them from happening. So, what do we do as teachers? We focus on controlling the classroom, on stuffing the students full of content. We extol the value of the content over the value of the learning. We fill the classroom time up so that there is no chance for any student to say anything that could question our authority or, even worse, ask a question that we wouldn't know how to answer! For many librarians, this is the biggest fear in teaching: "What happens if someone asks a question and I don't know the right answer?" In education, we are programmed to think of the teacher as the expert, the one with all the answers. Librarians historically have run organizations full of answers. To not know the right answer is chilling, so often we fill the class session up with words, more words, and more tips, rather than to enter a world of learning where mistakes occur every day and learning happens because of those mistakes.

## Reflection—Using Our Stories
### Monks
When I started teaching back in 1982, I was a newly-minted librarian who had taught piano to children and adults for seven years, but had only the vaguest notion of teaching as a librarian. My first professional position as a cataloger at a Benedictine Abbey in western Oregon did not require me to teach the young monks and scholars there. Yet, because of my undergraduate experience at Earlham College where librarians taught a session or two in almost every course I took, it never occurred to me that librarians don't teach. And, since there was no reference librarian at the abbey, I volunteered to teach basic research skills to the students. And what students they were! Studious, respectful, and attentive in their long robes, I was introduced to teaching in a world where questioning authority did not take place. I could teach the "right way" to do library research through the "right sources" to find the "right answers." And, I could focus upon the "rightness" without thinking much about who the students were (I was barely allowed to interact with them), much less think about what they were learning from me.

### Adult Learners
After two years of this classic authoritarian teaching, I then found myself at a new university standing in front of harried, tired adult learners at night and on the weekends, most of whom had no time, lots of life experience, and lots of questions. I was still a cataloger, but again, there was no reference librarian and I wanted to meet the students who used my catalog. These adult students demanded that I know who they were. Their life stories infused their college work

and brought a personal perspective to their learning that they demanded I hear. I did hear, and started reading and thinking about how to approach adult students and what exactly it was they needed from me in these library sessions. What they needed was clear: they had no time, they had little interest in most of the research, they needed answers fast, and they needed to know me as a person, not as a librarian. It had never occurred to me that anyone would be interested in who I was as their teacher. What a revelation! And it had not occurred to me before how knowledge became part of who I was as a student. I had thrived in schools and had not thought to question teachers and their approaches until I encountered some not-so-good examples in college and then in graduate school. But, until I stood in front of a classroom, I had not really thought about the sheer vulnerability of that act. All those eyes. All that potential judgment.

## College Students

Within five years I moved on to a traditional liberal arts college, and for the first time was actually in a public services position and so could focus on teaching. Again my audience shifted, and I was confronted with young, nice, but essentially disengaged students. They were taking a course, perhaps Asian Philosophy or Nineteenth-Century Romantic Music or Environmental Science, and they may have been interested in the content but by and large were not interested in how to find information within the library. Many of my faculty colleagues at Linfield complained about a general lack of engagement among these students, particularly in the lower division, general education courses. Again I started thinking, reading about learning rather than just about teaching, and I started going to whatever workshops I could find that focused upon teaching and learning. But, mostly, I talked with faculty at Linfield about their teaching, and I had the privilege of watching many of them teach and listening to their stories. It finally dawned on me that what connected students to their learning were their relationships with their faculty. And when I talked with my fellow Earlham alumni about what they remembered about their own learning, they first mentioned their favorite teachers and the relationship forged between teacher and student around the specific content.

Palmer's other tenet in *The Courage to Teach* is this: that to connect students with content, teachers first need to connect with students and forge a relationship between teacher and students, among students, and between students and the content. "Good teachers possess a capacity for connectedness. They are able to weave a complex web of connections among themselves, their subjects, and their students so that students can learn to weave a world for themselves."[5] Weaving this web begins with self-knowledge about yourself as a teacher, and reaching out to each student as a person rather than only as the content expert. Over time I did learn to self-disclose a bit about myself, often as part of a humorous incident involving other students or my children. I watched other faculty self-disclose, and noted their students' responses to the humanity of the moment. Students crave connections with others. Students are often amazed at faculty's human side. A recent survey at Linfield with alumni from the past ten years revealed the power of these connections between students and faculty.[6]

## Reflection

As you work on creating the connections with students, thinking about who you are as a teacher can be an exercise in frustration because it's not easy, and there is no one approach, no magic bullet. One approach is to think about good teachers in your life. Who were they? Why were they good? What was it about them that connected you to them and to their content? Doing this exercise with others is especially fruitful because to listen to others' stories about good teachers reveals that there is no one way to be a good teacher. Good teachers essentially vary widely in how they teach. They are alike only in their identity as teachers who are comfortable within themselves as teachers, a central Parker Palmer tenet. They have figured out their identity as teachers and are willing to share that self with others.

Another imaginative and less threatening way to talk about who you are as a teacher is to ask yourself to fill in this metaphor: teaching is like .... The variety of images that a room of teachers brings to this exercise is astounding. Is teaching like conducting a quartet where each player reads the score and pays attention to the conductor? Or is it more like jazz where improvisational riffs occasionally take over the main motif? Is teaching like growing a garden? Is teaching like building a house? The images range on and on with no limit because teaching and learning, to be effective, has to get under our skin, has to get personal. The academy can at times discount the sense of the importance of that personal connection. The emphasis on analysis and objectivity can impart to students and to faculty that knowledge is something "out there."[7] Good teachers know that knowledge becomes part of who students are. Palmer says, "Virtually every great scholar finds this way of appropriating knowledge, of living it and breathing it and bringing it so close to your heart that you and it are almost one. Objectivity and intimacy *can* go hand in hand."[8] The challenge for us in the academy, and in libraries in particular, is to show students the way to owning their knowledge. Libraries are full of books and articles, both print and electronic, that are written by people who care passionately about an idea, a person, an event, or a theory. Students can begin to see this connection within themselves when given the opportunity, to own their knowledge, when they pursue, for example, a topic of interest to their own lives. Or, they can begin to see this connection when they do collaborative research with a faculty member. They can begin to see the passion that drives the faculty member in his or her research. They can begin to see why this particular topic matters to themselves and to others.

Good teaching and good teachers develop over time, and with experience, gain knowledge of who they are as teachers and a sense that it's all right to fail sometimes. Giving up that fear of failure can result in classes that focus more on the students and what they need to learn. Focusing on the students and connecting with them as learners can free us from all the absolutes that we may think they need to know. The process can be messy. Mistakes can happen. Perfect searches can take on more realistic attributes that mirror students' searches. Conversations can happen within the class about why a search fails. Or, better yet, why it matters to think about why a search fails. Conversations about absurd Web sites can teach students, faculty and librarians about how each of us views our new webbed, instantaneous, pseudo-transparent world of knowledge. Knowing the right tool and all the bells and whistles won't be useful for teacher or student. Knowing how to *see* a record or a piece of information will be. Knowing how to ask *why* this matters will be. Rather than telling students what to see on an online index or a Web site, turn it around and *ask* them. Then wait. Ken Bain says that the best college teachers are those who "create a natural critical learning environment"[9] and who "help students build an understanding of concepts rather than simply perform their discipline in front of them."[10] A classroom with a "natural critical learning environment" is one where inquiry frames the method. Rather than telling students how to do the perfect search, work with them as you all do a search together, instead of offering something canned or predictable. Rather than filling the students' brains up with all the tricks and tips for a particular database, teach them how to think their way through such a source of information. Ask them what they see on the screen. Build your comments around their responses. If you teach the perfect, linear way to search, your search will not mirror what will happen to the students in their searches once they're in their dorm room at 2:00 a.m. Their world in education, and beyond that as adults, will not be about predictable results.

## Conclusion

So, relax, breathe, and think about who you are as a teacher. Who are you in front of the students? What story will you tell that will connect the students to you? How can you use humor to make a point? Or how can you use a still point of silence to do the same? And, keep the long perspective. Time matters as you teach and become a good teacher. Pay intentional attention to your teaching over the course of a year. Keep a journal in order to reflect on what you think went well, and more significantly, why. Ask the students what they learned and what they still don't understand, a quick assessment that reveals a lot. Think about how you give of yourself so that your students can dig deep into themselves. Do you ask the next question when revealing how best to search a particular source? Is searching not part of the thinking process? How do you demystify that process and yourself for your students? In the process of presenting yourself and your content to your students, how do you reveal both in order to connect with the students?

Why connect with students? Because Bain's work and Palmer's work and countless conversations with students about which teachers matter to them indicate that deep connections with the teacher as a person line the pathway to learning. As Palmer says, "connections made by good teachers are held in their hearts meaning heart in its ancient sense, as the place where intellect and emotion and spirit and will converge in the human self."[11] Libraries have long been about order and linearity. Today they are about connecting people with each other's ideas. Despite the technology-infused age we live in, students still want to connect with other students and with faculty. Give them and yourselves that chance.

## Notes

1. Ken Bain, *What The Best College Teachers Do* (Cambridge: Harvard: University Press, 2004), 15-21.

2. Parker J. Palmer, *The Courage to Teach: Exploring the Inner Landscape of a Teacher's Life* (San Francisco: Jossey Bass, 1998), 9-35.

3. Ibid., 17.

4. Jane Tompkins. *A Life in School: What the Teacher Learned* (Reading, MA: Perseus Books, 1996), 119.

5. Palmer, *Courage*, 11.

6. Jean Caspers and Susan Barnes Whyte, "Lifelong Learning: Making the Connection." Presentation at LOEX of the West Conference. Hilo, Hawaii, June 10, 2006.

7. Parker Palmer, "Community, Conflict and Ways of Knowing: Ways to Deepen our Educational Agenda," *Change* 19, no. 5 (Sept/Oct 1987): 22.

8. Ibid., 24.

9. Bain, *What the Best*, 99.

10. Ibid., 115.

11. Palmer, *Courage*, 11.

# Problem-Based Learning

*Alexis Smith Macklin*

Problem-based learning (PBL) is a learner-centered approach that empowers students to conduct research, integrate theory and practice, and apply knowledge and skills to develop a viable solution to a defined problem.[1] This approach to teaching and learning started at McMaster University in 1969 as curriculum reform for medical schools. It is now one of the most advanced instructional methodologies being used across disciplines today.[2] The problems are deliberately ill-structured (or open-ended) and are typically based on real-life simulations; they are designed for thoughtful and careful analysis to help improve critical thinking skills by applying the learner's own expertise and experience to data collection, analysis, and formulation of a solution.[3]

## How does PBL work?

The first step in developing a PBL activity is to find or create a problem or situation that needs a solution. Often some of the best resources of good problems are newspapers or popular magazines, such as *Time* or *Newsweek*, as well as radio or television. Using these kinds of sources, which are easy to find and adjust to specific learning objectives, is a great way to start building a PBL curriculum. Another tip to creating problems or activities is to stay current. Contemporary situations always seem to work best for writing problems that get and keep a learner's attention. The more recent or the more local a topic, the more relevant it will be in the students' everyday life experiences.

Some topics that work well for PBL activities:

- Binge drinking
- Academic integrity (cheating, plagiarism)
- Hazing
- Technology issues (i.e. piracy)
- Stem-cell research
- Environmental issues (nuclear energy as alternative fuel source)

## Criteria for Good Problems

*They are engaging.* People are more inclined to learn when they are interested in the subject. This does not necessarily mean developing problems based on popular culture; rather, it is the use of real-life situations to meet real-life information needs.

*They have structure.* While PBL uses ill-structured or open-ended problems, there are clearly identified learning objectives and expectations embedded into the learning process. In PBL, achieving the learning outcomes is the joint responsibility of both the instructor and the students.

Jonassen[4] identified the following characteristics of ill-structured problems:

- They possess multiple solutions, solution paths, or no solutions at all
- They possess multiple criteria for evaluating solutions, so there is uncertainty about which concepts, rules, and principles are necessary for the solution

*They are adaptable.* As problem-solving skills are developed, the learner will be able to see how one set of solutions for a situation can be applied to similar situations.

*They are collaborative.* Not everyone is an expert at everything. As learners engage in an information exchange, they will be able to build off of their own knowledge, evaluate others' interpretations of the situations presented, and arrive collectively at logical solutions.[5]

In the PBL activities, learners should be prepared to gather facts based on what is known, identify and ask questions about what is not known, formulate a problem statement and hypothesize about the solutions, locate information to support those ideas, and evaluate the materials they find.

## What is the Instructor's Role?

In PBL there is no teacher, *per se.* An expert facilitator replaces the traditional role of lecturer as the primary instructor. This person is responsible for helping the learners discover what they already know and guiding them to new knowledge through problem solving. The learning process is really about thoughtful trial and error. As students test out different solutions to the various problems, their knowledge base increases. A successful PBL facilitator must be able to draw out this evolving expertise by establishing a learning environment that is conducive to exploration, creative thinking, and continuous positive feedback and reinforcement. The following outlines the instructor's role more comprehensively:

- Sets up the problem/situation
- Balances student-direction with assistance
- Contributes knowledge and experiences
- Creates a pleasant learning environment
- Stimulates critical evaluation of ideas

The following is an example of a PBL activity developed for an introductory course in hotel, tourism, and management (HTM). The professor and librarian collaborated to write a problem that would present databases and journals specific to the HTM field. The scenario is a real-world experience addressed in the literature of the food industry:

> There are a growing number of reports on the popularity of *low*-carbohydrate *diets* among Americans. Dietary experts like Dr. Robert Atkins, developer of the Atkins diet, claim that a high-protein, low-carb diet changes the metabolism and allows for safe weight loss. Some nutritionists are concerned about the long term effects of these diets and want to find alternative ways of dealing with obesity and weight-related health problems. One thing is sure - the low-carb craze has had an effect on companies and food retailers that sell high carb food.

In order to stay on the cutting edge, even McDonald's is now offering a *low-carb* fare! "That's all well and good for the fast-food industry, but I make my living on pasta," says Tony Cillo, owner of That's Italian! on Main Street in downtown Lafayette, Indiana. He wants to investigate how other restaurant owners are working with their clientele to satisfy low-carb dietary needs—without radically changing his menu.

## Scaffolding Instruction

Scaffolding is a strategy or technique used to support learners engaged in the PBL process. These are especially important to use if there is limited instruction time to guide students through an activity. If you are only allotted one class session to teach critical information skills, and you decide to use a PBL approach, develop some materials to help bridge the gap for students. One strategy is to:

- Introduce new concepts by building on what the student already knows

For example, allow students to use search engines they are comfortable navigating, but create scaffolds (tutorials, worksheets, job aids) to teach the principles of preferred information tools, referencing similarities and differences to the one they commonly use. These scaffolds will help them transfer what they know from one search tool to another, and become more confident in their ability to use a variety of search engines.

An example of a scaffold used with the hotel, tourism, and management PBL activity included a list of questions on the topic of "low-carb menus." These were developed to generate a discussion about selecting the most appropriate information sources. Students often struggle to know when to use a book, versus a favorite search engine, etc. This scaffold was used, in conjunction with the PBL activity, to teach the importance of matching the resource to the information need. Incorporating this scaffold into the instruction time takes about twenty minutes. It can also be done as a take-home activity to assess (pre or post) skill level.

Pick ONE question to answer and find ONE information source that answers it:

A. Give some specific examples of how restaurants are dealing with the demand for low-carb food?
*Best source of information:* Book; Journal article; Newspaper; Google

B. How have some companies that manufacture high-carb foods reacted to this dietary trend?
*Best source of information:* Book; Journal article; Newspaper; Google

C. What are some of the nutritional issues regarding low-carb diets?
*Best resource of information:* Book; Journal article; Newspaper; Google

If you are integrating information skills into the curriculum using a problem-based learning approach, you may want to design scaffolds that will continue to build and test the students' understanding of the principles of information retrieval. One way to do this is to:

- Use instructional supports (concept maps, worksheets, dialog, peer mentoring) to help integrate new concepts into the student's existing knowledge bank

These types of scaffolds help the student analyze the problem by identifying relevant facts from the scenario. This process helps them to understand the problem, and then generate hypotheses about possible solutions; but it requires some serious collaboration. In this situation, the subject area faculty would provide the librarian with scenarios in which problem solving takes place in that discipline. For example, a forestry professor wanted to incorporate information skills into her course. She described some current issues in forestry that were adjusted for use as group problem-solving activities. To make it even more interesting for the students, the solutions were shared with forest rangers working with the Department of Natural Resources, who provided feedback and guidance to the groups. In this learning environment, students constructed their own understandings of the problem scenarios, and used the information they found to create workable solutions.[6]

## Is PBL the right choice?

Before embarking on the use of PBL to teach critical information skills, think about your needs, and the needs of your students. Do you have enough resources to adequately support you? Time is the most essential resource, and often the one most in demand. If you are only being allotted one class session, discuss your plans to use PBL with the faculty or instructor of record. Collaboration is essential for using PBL effectively to teach information skills. Ask for his or her input in the design of the problem, the scaffolding tools, and the assessment rubrics. Once you have buy-in, it's much easier to negotiate how to incorporate information skills to support the course content. You will also need to determine roles and strategies for delivering instruction. What will you do to teach information skills? What will the faculty member do to reinforce those skills?

Using PBL to teach information literacy skills:

- The facilitator introduces a problem
- The students analyze the problem for information—individually and collaboratively
- An information need is determined and possible solutions are proposed
- The facilitator introduces students to various information sources
- Students investigate the information sources and locate relevant information to support their hypothesis

## Writing Lesson Plans for the PBL Experience

PBL is student-centered and focused on the whole process of learning. While users of the traditional method of PBL are not necessarily interested in achieving a certain set of predefined performance outcomes and measurable behaviors, there are specific learning goals and objectives built into each information literacy problem. The concept of right and wrong answers is expanded to include more open-ended results, but there is still the expectation of a best answer—or at least clarification of why one answer might be better than another. Because the PBL methodology encourages freedom of thought, it is necessary to establish some clear boundaries through lesson planning, so that the experience does not become overwhelming and chaotic.

In the broadest sense of the idea, lesson plans are detailed outlines that provide the guidance needed to keep the teacher on track when creating and delivering instruction—even in a PBL environment. They are a great way to establish productive instruction time and to assess the learning in the process, without becoming inundated by the amount of content to cover. A well-constructed plan includes the following:

- Learning Goals
- Learning Objectives
- A step-by-step procedure for instruction
- An assessment tool for measuring the learning outcomes
- A self-evaluation of content and instruction

*Learning goals* should define the expectations of the learning experience. They are not meant to be all-inclusive, nor are they necessarily designed to be measurable. Rather, the goals are meant to keep the lesson plan focused. In a fifty-minute session, it is unrealistic to cover much more than two learning goals. If they are clear and concise, these goals will help build excellent learning objectives, which is the next logical step in writing a lesson plan. An example of two goals appropriate for an introductory level session:

- *Identify* important HTM resources
- *Practice* searching for HTM information sources

*Learning objectives* differ from learning goals because they measure behaviors and anticipated outcomes as a result of the instruction. They are much more detailed than learning goals, stating exactly what the learner will be expected to do. One way to think about writing learning objectives is a mnemonic device called "The A (audience), B (behaviors), C (conditions), D's (degree) of Writing Objectives." Here is what it looks like in practice:

Condition:   After completing the Library's online tutorial, and familiarizing themselves with the electronic resources and services available,

Audience:    the HTM 101 students will

Behaviors:    *Read* a given problem (individually)
              *Identify* an information need (small groups of 3-4)
              *Construct* a search strategy (small groups of 3-4)
              *Access* information from at least two different research databases
Degree:       *Select* one appropriate source and justify two reasons for the choice (individually)

In this example, the verbs recognize, read, identify, construct, access, and select are representative of intellectual activities and behaviors that are measurable.[7] Often when writing learning objectives, instructors tend to use the words "understand" or "appreciate" to say what the student will be able to do. These are vague terms and not easily measured. For the most effective assessment of the learning experience, the facilitator should use only measurable action verbs that clearly describe what is expected from the learner after the instruction is complete. By establishing a clear set of measurable performance expectations, the risk of grading and assessing subjectively is significantly reduced.

*A step-by-step procedure for instruction* in a PBL activity is not hierarchical in nature. Rather, it involves an iterative process that allows for investigation, evaluation, and collaboration with other learners. This approach underscores effective learning as a cycle or set of stages[8] proceeding from initial information retrieval skills, to more sophisticated, reflective understandings or information literacy:

- The perception of information needs
- The conceptual understanding of the organization of information
- The technical ability to use information technologies, and
- The cognitive ability to plan a search strategy, choose relevant information, and communicate ideas with others

To measure the outcomes of the PBL experience, require students to produce something tangible—a proposal, a design, charts, graphs, etc. to document and explain how they were thinking about solving the problem. As these products are tested and refined throughout the process, students will begin to represent (analyze and interpret) the problem. Like information retrieval, problem solving is an iterative process. Students may not understand the problem the first time. For every problem scenario, there is an individual level of interpretation that takes into consideration a learner's own experiences, domain knowledge, bias, etc. These all become part of the mental model. To evaluate the effectiveness of the model, learners must be trained to think about how they are thinking—a process called metacognition. The problem from the hotel, tourism, and management course is an example of how learners can be taught to document and explain their reasoning process, and refine critical thinking skills to produce workable solutions.

| Table I. Demonstrating measurable learning outcomes in PBL activities | | |
|---|---|---|
| **Learning Goal** | **Learning Objective(s)** | **Learning Outcome(s)** |
| *Identify* important HTM resources<br><br>*Practice* searching for HTM information sources | *Read* a given problem (individually)<br><br>*Identify* an information need (small groups of 3-4)<br><br>*Construct* a search strategy (small groups of 3-4)<br><br>*Access* information from at least two different research databases<br><br>*Select* one appropriate source and justify two reasons for the choice (individually) | *Interpret* problem<br><br>*List* key words/terms<br><br>*Recognize* known information from needed information<br><br>*Formulate* a search strategy using an appropriate resource<br><br>*Revise* the search/tool selection as needed<br><br>Evaluate information retrieved |

| Table II. Measuring targeted learning behaviors | | | |
|---|---|---|---|
| **Targeted Behaviors** | **Not Proficient** | **Low-Proficiency** | **Proficient** |
| Search for HTM information sources in appropriate resources | The user is not able to identify the information needed<br><br>The user has difficulty identifying which information resource to use to find information.<br><br>The user lacks the skills to access the appropriate information resources | The user has a limited understanding of the information needed<br><br>The user occasionally selects the correct information resource to meet the information need<br><br>The user is able to access the appropriate information resource, but has difficulty navigating within it | The user identifies the information needed<br><br>The user is able to access the libraries' Web site and navigate it beyond the orientation level skills |

*An assessment tool for measuring the learning outcomes* is essential for any lesson plan. Since we do not all process information exactly the same way, one standardized evaluation won't work in the PBL curriculum. This makes grading the activities a bit more time consuming, but much more relevant and meaningful to the individual learners. Although the PBL method is designed for self-directed learning, the process of reaching a particular goal or learning outcome needs to be logical and certain skills should be demonstrated as part of resolving the problem. When applying measurable outcomes and performance objectives to problem solving, the overall assessment plan needs to accommodate all possible paths arriving at the best result(s).

All activities and learning objectives should be clearly tied to measurable learning outcomes within the PBL curriculum. An important part of PBL is observing the transfer of skills from one learning experience to another. For example, the faculty member in HTM helped to coordinate an assessment rubric to measure the outcome of integrating information literacy as part of the PBL.[9]

## Conclusion

PBL is well suited to helping students become active learners because it situates learning in real-world problems and makes students responsible for their own learning. It has a dual emphasis on developing strategies for learning content, and skills, and constructing knowledge.[10] This is best accomplished in collaboration with faculty where the PBL approach builds the information literacy skills directly into the content—without the problem of finding additional time. The integration of information literacy education into any content using PBL, produces learning outcomes that can be seen in stronger problem solving skills and improved critical thinking. The immediate tie-in of these skills to the course-related content—and more importantly to a grade—is the key to success in establishing a stable and consistent information literacy program.

## Notes

1. John Savery, "Overview of Problem-Based Learning," *Interdisciplinary Journal of Problem-Based Learning* 1, no. 1 (2006): 9-21.

2. Barbara J. Duch, Susan E. Gron, and Deborah E. Allen, *The Power of Problem-Based Learning: A Practical "How to" For Teaching Undergraduate Courses in any Discipline* (Sterling, VA: Stylus Publishing, 2001).

3. David H. Jonassen, "Instructional Design Models for Well-Structured and Ill-Structured Problem-Solving Learning Outcomes." *Educational Technology, Research and Development* 45, no. 1 (1997): 65-94.

4. David H. Jonassen, *Learning to Solve Problems: An Instructional Design Guide* (San Francisco: Pfeiffer, 2004).

5. Alexius Smith and Joseph M. La Ropa, "Teaching Students to Think: How Problem-Based

Learning is Revolutionizing the Classroom" *Chef Educator Today* 1, no. 1 (2000): 25—27.

6. Alexius Macklin. "Theory Into Practice: Applying David Jonassen's Work in Instructional Design to Instruction Programs in Academic Libraries" *College and Research Libraries* 64, no. 6 (2003): 494-500.

7. Benjamin S. Bloom, *Taxonomy of Educational Objectives: the Classification of Educational Goals, by a Committee of College and University Examiners* (New York: Longmans, 1956).

8. David Jonassen, *Learning to Solve Problems.*

9. State Library and Adult Education Office. *RUBRICS for the Assessment of Information Literacy* (Denver: Colorado State Dept. of Education, 1996).

10. Cindy E. Hmelo-Silver, "Problem-Based Learning: What and How Do Students Learn?" *Educational Psychology Review* 16, no. 3 (2004): 235-266.

# Teaching as Performance
## Carla List-Handley

Teaching in a classroom is a performance activity. As such, it is difficult to expect someone to improve classroom performance by reading about it; it is much more a "practice, practice, practice" approach that will help beginning teachers. (Throughout this section, "librarians who teach" will be referred to as "teachers.") The discussion that follows focuses less on theory and more on the reality of teaching: action in the classroom. Read this section with a plan to go out and put the ideas into play as soon as possible. And then practice, practice, practice.

## Classroom Issues: Control and Confidence

A truism that few recognize is that control inspires confidence in many situations. Classroom teaching is one. Many new teachers are scared when they walk into the classroom for the first (or first dozen or first hundred) times. Much of their trepidation arises from a sense of lack of control. There are human beings under their purview in a classroom, when much of their previous experience had been working with silent, passive, malleable items such as words on paper or in a book. Human beings, college students in particular, are not inherently under a teacher's control. They talk when the teacher is talking, they use the computer while the teacher is explaining or demonstrating, they ask questions, sometimes unexpected ones. All of the above can contribute to the teacher's feeling that she or he is not in control. Since the students themselves are not and should not be expected to be controllable, the teacher's control of other elements can make the classroom manageable, and that leads to successful teaching. It is possible to use theatrical concepts to determine which classroom and performance elements she can control and then to control them.

## "Theatrical" Teaching

Teaching *is* performance. Even when a classroom teacher uses large segments of active learning activities in which she or he is speaking little as the students interact, the very act of giving students directions about how to complete an activity is performance. The teacher is the "performer" and the students are the "audience." To complete this analogy, the student desks/computers/worktable in the classroom become "the audience" in terms of space, while the whole room is the teacher's "performance space." Performance techniques that help actors can help teachers. And "rules" about performance space should be internalized by teachers to help make them more comfortable in their classrooms.

*Performance* is defined in the *Merriam-Webster Online* dictionary as "a public presentation or exhibition." Every time a teacher lectures, he performs. "I just hate speaking to groups," is a statement made by many. There are classes, online resources, and clubs to help the shy public speaker. There are acting classes for the aspiring actor. Both public speaking and acting offer suggestions that teachers can use, such as "Speak with confidence" and the basis of public speaking, "Tell your audience what you will tell them; tell them; and then tell them what you told them." But there are few resources for those who "perform" in a classroom. What follows is intended to address that need.

## Performance Aspects of Classroom Teaching
### Roles and Role-Playing

Performing/acting/teaching requires that the performer play a role, that of *the performer*. This is also true for the teacher. It is not as difficult as it may sound at first hearing. One plays roles throughout one's day: When a teacher rolls out of bed first thing in the morning, that may be the only moment that she is not taking on a role of any kind. Often within seconds that changes as she puts on the role of *spouse* or *partner* or *roommate, parent* or *animal owner.* The teacher at the breakfast table may be filling a role that is quite different, one might say at times unrecognizably so, from the role she plays on the morning commute. And often that role is shed as she enters the library and takes up the role of *the librarian.* Even as *the librarian,* she plays sub-roles, easily discernible from the differences in her behavior when conducting a meeting and when serving at the reference desk. Similarly, *the librarian* steps into the role of *the teacher* in the classroom. Underlining the existence of roles is the surprise often seen on a student's face when one encounters *the teacher* in a non-academic setting, for example, in the grocery store. Often the behavior of both the student and teacher revert temporarily into that appropriate for both their more familiar roles if a conversation ensues. Usually students are most comfortable dealing with *the teacher* as *the teacher* without having to learn a new role for and behavior to use with *the teacher* playing a different role.

### The Audience-Performer Contract

The above situation illustrates well the fact that students accept their role as students when the teacher is *the teacher*. It is acceptance of a part in a tacit *contract between audience and performer* that is entered into each time a person attends a performance or students attend a class. Under the contract, the audience agrees to be the audience while also agreeing to allow the performer to be the performer, and *vice versa*. The "contract" may seem to state the obvious but it is one of the great strengths that theatre can bring to the teacher. It is a mindset that is held by both sides, the audience member/student and the performer/teacher. A heckler in an audience is reneging on the contract, demanding to be the performer or, at the very least, not to let the performer be the performer. If the heckler refuses to let go of his or her attempt to become the performer, the rest of the audience often can be seen attempting to help the performer maintain his status. The student is involved in this performer-audience contract when she enters the classroom: she agrees to be the student and to let the teacher be the teacher. It may be underscored by observing behavior towards a "heckler" in the classroom: students do not appreciate a class member who is uncooperative or smart-alecky and will disassociate themselves from him or her. They object to a peer reneging on the contract they are a part of. The teacher benefits greatly from the theatrical contract between performer and audience and should learn to rely on it.

## Theatrical Concepts

The audience-performer contract provides strengths in other ways. It brings into play other theatrical concepts that involve space and actors and tools for both.

### *Performer Owns the Space*

As stated above, the whole classroom is the teacher's performance space. The audience agrees to that in the contract. This gives the performer "ownership" of the space, which means he can set rules for it. The teacher simply needs to tell the class that he has rules for her classroom, and then clearly state them. The rules should be commonsensical, involving courtesy towards one's peers and the teacher. A common example of a rule is the "no cell phone" rule; other familiar rules include bans on instant messaging during class, web surfing while the teacher is talking, talking while the teacher is speaking, etc. Such rules are actually appreciated by the members of a class, who usually follow them. But the teacher must *state* the rules clearly at the outset of the class; an assumption that students already know them is unreliable at best. And stating rules should be done as part of the "performance," with good humor—or true humor—so that they are seen for what they are, i.e., rules of courtesy, and not prison-style proscriptions.

In owning the space the teacher should take advantage of his ownership and use the space, as much of it as practical. Many good teachers walk through the classroom while speaking, just as many performances have actors using the audience space for entrances and exits. Not only does such movement demonstrate confidence on the part of the teacher, but it also gives (sometimes restless) students a chance to move in their seats. It can allow the teacher a chance to view student computer screens unobtrusively. A wireless mouse can contribute to the ease with which the teacher can move around the classroom while continuing to use the visual aids he has on a projection screen.

## Performer Tools for the Teacher

The contract described above provides tools that the teacher can take from the stage to the classroom. These include unexpected tools such as the audience and more familiar tools such as the voice.

### *The Audience*

A tool overlooked by many is a malleable audience. When an audience agrees to be an audience, its members allow themselves to be used by the performer if necessary. Many of us have seen performances in which a hapless audience member is taken by the performer onto the stage and asked to perform with him. While often very embarrassed, the audience member does what she is asked, and then gratefully returns to the anonymity of the audience. A roomful of students is no less pliable in the hands of the teacher. Instruction discussion lists have numerous posts about active-learning approaches that use the students in a class to become a database, rising and moving around the room as members of sets. Even uncooperative class members feel tremendous peer pressure to be part of the activity, and such lessons are reported by their teachers to be very successful. Those techniques work because the audience has agreed to be the audience and therefore to be directed by the performer. A teacher can to do almost anything within reason with a roomful of students and they will comply. An accommodating group of students is one of the teacher's best tools.

### *Actor's Tools*

Actors take classes in how to use the tools with which everyone is equipped: body and voice. The training they receive provides tips for teachers/performers.

### Body

The best thing about one's body as a tool is that it is simply impossible for the teacher to forget to bring it to class. And because an audience—students— pick up non-verbal cues so quickly, this tool can be put to very good use. This section focuses on three aspects of the body as a tool: movement, gesture, and voice.

## Movement

The picture of a timid teacher is that of one standing behind a podium or workstation, his or her white-knuckled hands gripping its sides or using the mouse. As stated above, with the whole room under his purview, the confident teacher gets out from behind that "shield" and moves while teaching. When walking through the classroom the teacher should remember to stop walking while a student is talking—asking a question or making a comment—to help focus the entire class' attention onto that student. The teacher wants to avoid pacing or other anxious movement, which can be more difficult than it sounds. One method for controlling nervous pacing movement is simply to move less, walking only occasionally during class. The teacher should use all of her body when moving; she does not aimlessly meander with slack movements (the bane of every director of community theatre!). She walks confidently, pausing to emphasize points she is making.

## Gesture

Gestures also can be used to emphasize points, or simply *to* point—to the screen, to another visual aid, etc. If the teacher is used to "talking with his hands," i.e., using gestures frequently when in conversation, he needs to use them only when they help him underline a point. Too many gestures become distracting. On the other hand, small, timid gestures can be equally distracting, demonstrating a lack of confidence rather than emphasizing a point. One key tip is for the teacher to get his elbows away from his body; tightly tucked elbows are as eloquent to students as arms crossed over her chest. While many teachers are familiar with the closed-mind message from crossed arms, fewer are aware that tucked elbows can indicate timidity, perhaps even fear of one's audience. To demonstrate to yourself, say a line of the lyrics to the anthem, *God Bless America*: "From the mountains to the prairies," in two different ways. First, keep your elbows tight against your body while you gesture with each hand to indicate the mountains on the left and the prairies on the right. Now do the same line with your arms outstretched. It is obvious that the country grows considerably when the line is said with elbows out! Outstretched arms indicate, above all, confidence. This simple change gives many a real boost in that respect.

Facial gestures also are important in the teacher's toolkit. Eye-contact is one part of performance that differs greatly between stage performers and teachers. Onstage, performers use eye-contact sparingly with a goal of not making eye-contact with any audience member unless such a gesture is important in the script. Teachers, on the other hand, should be making eye-contact with their students constantly. This is a communication mode for the teacher because he is often able to read confusion in students' eyes and faces. He can also use eye-contact to help with classroom control. Speaking directly to a student who is breaking of the rules of the classroom often can be the only disciplinary "action" needed to change that student's behavior. It can be a scary thing to do but usually stops the misbehavior as well as quickly winning the rest of the class over to the teacher.

A brief mention of the importance of smiling is necessary when speaking of performing in a classroom. A smile softens the announcement of a quiz as well as rewards a student for a relevant contribution. A smile can be used by the teacher to disguise the grumpy mood she was in before she enters the room; what surprises many is how self-fulfilling such an action is. When she smiles to the students to try and convey her enthusiasm, very often the teacher becomes more enthusiastic.

## Voice

Not only will a smile help the teacher's own mood, it will help his voice. Smiling lifts the soft palate and improves the way sound is generated in the mouth. Vocal clarity is important to the teacher; mumbled or indistinct speech causes even the most brilliant lesson to fail. The teacher may want to warm up his voice before class, especially if he has gone some time without speaking to anyone that day. An easy way to do this (in private, of course!) is for the teacher to sing some of his lecture beforehand. If this sounds too drastic, he can try speaking a few sentences in his lowest register, then in his highest. It's a simple matter of warming up the vocal cords. And to keep the vocal cords lubricated he can drink water during class, but not ice water—that will instead tighten them.

Any teacher needs to be aware of her own vocal patterns. She may be able to spot an annoying pattern in a news announcer without realizing that she has a speaking pattern of her own that irritates others. The easiest way to assess one's own speaking is to use a small, unobtrusive tape recorder while teaching. Many find listening to a vocal recording of themselves far less intimidating than viewing themselves on tape (not to mention the obtrusiveness of filming equipment). A tape recording should alert the teacher to vocal habits such as numerous voiced pauses—"er" or "uhhh"—or repetitive checks—"Okay?" Usually simple awareness of such habits enables the teacher to eliminate them.

A teacher needs to speak *slowly* enough to be followed—especially in ESL classrooms; *loudly* enough to be heard—ask for a microphone if necessary, and *with authority*—to be believed.

## Enthusiasm

Students who have been asked about what makes a good teacher frequently include *enthusiasm* near the top of their list of characteristics.[1] Enthusiasm can be demonstrated implicitly through body language such as smiles and gestures, and explicitly by the teacher telling students outright that he enjoys doing research and is happy to be a librarian. Even jaded students can become more interested when the teacher models good research behavior with enthusiasm.

## Expertise

A tool that is little discussed, especially among librarians who teach, is their own expertise. Librarians are research experts. While a departmental faculty member is a subject specialist, the librarian is the research specialist who can work with almost any subject field and retrieve information. The novice teacher is still an expert researcher. This alone should give the teaching librarian the confidence to enter any classroom.

## Humor

A tremendously important tool in the performing teacher's kit is humor. Much has been written about the use of humor in the classroom.[2] Teachers today must remember that students are very familiar with stand-up comedy and have come to expect their teachers to use humor, but teachers must also be careful not to use comedians as their role models in the classroom. Using humor in the classroom does not indicate a lack of respect for the student or the material being taught. For example, the teacher can state her classroom rules with humor and still be serious about them. The teacher can use funny examples in teaching a research technique and then segue into more serious topics that use the same technique. A teacher might try to create a clever mnemonic device knowing that humor makes many things more memorable for students. Humor and wordplay can be used frequently but being funny should not be more important than getting a concept across to students.

## Props

Anything other than his body and voice that the teacher uses can be considered a prop. This includes technology, which should not *be* the lesson—unless he is teaching an information technology workshop—but rather be used to convey the concepts of the lesson. Props, which could include a microphone and wireless mouse, require user preparation. What props is the teacher planning to use? An example of a simple prop and its preparation is an appropriate writing tool. Does the classroom have the necessary whiteboard markers—with enough ink!—or chalk? Proper preparation dictates that the teacher consider keeping a marker or chalk in a pocket just in case. Perhaps the most important preparation is a good grasp of how much time it will take to use any prop. Will an activity fail if it takes too long to distribute the necessary handouts? If he has students using computers during class, will they have time to find the correct site and do the activity? When thinking of props, the teacher must also think of *planning*.

## Sightlines and Acoustics

As stated earlier, the performance space, i.e., the classroom, belongs to the teacher. There are parts of the space that she can control and parts he cannot. What are the sightlines for the students in the classroom? This is an element that usually cannot be changed, but the teacher can adapt to it. If there is no way to walk completely around the classroom, allowing all students to see her, the teacher should use as much of classroom's sightlines as possible. Can all students see a screen at the front of the room? If not, the teacher needs to think of a way that they can, or perhaps also use handouts of the screens.

How are the acoustics in the room? Even a teacher whose voice carries easily to the back of the room should use a microphone if he will be speaking for any length of time, i.e., more than one fifty-minute period. And one whose voice does not carry should definitely use a microphone. He should not be at all embarrassed by such a need; if a lesson is not heard by all students it is doomed to failure. It is important for the teacher to request a microphone and to be somewhat familiar with using one; if the microphone is wired it may inhibit movement and he will need to be prepared for that.

## Conclusion

Teaching can be fun. It never will be supremely enjoyable for every librarian who steps into a classroom, but it can be survivable by using some of the performance tips above. The greatest reward is having even one student appear at the reference desk following a class and make an offhand remark about having learned how to do this or that part in a librarian-taught class. Looking at the act of teaching as a theatrical activity allows the teacher to use tools from that field to help teach successfully, so that students will learn successfully.

## Notes

1. Thomas F. Cravens, *Students' Perceptions of the Characteristics of Teaching Excellence.* National Social Science Conference, Reno, NV, March 27-29, 1996. ERIC, ED393478; Kansas State University, Center for Advancement of Teaching and Learning, "Characteristics of the Superior College Teacher from Principles of College Teaching." Available online from http://www.k-state.edu/catl/effectv.htm [Accessed 14 April 2006].

2. Billie E. Walker, "Using Humor in Library Instruction," *Reference Services Review* 34 (2006): 117-128.

## Additional Recommended Resources

Advanced Public Speaking Institute, "Public Speaking: Stage Fright Strategies." Available online from http://www.public-speaking.org/public-speaking-stagefright-article.htm. [Accessed 18 April 2006].

American Library Association. Library Instruction Round Table Research Committee. "Library Instruction Teaching Tips." June 1999. Available online from http://www3.baylor.edu/LIRT/lirtpres.pdf [Accessed 21 September 2006].

Jerrie S. Cheek, "Speech and Public Speaking" *Educational Technology Center—KSU*. 16 August 2005. Available online from http://webtech.kennesaw.edu/jcheek4/speech.htm [Accessed 17 April 2006].

Laura A. Ewald, "Commedia Dell'Arte Academica." *College Teacher* 53 (2005): 115-119.

"Free Self-Help Articles," *The Leadership Institute* 2001. Available online from http://www.leader-sinstitute.com/self-help-articles.html [Accessed 17 April 2006].

Ka Leo Kumu, "The Public Speakers' Page," *University of Hawaii Maui Community College Speech Department,* 23 August 2005. Available online from http://www.hawaii.edu/mauispeech/ [Accessed 17 April 2006].

Kenneth A. Feldman, "The Superior College Teacher from the Students' Point of View" *Research in Education* 5 (1976): 243–288.

Peter G. Filene, *The Joy of Teaching: A Practical Guide for New College Instructors* (Chapel Hill: University of North Carolina Press, 2005).

Sabin R. Epstein and John Harrop, *Basic Acting: The Modular Acting Process* Boston: Allyn and Bacon, 1996).

Robert T. Tauber and Cathy Sargent Mester. *Acting Lessons for Teachers; Using Performance Skills in the Classroom* (Westport, CT: Praeger, 1994).

The University of Arizona Library, "TAR 100 & 149—Acting—Library Research Guide," 19 August 2005. Available online from http://www.library.arizona.edu/help/tutorials/courses/tar/100/TAR100149_8.html [Accessed 17 April 2006].

# Motivation
## Trudi E. Jacobson

One of the things teachers often worry about when facing a class is, "Will the students pay attention?" As anyone who has taught a group that isn't engaged knows, it is extremely discouraging. We tend to blame ourselves when students are disengaged and ask ourselves why they aren't motivated to learn. Students in course-related instruction sessions may wonder why they should pay attention, perhaps not understanding the connection between this class and the goals for their course. Librarians and faculty members work hard to counter this scenario by developing and scheduling instruction sessions directly related to assignments, but often more direct attention to the problem is needed to motivate students.

This chapter will examine techniques you can use to help to motivate students. It will address both those that pertain to all teaching situations, including sign-up or drop-in classes, course-related sessions, and credit courses. But because there is much greater scope for motivating students in courses where the librarian is the course professor, the chapter ends with a brief section containing additional ideas for those situations, whether the course is taught in person or online.

## Types of Motivation

Think back to a course that you took as a student, one that you really enjoyed. Can you remember what it was that motivated you in that course? And was it an extrinsic or an intrinsic motivator? Extrinsic motivators include awarding students candy or even a good grade for work well done. Extrinsic motivators do not originate with students themselves, but are external. Intrinsic motivators, on the other hand, capitalize on "the desire to learn—to discover, to comprehend, to synthesize, to develop—[which] is an intrinsic part of human nature...."[1] In the short term, intrinsic motivators may seem more challenging to introduce into the classroom, but they are more lasting, more effective motivators, and they will be the focus of this chapter.

Forsyth and McMillan introduce a number of methods for building intrinsic motivators into a class, including:

• Introducing the course and each topic in an interesting, informative, and challenging way.

• Presenting material at a challenging level that communicates respect for your students and their abilities.

• Using varied and creative styles of teaching to avoid monotony and keep students' interest high.

• Focusing on higher order learning outcomes, such as application, analysis, synthesis and evaluation, rather than on lower-order outcomes such as knowledge and comprehension.

• Modeling enthusiasm for the course content and for learning itself.

• Giving responsibility for learning back to the students.[2]

While it may appear at first glance that some of these methods, which will be discussed further later in this chapter, are more appropriate to a full course than to a single instruction session, it is actually possible to adapt and incorporate each of these in a class that lasts only one hour. Before we start to examine methods for building intrinsic motivation in more detail, let's consider a motivation model that will provide the foundation for the techniques that will be addressed in this chapter.

## ARCS Model

John M. Keller developed a model that helps us focus on key elements connected to intrinsic motivation and also methods for addressing them.[3] The model is composed of four requirements that need to be met so that students will be motivated to learn, with accompanying practical strategies. These are:

**A**ttention: It is critical to obtain and sustain the students' attention.

**R**elevance: Students expect the material that you teach to be connected to their own goals.

**C**onfidence: In order for students to succeed, it is important that they be neither too fearful of the class material, nor over sure of their own knowledge.

Satisfaction: In order for students to want to continue learning, they must feel satisfied with the process or the results of the learning experience. Satisfaction can arise from either intrinsic or extrinsic factors.[4]

Keller stresses that these factors are connected to two important questions: "First, what will you do to make the instruction valuable and stimulating for your students? Second, how will you help your students succeed and feel that they were responsible for their success?"[5] These are important questions to keep at the forefront of your mind when you are designing an instruction session, either in conjunction with the course professor or on your own. When developing a new class, it is critical not to leave these elements until last, but to consider them throughout the planning process. If you would like to include more motivators in an existing class, be ready to alter a variety of aspects of the class, perhaps, over time, dramatically. It is a good idea to start slowly when you make changes, only making additional ones when you are confident about the initial changes.

Focus on Keller's two questions and these four elements whenever you plan instruction, and soon incorporating them will become second nature.[6]

## Teaching Techniques that Enhance Motivation
### All Classroom Settings

Many librarians teach a variety of types of instruction sessions, including course-related, course-integrated, and perhaps sign-up or drop-in classes, for students who would like to take advantage of learning opportunities outside the classroom setting. Some librarians also have the opportunity to teach credit courses. The latter offer expanded scope for integrating motivational techniques. However, even if you meet with a group of students just once or twice, there are a number of motivational tools available to you.

### Teaching Behaviors

Both the attitudes and behaviors of an instructor can have a profound influence on student motivation. Imagine a teacher who is dismissive of the students or bored by the subject material—would you find this person motivating? But genuine interest in the students and their project and real enthusiasm about the class topic would produce a very different reaction in students.

In the ARCS Model, the first element is to gain and hold students' attention. Enthusiasm aids this goal. You can show enthusiasm by speaking clearly, gesturing, moving around the classroom, maintaining eye contact with students, and using evocative facial expressions. Be careful if you are using notes—you do not want to be so focused on reading them that you lose sight of your students.[7]

Forsyth and McMillan stress modeling enthusiasm for the course content and for learning itself. As a part of this, show enthusiasm for what you are teaching in any given class. While you do not have a syllabus and an entire course to introduce to students, you do have a class period, or perhaps more than one. However, students may not really understand why you are teaching them. Forsyth and McMillan encourage teachers to "highlight the stimulating intellectual tasks to be accomplished, pique students' curiosity, challenge traditional views, and hint at inconsistencies to be resolved."[8] An example that many librarians use is to challenge students' reliance on searching the Web for research materials. Setting up dilemmas or inconsistencies and then resolving them, when possible, focuses students' attention and has the potential to be directly relevant to the skills that they bring to this and future information-seeking.

Clarity is another important teaching behavior. Unfocused or confused classes will not engage students. Strive for clarity in all of the following:

- Speaking
- Method of presentation
- Outline
- Focus on major points
- Use of examples to illustrate key points
- Use of visual aids, and
- Review and summary of the class material.[9]

Some of these items may seem self-evident. However, even experienced teachers occasionally forget. It is easy to decide that many topics need to be covered during a class so students will learn all they need to know; it is much harder to select the smaller number of critical points that students must know and focus clearly on them. Help your students by providing scaffolding in a variety of forms that will enable them to understand how the class material is structured and connected.[10] Share your outline with them, either by distributing paper copies or showing it on a screen or board. You might want to provide other "advance organizers" to help students follow the class material as well.[11] In addition, use good examples to illustrate important points. The examples you use may be vital in helping students understand a concept. Before class starts, consciously choose good examples that resonate with students: don't trust that the perfect example will come to you as you teach. And provide visuals to help students who learn more easily through their eyes than through their ears. Don't forget to summarize the class material at the end, which will help students to relate what they have learned to what you identify as the key topics of the class. It will also remind them of elements they had already forgotten.

Bringing clarity to these aspects of a class addresses three of Keller's four motivational requirements: attention, relevance, and confidence. Students who are uncertain about where the class is heading, or who don't understand the material that is being presented, will certainly not feel confident. And if the material being taught is not relevant to their needs, some will not understand why they should bother to learn it.

Your interaction with students can be a strong motivator. It is unrealistic to expect that you will learn students' names if you are only meeting with them once, though you might ask them to identify themselves if they ask a question or if you ask them to participate. Then use those names that you remember. Encourage students to ask you questions and ask questions of them. Provide positive feedback for good responses. If a student's response is not correct, be gentle in the way you respond. Treat students as your equals: be careful not to talk down to them. Treating them with respect also means that you will present them with challenging material. Do so carefully, however, so that you don't move too quickly and cause students to become confused.[12] Through your interactions with students, you are addressing relevance, confidence, and satisfaction.[13] Relevance will come through the participation you encourage, while "techniques such as asking students for opinions and comments show your respect for and confidence in the students, which help them to become more confident."[14]

## Active Engagement/Active Learning

Actively engaging students in the classroom strongly motivates many of them. You are providing them with an opportunity to grapple directly with the class material; to think independently and perhaps express their knowledge and opinions to others in small groups or the class as a whole; and to apply what they have learned to their own topics. The attention spans of adult learners can be quite short. After 15-20 minutes of one type of activity, and particularly lectures, their attention begins to drift.[15] If you are teaching a 50-60 minute class, you have the opportunity to use several different teaching techniques to keep students' attention. However, these techniques, used judiciously, also provide the opportunity to address the relevance of the material to the students, bolster their confidence, and provide opportunities for satisfaction with what they have accomplished.

Many methods have been developed for incorporating active learning in the classroom. Some, such as small group debates and role playing, admittedly work better in the setting of a full course. However, librarians teaching course-related sessions use a number of other techniques that fit comfortably into the time they have available.[16]

### Discovery Learning

Discovery learning is an excellent method of encouraging students to become intellectually engaged. It gives them the chance to explore a topic before they learn it formally, or the chance to expand upon what they have just been taught. Worksheets can be developed to guide students as they work. Depending upon how the exercise is structured, it might be possible to allow students to explore using their own topics, adding to the relevance of the assignment. One example of a discovery learning opportunity is to ask students to compare their results for a topic that they search both in a Web search engine and in a database. While some students may be unfamiliar with database searching, they will be able to do the exercise if you provide enough information to get them into the database. Their relative inexperience with these research tools adds to the challenge of the task, keeping their interest and attention. The questions you pose should be structured to encourage students to analyze the difference between the results, and to evaluate those results for their own needs. Consider Forsyth and McMillan's admonition to "introduce ... each topic in an interesting, informative, and challenging way."[17] Which would be more interesting to you: a lecture on the differences between search engines and research databases, or this opportunity to explore those differences based on your own topic? Not only would the exploration be more interesting, but it would also be more relevant and would serve to build confidence.

An article by Bicknell-Holmes and Hoffman provides a much fuller treatment of discovery learning.[18] One of the categories they address is simulation-based learning. A subset of simulation-based learning is problem-based learning, which was previously covered by **Alexis Smith Macklin** in this chapter.

### *Writing to Learn*

Writing to learn activities provide opportunities for reflection, allowing students to begin to incorporate what they are learning with what they already know. Students find the occasions when they are asked to do the following relevant to their own needs:

- Write a paragraph on what you recall about the material covered in class today.
- Identify one or two questions you still have (this can be done either at the end of the class and cover all the material, or at the end of a particular topic).
- Discuss the most important concept of the session.[19]

Writing to learn exercises provide the instructor with excellent feedback about the clarity and success of a given class. These exercises can also provide an immediate opportunity to gauge student learning and address points students find difficult. If you ask students to jot down one question they still have after a more challenging topic, you can collect and read their questions and address them right then. By asking all students to write down a question, you provide the opportunity for each of them to reflect upon what he or she has learned. If you had just asked students if there are any questions, most will not mentally review the material in the same manner. Students appreciate that you would like to make sure that they all understand before you move on to the next topic.

Actively engaging students in the classroom has a powerful effect on their motivation to learn. You will capture and hold their attention if the techniques you use are well designed and appropriate to the content of the class. You are able to increase relevance and ensure that students gain confidence by allowing them to grapple with the tools and concepts they will use outside of class. This will lead to their gaining a sense of satisfaction.

### Credit Courses

If you teach a credit-bearing course, you will have additional opportunities to enhance student motivation. A number of these areas are mentioned just briefly below, but more information is available in the two resources by Jacobson and Xu, and in the materials cited therein.

### Course Design

When you are developing a new course or revising an existing one, consider motivational techniques from the outset. This will include the way you develop the syllabus and the language you use, the topics you include, the course goals and objectives, the assignments you give, the opportunities you provide for students to make choices, and the instructional and assessment methods you will use. All four of the ARCS elements come into play with course design. Don't expect to get it all right the very first time you design a course—as with all teaching, trial and error is a significant learning tool.

### Autonomy

One quick way to get students' attention is to provide them with opportunities to make choices in your class. Students are not given such opportunities frequently. When they do occur, they are often connected with paper topics. Consider expanding the options to course content, activities, assignments, policies, and assessment methods.[20] For example, in order to increase students' confidence, you might want to provide two assignment choices that meet your goal for a particular objective. These assignments might be quite different, allowing students to select the one at which they feel they will do best. Or you might discuss the topics you plan to cover during the course in the first class period, asking students if there are others that they would like included, or some that they feel they already understand. Since you will not want to take such assertions on faith, explore their knowledge further to decide if you might de-emphasize particular topics. Allowing students such autonomy can be nerve-wracking even to experienced teachers, not to mention newer ones. Tread carefully, and only incorporate those techniques to enhance autonomy with which you feel comfortable.

### Authentic Assessment

Traditional assessment methods, such as exams and term papers, can reduce student motivation. They have the potential to:

- Lack a clear explanation of grading criteria;
- Lack an opportunity for feedback before the grade is assigned;
- Ask only for recall of discrete pieces of knowledge;
- Lack a connection to what students will do in the real world; and
- Be based on a curve.[21]

Authentic assessment methods, such as rubrics, concept mapping, minute writing, case studies, and portfolios, on the other hand, ask students:

> to demonstrate, in a meaningful way, what they know and are able to do. Rather than measuring isolated skills, authentic assessment emphasizes the application and use of knowledge. Authentic assessment includes holistic performance of meaningful, complex tasks in challenging environments that involve contextualized problems. Authentic tasks are often multidimensional and require higher levels of cognitive thinking such as problem solving and critical thinking.[22]

Authentic assessment is effective in enhancing student confidence and satisfaction. For example, if you give students a grading rubric for an assignment, they feel much more in control than they would otherwise. Asking students to submit parts of an assignment before the entire assignment is due allows them to receive feedback and to strengthen their work, which also contributes to their sense of confidence, and ultimately, their satisfaction level. See the chapter on assessment in this volume for a fuller treatment of the topic.

### Online Courses

Courses that are taught partially or fully online provide their own motivational challenges. Many of the techniques discussed in this chapter will be applicable to the online setting, but there are others that will be important for motivating students in this environment.[23] Grabowski and Curtis apply the ARCS Model to the hypermedia environment. While that environment was in its infancy at the time they wrote, their article is still useful for thinking about today's online classes. Their adaptation of Keller's model reformulates the four requirements:

- Interest in or attention to the information and the technology;

- Perceived relevance of the information;
- Self-confidence in the ability to access and use the information; and
- Resulting satisfaction from successful access to and usefulness of the information.[24]

Grabowski and Curtis's interpretation of Keller's model for the online environment emphasizes the importance of students' ability to use the technology successfully, and their interest and confidence in doing so. Beyond technology issues, online instructors need to engage and motivate students who are not in the same room as the instructor or the other students. An online instructor's active engagement toolbox needs to include adaptations of the tools mentioned earlier in this chapter.

Clarity in instructional materials in particularly critical, since students will be on their own when they first look at these items. Tell students exactly how you will be in touch with them, and how they should contact you. Let them know how and when assignments will be made available to them. Make sure that you use a variety of instructional methods, and provide plenty of opportunities for students to apply what they are learning. Course material must be as relevant to the students as possible. Students in online courses may decide that the course is insufficiently connected to their needs, and stop making time to complete the course requirements.

As the instructor, you must be a visible and accessible presence to your students. Bischoff explains in more depth the types of messages that are most successful in achieving this.[25] She also addresses ways to give feedback, both to the class as a whole, and to individuals, that can be extremely motivational to distance learners. Authentic assessment methods work extremely well as motivators for students in online courses.

Electronic discussions are a frequent component in online courses, as a way to encourage student involvement and to gauge student learning. Lang addresses online discussions as a venue for furthering critical thinking by students, and provides a number of ways to enhance such thinking.[26] This echoes Forsyth and McMillan's recommendation to provide challenging material for students, and to focus on higher order thinking skills.

Beyond reading the appropriate literature about best teaching practices in the online environment (which will lead to enhancing student motivation), new online instructors find that learning from others who have taught such courses can be invaluable. Some campus teaching centers will include the topic in their workshop or brown bag series, or you may seek out other individuals who have taught online courses. They can tell you what has and has not worked in their courses, giving you some ideas about how to structure your own course. Many instructors and institutions are sharing materials with others on the Web. One good source of such material is the Instructional Design section of the Distance Education Clearinghouse.[27]

## Conclusion

Sometimes addressing student motivation feels like a juggling act, with four of the balls representing Keller's requirements for motivation, while other balls represent the time available to you, the desires of the faculty member for a course-related class, and even the personality of the class and your energy level on any given day. However, to continue the simile, the conjunction of motivational techniques with good teaching practices reduces the number of balls. As you become more proficient as a teacher, many of the techniques mentioned in this chapter will become second nature to you. Yet it is a good idea to periodically review Keller's elements of attention, relevance, confidence, and satisfaction, and your evolving strategies for meeting these requirements for motivation.

## Notes

1. Donelson R. Forsyth and James H. McMillan, "Practical Proposals for Motivating Students," *New Directions for Teaching and Learning* no. 45 (1991): 53.

2. Ibid., 54-55.

3. John M. Keller, "Strategies for Stimulating the Motivation to Learn," *Performance & Instruction* 26 (October 1987): 1-7.

4. Ibid., 1.

5. Ibid., 2.

6. For a more complete treatment of both motivating techniques and how they apply to Keller's model, see Trudi E. Jacobson and Lijuan Xu, *Motivating Students in Information Literacy Classes* (New York: Neal-Schuman, 2004) and Trudi E. Jacobson and Lijuan Xu, "Motivating Students in Credit-based Information Literacy Courses: Theories and Practice," *portal* 2 (July 2002): 423-441.

7. Jacobson and Xu, *Motivating Students in Information Literacy Classes,* 44.

8. Forsyth and McMillan, "Practical Proposals," 54.

9. Jacobson and Xu, *Motivating Students in Information Literacy Classes,* 48.

10. A number of the succinct POD—IDEA Center Notes, written in collaboration with and available from the Professional Development Network in Higher Education, address motivational areas raised in this chapter. As an example related to issues of clarity, see Michael Theall, "IDEA Item #6: Made It Clear How Each Topic Fit the Course," (July 2004). Available online from http://idea.ksu.edu/podidea/. See also Mary Deane Sorcinelli, "IDEA Item #10: Explained Course Material Clearly and Concisely," (July 2005). Available online from http://idea.ksu.edu/podidea/.

11. Daniel Callison, "Key Words in Instruction: Organizers." *School Library Media Activities Monthly* 16 (Jan. 2000): 36-39.

12. Forsyth and McMillan, "Practical Proposals," 54.

13. Jacobson and Xu, *Motivating Students in Information Literacy Classes,* 55.

14. Ibid., 63.

15. Joan Middendorf and Alan Kalish, "The Change-Up in Lectures," *The National Teaching and Learning Forum,* 5 no. 2 (1996): 1-4. Available online from http://www.ntlf.com/html/pi/9601/v5n2.pdf.

16. For many other active learning ideas designed specifically for library-related instruction, see Gail Gradowski, Loanne Snaveley, and Paula Dempsey, eds., *Designs for Active Learning* (Chicago: Association of College and Research Libraries, 1998); Trudi E. Jacobson and Timothy H. Gatti, eds., *Teaching Information Literacy Concepts: Activities and Frameworks from the Field* (Pitts-

burgh: Library Instruction Publications, 2001); and Carol Anne Germain and Deborah Bernnard, eds., *Empowering Students II: Teaching Information Literacy Concepts with Hands-on and Minds-on* (Pittsburgh: Library Instruction Publications, 2004). Although it is not specifically designed for library-related instruction, Linda B. Nilson's *Teaching at Its Best: A Research Based Resource for College Instructors* (Bolton, MA: Anker, 1998) provides chapters on discovery learning and writing to learn activities, as well as a variety of other chapters about actively engaging students.

17.  Forsyth and McMillan, "Practical Proposals," 54.

18.  Tracy Bicknell-Holmes and Paul Seth Hoffman, "Elicit, Engage, Experience, Explore: Discovery Learning in Library Instruction," *Reference Services Review* 28 (November 2000): 313-322.

19.  Jacobson and Xu, *Motivating Students in Information Literacy Classes*, 73.

20.  Maryellen Weimer, "Let Students Make Classroom Decisions," *Teaching Professor* 15 (January 2001): 1-2.

21.  Jacobson and Xu, *Motivating Students in Information Literacy Classes*, 101.

22.  Kathleen Montgomery, "Authentic Tasks and Rubrics: Going Beyond Traditional Assessment in College Teaching," *College Teaching* 50 (2002): 35.

23.  John M. Keller, "Motivation in Cyber Learning Environments," *International Journal of Educational Technology* 1 (1999): 7-30.

24.  Barbara L. Grabowski and Ruth Curtis, "Information, Instruction and Learning: A Hypermedia Perspective," *Performance Improvement Quarterly* 4 (1991): 2-12.

25.  Anita Bischoff, "The Elements of Effective Online Teaching: Overcoming the Barriers to Success" in *The Online Teaching Guide: A Handbook of Attitudes, Strategies, and Techniques for the Virtual Classroom*, edited by Ken W. White and Bob H. Weight (Boston: Allyn and Bacon, 2000).

26.  David Lang, "Critical Thinking in Web Courses: An Oxymoron?" *Syllabus* 14 (September, 2000): 20-21, 23-24.

27.  University of Wisconsin-Extension, "Distance Education Clearinghouse." Available online from http://www.uwex.edu/disted/index.html [Accessed 28 August 2007].

# CHAPTER 4

# *Collaboration*

Hannelore B. Rader

Partnerships between faculty and librarians can be built through a variety of activities, with robust liaison work serving as a cornerstone of collaborative efforts. Many academic librarians work with their counterparts among the faculty to build the library collections and to cooperate in research initiatives. Librarians also partner with faculty in curriculum planning and support, in instructional activities to teach students information skills and in building partnerships for faculty development. Librarians are in a unique position to become partners with faculty in curriculum reform and achieving resource-based learning for students. However, to make the most of this role, librarians will have to break out of their more traditional reactive mode and become proactive leaders and innovators in their interactions with faculty.[1]

Another area of natural collaboration is resource-based learning, which involves active learning environments where students under the supervision of teachers and or facilitators utilize a variety of information resources to solve problems. Librarians are uniquely qualified to partner with faculty to provide resource expertise and instruction in the application and use of resources. They are prepared to instruct students in finding, evaluating, organizing and applying information to approaches required to locate and use electronic information sources effectively.[2]

Librarians have long collaborated with faculty in instructional development through national initiatives such as:

- EDUCAUSE[3]

This national learning infrastructure initiative focuses on advancing higher education by promoting the intelligent use of information technology through cooperative ventures (meetings, programs and publications) by faculty, librarians and technologists.

- CNI (Coalition of Networked Information)[4]

This partnership involves ARL (Association of Research Libraries) and EDUCAUSE and includes more than 200 institutions representing higher education, publishing, telecommunication and information technology in support of networked information technology for the advancement of scholarly communication and the enrichment of intellectual productivity.

- AAUP (American Association of University Presses) and ARL (Association of Research Libraries)[5]

Collaborative efforts between academic libraries and university presses have produced many innovative projects, particularly related to scholarly communication and to the digitization and archiving of information.

These are but a few national collaborative group endeavors in higher education, which provide opportunities for librarians and faculty members to work together in rethinking and advancing teaching and learning.

Librarians have been able to build on earlier projects, such as sponsoring subject- specific Internet seminars on their campuses which introduced faculty to continually evolving information sources, to becoming partners in designing and populating course spaces in Blackboard or WebCT. Librarians have also taken on integral roles in first-year experience programs and have taken part in activities sponsored by campus centers for teaching and learning. At some institutions, like Purdue, librarians have been tapped for their expertise in knowledge management, and have become partners in substantial grant-funded projects in the sciences.

Thanks to these activities librarians are emerging within their universities as leaders in the information environment where continually evolving formats of information and knowledge continue to have a great impact on learning, teaching and research.

## Collaboration for Instructional Programs

Dynamic librarian-faculty interaction is most important to build strong and collaborative instruction programs. Throughout the academic community in the United States there are many noteworthy efforts describing faculty-librarian partnerships in the library and higher education literature. In particular, small liberal arts colleges have made substantial progress in forming successful partnerships.[6]

Team teaching a course by a librarian and teaching faculty is an excellent way to collaborate. A good description of such an endeavor can be found in an article describing Florida Atlantic University's course on grantsmanship.[7] Technology can be another challenging way of building partnerships between librarians and faculty related to teaching and information access in the electronic environment.

Along with more traditional classroom approaches, librarians are finding great opportunities to advance their information literacy instruction goals by reaching more students directly through student and academic advising services. Opportunities abound to meet with transfer students, returning adult students, students in interdisciplinary first-year experience programs, and with first-generation or minority students who are involved in various campus programs that offer them academic transition support. Other programs that cross disciplinary boundaries, such as writing centers or academic support programs for student athletes, are also natural partners for information literacy and library orientation services.

Distance education also provides many opportunities for librarians to collaborate with faculty. While planning distance courses, librarians need to work with the instructors of such courses in planning the physical and electronic document delivery of information resources and must work with faculty to create appropriate Web pages and/or Web-based resources.

Based on the various experiences described in the library literature librarians need to consider the following when collaborating with faculty:

1. Become acquainted with the faculty and understand the university curriculum

2. Remember the faculty's central role in the curriculum to ensure success

3. Understand course content and how information resources and information skills instruction will fit into it

4. Utilize individual competencies in collaboration endeavors

5. Start small through the use of pilot projects

6. Utilize evaluation and feedback to make revisions

In the current technology environment librarians have to increase their scholarly understanding of the disciplines they support in order to best obtain and apply different types of historical and electronic information.[8]

ACRL has built a number of toolkits that can assist librarians in building connections with faculty on particular issues, such as the information literacy competency standards and scholarly communication.[9] The University of Connecticut also has a liaison toolkit that provides links to services that faculty often request.[10] Many libraries have borrowed this approach to build local pages for their own faculty.

Librarians may find that their collaborative efforts increasingly dovetail with marketing and public relations work that may or may not be done by others in the library. Jill Glover of Virginia Commonwealth University hosts a blog about efforts to increase the library's visibility and partnerships on campus; her efforts were also outlined in a recent *Library Journal* article.[11] These types of tools can be useful, particularly if you are just beginning a liaison program or need to refresh your existing partnerships.

## Rethinking the Curriculum

Educational reforms have been in process for several years and faculty have been concerned about students' acquisition of knowledge and skills to enable them to think critically and to solve problems. Progress in educational reform to address these issues has been slow in part because faculty have needed to prepare themselves for teaching with the most up-to-date instructional technology. In addition, many faculty need training and assistance to integrate electronic information into their teaching.

There is much pressure on faculty to restructure the academic curriculum in order to meet newly evolving learning needs of students. This is a very challenging environment for academia where curriculum development has always been the sole responsibility of faculty. The educational enterprise is looked upon as a process of heuristic inquiry fostering programs for further investigation. If education is to become true to its mission it must utilize access to all types of information resources throughout the learning process. Sharing of information and collaborative learning projects should become an integral part of every classroom experience.[12]

Resource-based learning in all disciplines will depend on incorporating information resources in print and electronic formats into the learning environments, and this will create many new opportunities for librarians to partner with faculty in order to become involved in teaching information skills to students in close collaboration with faculty. Thanks to their rich experiences within the electronic information environment and their excellent experience in teaching information skills librarians are emerging within universities as leaders to deal with new formats of information and knowledge and they are making an impact on learning, teaching and research.

Academic librarians already had to rethink their own processes and their new role in the university.[13] This experience is now helping them to assist faculty in the acquisition of new electronic information skills and in rethinking teaching in a collaborative instructional setting. As pointed out earlier, there is pressure on faculty to increase their productivity and to change instructional strategies. Such demands can be accomplished if instructional collaborations between librarians, technologist and teaching faculty become a strong reality. Involvement in such collaboration will provide librarians with an opportunity to:

- Facilitate the integration of electronic information into the curriculum
- Offer their expertise in teaching information and critical thinking skills to students
- Help faculty become knowledgeable about electronic information formats
- Provide up-do-date physical learning facilities for students

In the future, the quality of academic librarians will be assessed on the basis of how successfully they connect their customers to electronic information resources. They will also be assessed in terms of how well they meet the information and learning needs of the students and the research needs of the campus community. They will be seen as instructional partners with faculty to help students become effective consumers of information.

## Integrating Information Skills Instruction throughout the Curricula

Academic librarians need to build strong relationships with deans, department chairs and faculty in curriculum development. Some of the liaison activities between librarians and faculty can produce important results such as getting librarians on curriculum and accreditation committees. Librarians must actively reach out to the faculty and participate in academic initiatives, such as faculty development on campus, to ensure that everyone understands the importance of integrating information and critical thinking skills instruction into the undergraduate and graduate curricula. On many campuses librarians are members of curriculum committees and teach regular courses in various disciplines. Such activities result in high visibility for librarians among the faculty and the students.

## Creating Successful Learning Environments

A user-friendly physical environment will enhance the learning processes at a university as well as the library. Comfortable furniture, wireless computing, the latest technology equipment, state-of-the-art information access, and friendly experts to advise and help students and other campus personnel are requirements, as is strong library support for distance education and electronic learning. Such environmental conditions will encourage the development of dynamic faculty-librarian interaction and collaborative activities while contributing to a successful learning environment.

## Examples of Faculty-Librarian Collaboration

There are numerous examples of faculty-librarian partnerships in higher education. They vary tremendously in complexity and scope but demonstrate that different types of collaborations can be highly effective for everyone who participates. These partnerships do require a certain amount of entrepreneurship and creativity on the part of librarians who need to reach out to the faculty to initiate cooperative ventures. Listed below are a few examples of such partnerships.

### University of Washington
The UWired program demonstrates how collaboration between librarians, computing, communications, and University Extension can result in campus-wide initiatives on teaching and learning. It was founded as a collaboration between librarians, faculty and information technologists and prepares incoming fresh-

men for using new information technologies and provides a framework for the instruction and assessment of information literacy.[14]

### Kentucky Virtual University

The Kentucky Virtual University (KYVU) and the Virtual Library (KYVL) have been developed to bring education and information to all citizens in the state. KYVU aspires to create a technology-supported, lifelong learning environment that results in better lives for Kentucky's people. It is their mission to serve as statewide advocate for access to learning through technology, a convener of partners that use resources effectively, and a catalyst for innovative and excellence in e-learning. The Kentucky Virtual Library (KYVL) features access to electronic information, print information, digitized special collections, and reference services for all state citizens. Additionally, this virtual library offers several useful Web-based interactive tutorials, developed through various collaborations between academic, public, K-12 and special librarians, to teach students and citizens necessary information skills.[15]

### University of Louisville

The University of Louisville has been building partnerships with faculty in all disciplines through collection development and collaborative efforts to integrate information literacy throughout the curriculum. Librarians, faculty and technology experts are partnering to teach not only the required general education and honor courses but also to teach information and critical thinking skills to undergraduate and graduate students. Other initiatives involve active partnerships in faculty development activities.[16]

### California State University-Fullerton

The librarians at California State University offer another great example of faculty librarian partnerships to provide information literacy instruction for students through a "library survival skills" module to teach students how to find print and electronic information, how to use the library catalog successfully.[17]

### Washington State University

The Library Instruction Department has been particularly active on campus, with partnerships in the Freshman Seminar Program, the new Freshman Focus program, and with providing information literacy instruction to groups affiliated with student support services, such as McNair Scholars, transfer students and TRiO program participants.[18] This visibility led to involvement in academic integrity endeavors, as well, including the Libraries' playing a role in a campus-wide Web site on academic integrity issues, several librarians serving on campus committees that dealt with reframing policies and procedures, and with librarians now teaching a mandatory workshop on academic integrity issues for students who have violated the university policies.[19]

### *An Example of Collaboration for Information Literacy*

The University of Louisville Libraries are a good example of how an organization such as an academic research library can become more successful in the educational enterprise by providing an environment that aids in transforming student learning through cooperative ventures. Utilizing effective leadership and creativity, library faculty and staff have achieved outcomes never imagined in the past.

During the past several years, the libraries have experienced considerable growth in collections and expansion of user services through cooperation with other academic units on campus and in the state of Kentucky. The Libraries' goal has been to become the center for information searching, intellectual discovery, research skills development and social interaction on campus as well as in the community.

Information skills instruction is also a major component of the distance education support provided by Distance Learning Library Services (DLLS).This department was created several years ago to provide off-campus library support for students in the distance education program nationally and internationally. Success indicators of the instructional endeavors have been strong, and demand for instruction sessions given by librarians has continued to increase. Librarians were invited to participate in a newly created Undergraduate Council as well as undergraduate curriculum committees.

## Creative Collaborations

Librarians need to establish strong relationships with other academic departments and partner with faculty in student learning and research endeavors on campus. This will result in cooperative collection building, teaching and research initiatives related to information literacy.

Initiatives such as a collaborative discussion series between faculty and librarians can also be most successful. An example for such a discussion theme can be scholarly communication allowing participants to become more knowledgeable about complex evolving scholarly issues. Such an event can be followed by other symposia and events on educational and scholarly topics.

Librarians can also teach credit courses within the university related to their subject specialties. These experiences offer librarians opportunity to collaborate effectively with the teaching faculty and thus become highly visible in the instructional environment. Success indicators of such collaborations are that librarians become included in departmental decision-making on course development and evaluation.

## Successful Social Interactions

Many academic libraries have broken the food and drink barrier in libraries by providing coffee bars in their building. Despite some skepticism and opposition, all libraries have found the coffee bar to be an instant success, and many have been able to expand hours and services for the increased flow of patrons venturing into the library for coffee and staying for other reasons. Students, faculty, and university staff who might not otherwise see the library as a place for social interaction are coming to the libraries to take a break from their research activities. These endeavors are especially important on urban campus with severely limited social spaces. Thus libraries and their cafes provide opportunities for conversation and interaction between faculty and students outside the classroom. Indicators of success usually show a major increase in the number of persons visiting the library and a substantial growth in library use statistics.

Libraries are building collaborative efforts by making the spaces more comfortable and adaptable to student and faculty needs. In addition to creating more friendly spaces, libraries are also increasing programs such as book exchanges, free coffee and cookies during finals week, and sponsoring readings and lectures that bring in more people from the campus and from the community.[20]

## State-of-the-Art Technology Environment

Many academic libraries are cooperating with their information technology departments to created state-of-the-art digital information environments. Research libraries can successfully transform themselves into a dynamic and interactive teaching and research units on campus prepared for the challenges of the expanding and changing information environment, thanks to various collaborative ventures with other university and community units. Based on the variety of information and research needs of the campus, libraries can emerge as the center for teaching, learning and socializing for students and faculty.

## Conclusion

Higher education and academic libraries are in a changing technology and information environment. Teaching and learning are undergoing major revisions and opportunities abound for librarians to collaborate with faculty in changing the higher education curriculum and learning environment. To be successful, librarians need to be alert, creative and informed about what is happening on their university campus. Many examples of productive faculty-librarian partnerships are already in existence and new ones are created on a regular basis. Librarians at many universities are working with faculty to incorporate information and critical thinking skills instruction into the curriculum so that students can gain fluency in using information effectively and successfully. Librarians who started a few years ago by offering faculty Internet workshops and technology instruction are sought out by faculty for advice and help in rethinking teaching. This is the environment in which librarians and faculty can collaborate to ensure that students are successfully educated and prepared to function effectively in the information environment.

In the changing higher education environment, collaboration between librarians and faculty to teach students information and critical thinking skills will continue to ensure that students will become effective in their future work environments through the use of cultural, visual, computer, technology, research and information management skills.

## Notes

1. *The Evolving Education Mission of the Library* (Chicago: American Library Association, 1992). 90-108.

2. Hannelore B. Rader, "Information Literacy and the Undergraduate Curriculum," *Library Trends* 44 (Fall 1995): 70-78.

3. EDUCAUSE. Home page. Available online from http://www.educause.edu/. [Accessed September 8, 2007.]

4. Center for Networked Information. Home page. Available online from http://www.cni.org. [Accessed September 8, 2007.]

5. Association of American University Professors. Homepage. Available online from http://aaupnet.org/arlaaup/projects/list.html. [Accessed September 8, 2007.]

6. Donald H. Dilmore, "Librarian/Faculty Interaction at Nine New England Colleges," *College and Research Libraries* 57 (May 1996): 274-284.

7. Paul G. Kussrow and Helen Laurence, "Instruction in Developing Grant Proposals: A Librarian-Faculty Partnership," *Research Strategies* 11 (Winter 1993): 47-51.

8. Stanley Chodorow, "The Medieval Future of Intellectual Culture: Scholars and Librarians in the Age of the Electron." Address at the 1996 ARL membership meeting.

9. Association of College and Research Libraries, *Professional Tools*. Available online from http://www.ala.org/ala/acrl/acrlproftools/professional.cfm [Accessed September 25, 2007].

10. Scott Kennedy and Kate Fuller, University of Connecticut Libraries. *Liaison Working Tools*. Available online from http://www.lib.uconn.edu/using/services/liaison/workingtools.html [Accessed September 25, 2007].

11. Jill Glover, "Coffee Klatch," *Library Journal* March 15, 2006. The blog, *Library Marketing: Thinking Outside the Book*, is available online from http://librarymarketing.blogspot.com/ [Accessed September 25, 2007].

12. Mihai Nadin, "The Civilization of Illiteracy," *Educom Review* 33, no. 51-52 (March/April, 1998): 50-53.

13. Charles A. Schwartz, *Restructuring Academic Libraries*. Chicago: ACRL, 1997. ERIC Document ED 414942.

14. University of Washington, UWired. Available online from http://www.cac.washington.edu/uwired/ [Accessed September 8, 2007.]

15. Kentucky Virtual Library. Available online from http://www.kyvl.org/html/tutorial/research/ [Accessed September 8, 2007.]

16. University of Louisville, Information Literacy. Available online from http://www.louisville.edu/infoliteracy [Accessed September 8, 2007.]

17. California State University-Fullerton Available online from http://guides.library.fullerton.edu/introduction/ [Accessed September 8, 2007].

18. Lara Ursin Cummings, "Bursting out of the Box: Outreach to the Millennial Generation through Student Services Programs." *Reference Services Review* 35.2 (2007): 285-295; Scott Walter, "Moving beyond Collections: Academic Library Outreach to Multicultural Student Centers." *Reference Services Review* 33.4 (2005): 438-458.

19. Beth Lindsay, personal correspondence, September 25, 2007.

20. See, for example, Mark Sanders, "Paperbacks and a Percolator: Fostering a Sense of Community in the Academic Library," *Mississippi Libraries* 69.1 (Spring 2005): 5-6; Mary Wise, "Books, Hot Coffee and a Comfortable Chair," *Alki* 21.1 (March 2005): 11-12; and Laura Wight, "Free Coffee and Donuts for Finals Week," The Unabashed Librarian no. 129 (2003): 6-7. There are a number of articles from the late 1990s on how public libraries used the café approach to build customer relations.

# CHAPTER 5

# Curriculum Issues in Information Literacy Instruction

Barbara Fister and Thomas Eland

Through our profession's movements from bibliographic instruction to library instruction to information literacy instruction and all points along the way, one topic has continued to raise discussion and debate. Regardless of what technology is used, or which learning styles are addressed, or even what we call what we do, the question of where we deliver information literacy instruction remains. The question of what's most effective—teaching some number of sessions integrated into subject courses or teaching information literacy as a separate concept—is one that never seems to be fully resolved. When this topic comes up on ILI-L (the online discussion list focused on information literacy instruction), two voices often emerge with the clearest, most passionate arguments for these two curricular approaches. This chapter provides insights from those two voices, Barbara Fister and Tom Eland.

## Course-Related Instruction
### Barbara Fister

The debate about how best to teach information literacy is as old as the argument that it should be taught. To date, the most common framework academic libraries use for providing information literacy instruction in higher education is for librarians to collaborate with faculty in the disciplines by providing course-related instructional sessions and materials, usually meeting with the class in the library for a single period to acquaint students with the library resources and search strategies most helpful for a particular research assignment.[1]

The vernacular shorthand for this approach—the "one-shot"—points to its structural limits. If librarians only have a fifty-minute window of opportunity to reach students, and if those sessions are dependent on individual faculty inviting librarians to be involved without any overall vision of how it fits into the curriculum, it is difficult to build a systematic program for developing sophisticated information literacy skills. Librarians become an adjunct to the course instructor, a guest who rarely sees how the skills they are trying to teach are applied by the students they are trying to teach. Too often, librarians given such a short amount of time end up focusing on research tools and "how the library works" rather than on the more challenging processes of refining a research question, evaluating the results of a search, and understanding the context and content of sources. But the "one-shot," with all its limitations, embraces a fundamental assumption of course-related instruction: that faculty in the disciplines are key players in information literacy instruction and that they share with librarians the responsibility of making it a significant part of the curriculum. In fact, it assumes the single "shot" a librarian has with the students is accompanied by a far more thorough exposure to research skills provided by the instructor throughout the course.

There are pragmatic reasons that course-related instruction has been more widely adopted by libraries than credit-bearing courses. Proposing a course means its value must be articulated and accepted, first by the faculty and then by students. How difficult that may be depends on the campus climate and the local political economy for developing and marketing course offerings. If a course is offered as an elective, it may fail to enroll many students; a library may well decide it's a better use of time to meet for a few hours with as many students as possible in a variety of contexts rather than to spend several hours a week with a small number of students. Making an information literacy course a graduation requirement would reach all students, but it requires a great deal of curricular negotiation and significant staffing, puts a bulk of instructional resources into a single-semester experience—and there still is no guarantee students will believe it is worth their time and tuition dollars. In contrast, developing informal relationships with individual faculty members is relatively easy. It does not require campus-wide acceptance and can be built and nurtured incrementally, as time, staffing, and energy permit. And students are more likely to be motivated to learn material if it has the immediate and obvious benefit of helping them complete a particular assignment successfully.

But there are also philosophical arguments to be made that course-related instruction is a sound approach. Proponents believe information is inevitably embedded in a variety of social and epistemological contexts. Though there is much to learn about finding, evaluating, and using information generally, information is always *about* something, and it can be argued that those skills are best learned in the context of course content rather than in the abstract. Further, what "research" looks like differs from discipline to discipline and how one conducts it will vary depending on the specific task. There is no single process for conducting inquiry, nor is information literacy itself generally considered a specialized body of knowledge that exists apart from the disciplines in which it is embedded.[2] Information literacy should address the broader issues of how knowledge is produced, circulated, and acted upon in society, rather than treating information as discrete bits of material to be gathered and manipulated using standardized rules and processes. In short, it can't be taught effectively as a set of distinctive skills without reference to content or context.[3]

The course-related instruction approach assumes that the entire faculty should be involved in teaching principles of information literacy (though faculty in other departments may not call it that). It takes the position that faculty are already invested in this kind of learning, and are willing to draw on librarians' expertise to improve students' ability to find and use information across the curriculum. It views information literacy as a skill so fundamental it can't be taught by a single department and must be threaded throughout the student's career, building skills incrementally through application in a variety of settings.

## Historical Roots

Though the phrase "information literacy" is relatively new, the notion that academic libraries should be a laboratory for independent learning has a long history. Justin Winsor made the argument in 1880 that librarians should be teachers, "not with a text book, but with a world of books.[4]" In the 1960s Patricia Knapp explored the concept of the "library-college," in which learning would be project based and library skills would be practiced and developed throughout the students' entire education.[5] Though she argued that library skills were best learned in context, taught by librarians and disciplinary faculty in collaboration, her experiment uncovered the very problem that perplexes librarians today: how to ensure information literacy would be taken seriously enough by faculty in the disciplines that it would be explicitly and permanently embedded throughout the curriculum. In the 1970s, Earlham College, under the directorship of Evan Farber, developed a vibrant and much-imitated program of course-related instruction; indeed, course-related instruction that is provided by librarians in collaboration with faculty is often called "the Earlham model.[6]" It is probably no accident that the model was developed at a liberal arts college. A study of libraries' contributions to student engagement found that students at liberal arts colleges are more likely than those at research institutions to report involvement in library research and for that involvement to correlate with other factors contributing to engagement, such as working closely with faculty and discussing ideas with other students out of class.[7] The residential nature and size of such colleges may be a factor, as may be the focus of their libraries on undergraduate education rather than on supporting advanced research with large and complex collections.

In 1989 Patricia Breivik and Gordon Gee published *Information Literacy: Revolution in the Library*, a book that boldly suggested librarians could lead the way in higher education reform, arguing that libraries offer an interdisciplinary laboratory for the development of skills necessary for the modern age and lifelong learning.[8] This book appeared on the heels of Ernest Boyer's influential *College: The Undergraduate Experience in America*, that urged a number of reforms for higher education, including making better use of libraries in developing habits of independent inquiry.[9] Certainly, the notion that information literacy is a basic and essential skill that demands the attention of the entire faculty is one of the chief distinctions between earlier efforts at collaboration—one faculty member and one course at a time—and the more complex and demanding set of skills outlined in the 2000 ACRL Information Literacy Competency Standards for Higher Education.[10]

It's encouraging to note that these standards were endorsed by the American Association for Higher Education, demonstrating recognition beyond libraries and librarians. As the emphasis in accreditation has shifted from teaching to learning, the assessment of libraries' contributions to institutional strength has likewise focused less on inputs and outputs and more on what difference libraries make in student learning, often specifying collaboration between faculty and librarians as an indicator of quality.[11] More recently, information literacy was identified as one of six intellectual and practical skills promoted by liberal learning by the Association of American Colleges and Universities in their *Greater Expectations* report and their 2005 follow-up report on student achievement.[12] Another indicator that information literacy has achieved mainstream acceptance as an educational goal for institutions is the development by the Educational Testing Service of a standardized exam to test information and communication technology literacy that measures not just technological proficiency, but interpretive, communication, and critical thinking skills.[13] Such developments reinforce what proponents of course-related instruction have said all along: that information literacy is a learning outcome shared across campus, not a subject to be taught primarily by librarians.

## Approaches to Integration

The structure a particular library will adopt in designing support for a course-integrated information literacy program depends on resources, strategic alliances, and campus priorities. There is no single roadmap for integrated learning that will work at all institutions, but most academic libraries try to balance the need to teach new students lower-level competencies with meeting the needs of more advanced students whose understanding of how information works has deepened through their exposure to academic work within a particular discipline. The following list covers some of the most common frameworks for instruction.

• *The First Year Experience.* Many libraries form alliances with faculty and staff responsible for courses commonly taken by first year students.[14] This may be a required introductory writing or public speaking course, a first term seminar, or learning communities designed to introduce students to the academy. These courses typically include an introduction to scholarly modes of communication, practicing argument from sources and documentation rules; libraries often use this activity to introduce basic library skills so that students will be able to use the institutions' resources in future. Students at this level are typically focused on practical needs rather than more sophisticated processes of evaluating sources and understanding the social and cultural contexts of information; their assignments are often focused on practicing skills rather than the content of the sources they select, and as a result students often fail to engage with the material.[15] At universities with large enrollments (those that, ironically, have the most complex libraries) a single introductory session may be the only predictable point of contact librarians have with students in the classroom. In some cases, classroom meetings are highly scripted or are replaced by online tutorials.[16] One potential drawback to designing a program that emphasizes reaching every student in their first year is that faculty may mistakenly assume their students have learned in their first semester all they need to know to use the library and other information resources well. In fact, students who may not tackle a significant research project in their sophomore year are likely to have forgotten most of the basic skills they were taught.[17] Further, if faculty decide whether or not to build on basic skills based on students' reports of their own competency, they are likely to be misled.[18]

• *Course-related instruction on demand.* Librarians often develop collaborative relationships with individual faculty across the curriculum, providing instruction for a variety of courses when asked. Sometimes these relationships are built through department liaison programs, with librarians and faculty collaborating on collection development as well as instruction. At other times they are ad hoc connections forged through more informal interactions. These instruction opportunities often offer the advantage of being more closely tied to course content than first year experience courses tend to be. They also typically focus on research tools and strategies that are specific to a discipline and go beyond generic skills. One drawback to this form of instruction is that students are not all at the same level of proficiency, so there tends to be a certain amount of repetition of information, and the only students who benefit are those whose teachers believe in its importance. Because coverage is spotty, some students will complain they have too many library sessions covering the same information, while others may graduate without having any. And carefully nurtured collaborations fall apart when a faculty member moves on.

• *Sequenced instruction embedded in a department's curriculum.* In this scenario, students in a particular program learn research skills in a sequence that builds from course to course, from basic skills in an introductory survey to the integration of an entire repertoire of skills in a senior capstone project. This may seem an obvious solution to the problems raised above, and yet it is far less common than one would expect for a couple of reasons. First, the faculty in a department must agree that some required courses in their major will include research skills in an agreed-upon sequence. The independence many academics cherish in their teaching seems to work against such brokered agreements. Second, the major must *have* a sequence of courses. In the sciences this is common, but in the social sciences and humanities courses aren't always taken in a prescribed order. Further, it is relatively easy for individual faculty to buy into the importance of information literacy as a learning outcome that matters and to build it into their courses. For an entire department to make such a commitment requires a negotiation of values in which information literacy may be placed in competition with other outcomes such as civic engagement, quantitative literacy, global awareness, or new disciplinary content. Finally, librarians who have been involved in such intentional curricular design report it can take years to build up and maintain the level of trust and awareness that it takes for a department to take the leap.[19]

• *Team-teaching.* In some cases librarians meet multiple times with a particular class or even play an equal role with a faculty member in a discipline in designing, teaching, and evaluating student work for a course. Though there are reports that such teaching is effective[20] it is something of an anomaly, perhaps because interest in collaboration is asymmetrical; librarians are deeply invested in collaborating with faculty in the disciplines and believe that their goals for student learning will be enhanced through collaboration; faculty in the disciplines are less aware of librarians' role in teaching and learning and have far less investment in collaboration.[21]

• *Faculty development.* Some librarians have argued that our energies should be placed in preparing the faculty to do a better job of teaching information literacy[22] and many libraries have conducted workshops and other programs to encourage faculty to embed research skills more effectively into their courses.[23] Yet to date, there is no strong movement for faculty development programs to replace the sort of course-related instruction that has been a mainstay in libraries since the 1970s. In part, this may be due to a recognition that libraries have grown more complex than ever with the emergence of electronic resources. It may also be a symptom of librarians' relative lack of social standing that they aren't more often tapped to lead faculty development events. Yet there is some irony in the fact that highly-trained faculty who conduct research routinely aren't considered sufficiently expert to teach information literacy skills to their students—or, if they are not competent to do so, that librarians don't take on improving information literacy among the faculty as a cause as pressing as that of improving students' skills, even though there is some evidence faculty would be receptive.[24]

- *Creating a learning commons.* In the past few years there has been a surge of interest in designing library facilities in ways that encourage learning.[25] This rejuvenation of the cultural capital of libraries recognizes that, in spite of remote access to electronic materials and the ubiquitous web of information available on the Internet, there is a social dimension to learning that values the symbolic common space occupied by the library. Librarians should explore the opportunities for learning through informal social interaction in the library—and through online social networks. They would do well to reexamine ways that both traditional library services such as reference and new technological tools can become more effective sites for integrating information literacy into student learning.[26]

## Conclusion

Though course-related instruction has been a primary means for libraries to promote information literacy, the challenges noted early on by Patricia Knapp remain persistently vexing. Tom Eadie caused a stir in 1990 when he asserted flatly that "user instruction for students does not work." More recently, an essay by Stanley Wilder in *The Chronicle of Higher Education* argued that the information literacy movement is actually "harmful."[27] Both critics described librarians' attempts to integrate research skills into the curriculum as programs that focused on training students in the fine points of search tools without questioning whether students actually needed or wanted those skills. Both suggested that librarians would spend their time more fruitfully reducing barriers to finding information than in teaching students how to overcome those barriers. Though many librarians faulted their characterizations of library instruction as inaccurate, we do not have strong and consistent evidence that course-related instruction has a positive effect on student learning, even though it has been a fixture of academic libraries for over thirty years.

However, there is some recent evidence that information literacy may be gaining wider acceptance outside the field of librarianship. As the focus of accreditation turns from teaching to learning and from inputs to outcomes, and as organizations such as the American Association of Colleges and Universities articulate information literacy as a fundamental outcome of a liberal education—in short, as information literacy becomes a cause for higher education generally rather than a library-driven movement—librarians may find the urge to collaborate less one-sided than it has been since the 1970s, with faculty growing more willing to share leadership with librarians for making information literacy a common goal for higher education.

## Notes

1. Surveys of library instruction methods conducted between 1973 and 1997 indicate that while the number of academic libraries with instruction programs grew, the percentage offering credit-bearing courses dropped, according to Edward K. Owusu-Ansah in "Information Literacy

and Higher Education: Placing the Academic Library in the Center of a Comprehensive Solution," *Journal of Academic Librarianship* 30.1 (January 2004): 3-16; Owusu-Ansah argues in favor of reversing that trend by replacing introductory course-related instruction with a required credit-bearing course. A Canadian survey found less than 9% of Canadian academic libraries offered credit courses; see Heidi Julien, "Information literacy instruction in Canadian academic libraries: Longitudinal trends and international comparisons," *College and Research Libraries* 61.6 (November 2000): 510-523.

2. Sheila Webber and Bill Johnston have gone against the grain by arguing that information literacy does, indeed, constitute a distinct discipline with its own theory and practice in "Conceptions of Information Literacy: New Perspectives and Implications," *Journal of Information Science* 26.6 (2000): 381-397.

3. For a critique of information literacy as a concept that reifies and commodifies information and neglects its context and content, see Christine Pawley, "Information Literacy: A Contradictory Coupling," *Library Quarterly* 73.4 (2003): 422-452; for an argument that it should focus on learning rather than information, and on sociotechnical fluency rather than literacy, see James Marcum, "Rethinking Information Literacy," *Library Quarterly* 72.1 (January 2002): 1-26. Both authors argue for a broader yet more focused understanding of the phrase.

4. Justin Winsor, *College Libraries as Aids to Instruction*, quoted in Evan Farber, "College Libraries and the Teaching/Learning Process: A 25-Year Reflection," *Journal of College and Research Libraries* 25.3 (May 1999): 171. Farber also traces the argument about whether librarians or faculty in the disciplines are better prepared to teach the use of the library back to the 1930s. Harvie Branscomb contended that faculty should bring their classes to the library, while Louis Shores proposed the "Library College" in which librarian-bibliographers would teach academic subjects. See Farber's "Faculty-Librarian Cooperation: A Personal Retrospective," *Reference Services Review* 27.3 (1999): 229-234.

5. Patricia Knapp, *The Monteith College Library Experiment* (New York: Scarecrow, 1966); for an assessment of Knapp's work, see Diane Worrell, "The Work of Patricia Knapp (1914-1972): Relevance for the Electronic Era," *The Katharine Sharp Review* 3 (Summer 1996). Available online from http://alexia.lis.uiuc.edu/review.old/summer1996/worrell.html [22 April 2006.]

6. Larry Hardesty, Jamie Hastreiter, and David Henderson, eds., *Bibliographic Instruction in Practice: A Tribute to Evan Ira Farber* (Ann Arbor: Pierian, 1993).

7. George D. Kuh and Robert M. Gonyea, "The Role of the Academic Library in Promoting Student Engagement in Learning," *College and Research Libraries* 64 (July 2003): 256-281.

8. Patricia Senn Breivik and E. Gordon Gee, *Information Literacy: Revolution in the Library* (New York: American Council on Education, 1989).

9. Ernest L. Boyer, *College: The Undergraduate Experience in America* (New York: Harper and Row, 1987).

10. Association of College and Research Libraries, *Information Literacy Competency Standards for Higher Education,* 2000. Available online from http://www.ala.org/ala/acrl/acrlstandards/informationliteracycompetency.htm [22 April 2006].

11. Larry Hardesty, "Academic Libraries and Regional Accreditation," *Library Issues: Briefings for Faculty and Administrators* 21.4 (March 2001); see also the Association of College and Research Libraries' recently revised *Standards for Libraries in Higher Education* (2004) <http://www.ala.org/ala/acrl/acrlstandards/standardslibraries.htm> (22 April 2006).

12. American Association of Colleges and Universities, *Greater Expectations: A New Vision for Learning as a Nation Goes to College,* 2002, <http://www.greaterexpectations.org> (22 April 2006); for a focus on progress and assessment measures, see *Liberal Education Outcomes: A Preliminary Report on Student Achievement in College,* 2005, <http://www.aacu.org/advocacy/pdfs/

LEAP_Report_FINAL.pdf> (22 April 2006).

13. Background on the test and its development can be found under the link to ICT Literacy Assessment through the Educational Testing Service portal, <http://www.ets.org> (22 April 2006).

14. Collen Boff and Kristin Johnson report that most FYE courses taught in the U.S. include a library component, but what that means varies widely; see "The Library and First-Year Experience Courses: A Nationwide Study," *Reference Services Review* 30.4 (2002): 277-287.

15. Richard Larson offered a classic critique of this problem in "The 'Research Paper' in the Writing Course: A Non-Form of Writing," *College English* 44.8 (December 1982): 811-816.

16. Jerilyn Veldorf describes a process for developing reproducible session plans in *Creating the One-Shot Library Workshop: A Step-By-Step Guide* (Chicago: American Library Association, 2006); William A. Orme describes the use of an online tutorial in "A Study of the Residual Impact of the Texas *Information Literacy* Tutorial on the *Information*-Seeking Ability of *First Year* College Students," *College & Research Libraries* 65.3 (May 2004): 205-215.

17. This observation is based on anecdotal evidence; however a survey conducted in 2000 found that students were not retaining what they learned and, in fact, there was no correlation between amount of instruction and skill level. See Honora F. Nerz and Suzanne T. Weiner, "Information Competencies: A Strategic Approach," in *Proceedings of the 2001 American Society for Engineering Annual Conference & Exposition*, <http://eld.lib.ucdavis.edu/fulltext/00510_2001.pdf> (10 June 10, 2006).

18. A UC Berkeley study found that students' evaluation of their basic information literacy skills were out of kilter with their actual abilities; see Patricia Davitt Maughan, "Assessing Information Literacy Among Undergraduates: A Discussion of the Literature and the University of California-Berkeley Assessment Experience," *College and Research Libraries* 62.1 (January 2001): 71-85; see also Diana G. Oblinger and Brian L. Hawkins, "The Myth about Student Competency," *Educause Review* 41.2 (March-April 2006):12-13.

19. For a thorough discussion of the issues see Beth Christensen, "Warp, Weft, and Waffle: Weaving Information Literacy into an Undergraduate Music Curriculum," *Notes* 60.3 (March 2004): 616-631.

20. Molly Flashpoler reports first year seminar sections that had an enhanced information literacy component with multiple sessions had stronger information literacy test results than sections with a single library session in "Information Literacy Program Assessment: One Small College Takes the Big Plunge," *Reference Services Review* 31.2 (2003): 129-40. Michael R. Hearn also describes a multiple-session experience in "Embedding a Librarian in the Classroom: An Intensive Information Literacy Model." *Reference Services Review* 33.2 (2005): 219-227.

21. Lars Christensen, Mindy Stombler, and Lyn Thaxton, "A Report on Librarian-Faculty Relations from a Sociological Perspective," *Journal of Academic Librarianship* 30.2 (March 2004): 116-121.

22. Risë L. Smith argues that librarians could have an impact on more students through faculty programming in "Philosophical Shift: Teach the Faculty to Teach Information Literacy," in *Choosing Our Futures: Proceedings of the 8th National Conference* (Chicago: Association of College and Research Libraries, 1997) <http://www.ala.org/ala/acrl/acrlevents/nationalconference/97authorindex.htm>; Patricia Iannuzzi provides an overview in "Faculty Development and Information Literacy: Establishing Campus Partnerships," *Reference Services Review* 26 (1998): 97-102.

23. "Enhancing Developmental Research Skills in the Undergraduate Curriculum" is an example of a faculty development program funded by a two-year Institute of Museum and Library Services National Leadership Grant in 1999; more information, including details of the workshop and the grant proposal can be found at <http://www.gustavus.edu/oncampus/academics/library/IMLS/> (22 April 2006).

24. Gloria Leckie and Anne Fullerton, "Information Literacy in Science and Engineering Education: Faculty Attitudes and Pedagogical Practices," *College and Research Libraries* 60.1 (January 1999): 9-29.

25. Scott Bennett provides a compelling argument for designing libraries around student learning needs rather than library services in *Libraries Designed for Learning* (Washington, DC: Council on Library and Information Resources, 2003); see also *Library as Place: Rethinking Roles, Rethinking Space* (Washington, DC: Council on Library and Information Resources, 2005).

26. For an examination of the potential of the reference desk, see James K. Elmborg, "Teaching at the Desk: Toward a Reference Pedagogy," *portal: Libraries and the Academy* 2.3 (July 2003): 455-464; for a broad perspective, see Jean Galvin, "Alternative Strategies for Promoting Information Literacy." *Journal of Academic Librarianship* 31.4 (July 2004): 352-357.

27. Tom Eadie, "Immodest Proposals: User Instruction for Students Does Not Work," *Library Journal* 115 (15 October 1990): 42-45; Stanley Wilder, "Information Literacy Makes All the Wrong Assumptions." *Chronicle of Higher Education* January 7, 2005: B13.

# A Curriculum-Integrated Approach to Information Literacy

*Thomas W. Eland*

Much has been written about course integrated information literacy. The goal of course integrated information literacy is to make information literacy instruction relevant to students by contextualizing instruction within disciplined-based courses that require some sort of research project. Proponents of course integrated information literacy instruction generally argue that it produces a collaborative approach to teaching the research process. The Association of College and Research Libraries (ACRL) information literacy standards and best practices material demonstrates a bias towards this model of instruction, urging librarians to develop a cooperative model with teaching faculty for the delivery of information literacy instruction. Much of the information literacy literature implies that "teaching faculty" are to take the lead in instructional delivery, with librarians acting in a consultative role.

While there is much that is commendable about this model—collaboration is often a desirable educational goal, and in an ideal educational environment would be the norm, ensuring that the expertise of everyone is utilized—there are practical reasons why the model has not and ultimately will not work in higher education. Students and librarians would be better served by the development of a curriculum integrated model.

## What is the Desired Outcome of an Information Literacy Program?

The first question that we must ask as a profession is: "How many students do we wish to reach with information literacy instruction?" Is the goal of information literacy instruction to teach and assess every student who graduates from our colleges and universities? Or is it simply to reach a small percentage of students? The answer to these questions will shape how we develop an information literacy program.

We need to address and answer these questions before we can begin development of an information literacy program. Unfortunately these questions are not seriously addressed by most of the information literacy literature. If we are serious about information literacy, then our goal should be to provide in-depth instruction that is taught and assessed at multiple points in the curriculum to every student who graduates from our institutions. Anything less demonstrates that we are not truly serious about information literacy instruction. So, how do we accomplish this task?

## Traditional Course Integrated Instruction Cannot Achieve Our Goal

There are many reasons why the traditional course-integrated information literacy model will never produce consistent, coherent, and sequential information literacy instruction and assessment that reaches all students. First, it provides no ownership of the information literacy curriculum. The traditional model advances the idea that teaching faculty should be the ones with primary responsibility for teaching and assessing information literacy within their discipline classes. However, the advancement of a field of study, and the teaching of knowledge in that field, is done by faculty who hold credentials in the field and are given authority by the institution to teach and assess student knowledge in that field. But faculties in the various academic disciplines do not consider information literacy as part of their academic discipline. Information literacy was developed by academic librarians, and most of the research and literature concerning information literacy has been written by librarians and library educators. This tells us that information literacy is seen by all involved as residing in the field of library and information studies. So what makes librarians think that disciplinary faculty have the professional interest or energy to advance a field of study and teaching to the point where it reaches all students graduating from our institutions? What academic or professional incentives or rewards would subject faculty have to develop, teach, and assess information literacy in an institutionally significant way?

Secondly, the philosophy behind the course integrated approach does not provide academic librarians with the status necessary to advance the study, teaching, and assessment of information literacy in academe. Academic librarians, even on campuses where they have faculty status, are viewed as playing a support role to the curriculum and to the teaching and research done by the faculty. The faculty see their role as the primary one in higher education, with all other positions existing to support their teaching and research. I do not take issue with this viewpoint; in fact I find it to be essentially correct. Academic librarians can be proud of fulfilling their support role in the teaching and learning process. We build useful collections that support the curriculum and research needs of students and faculty, provide quality reference services, and produce well functioning and easy to use catalogs and indexes. The one thing that academic librarians cannot do from this support position is advance and coordinate a meaningful information literacy teaching and assessment program. The faculty and academic administration at most institutions will never allow support staff to play an institutionally significant role in the teaching and assessment of knowledge. To successfully advance comprehensive information literacy instruction and assessment, librarians must adopt the mindset that they are qualified experts with the appropriate academic credentials to teach and assess information literacy. Therefore, academic librarians must claim information literacy as their discipline.

Lastly, the traditional course integrated approach uses a flawed economic model. While collaborative teaching is a noble goal, and should be pursued when appropriate, it is not the model generally used on college campuses. When collaborative teaching is done, it is done in a very different way from the model of collaboration proposed by those who advocate course integrated information literacy. When faculty collaborate to team teach courses, each faculty member is assigned a specific percentage of the total course credits. Ideally each faculty member would offer the amount of instruction based upon the credits they are assigned, but often team taught courses require faculty members to put in much more time than they would in a traditional course. This is one reason why team taught courses are so rare in the curriculum. But even though team taught courses require more time, they are based upon the standard economic model used by colleges. Faculty members are assigned credits to teach courses, and the cost of instruction is subsidized by the tuition generated. Departments hire and fire faculty based upon the demand for their courses, and the ability of departments to fill class sections with enough students to cover the cost of instruction. But course integrated information literacy instruction completely ignores this economic fact. In the standard course integrated model, librarians are told to offer their collaborative teaching services for free. The model provides no funding mechanism for librarians to recapture the cost of their instructional services. As a result, one of the worst outcomes of this standard model is success. Librarians who were able to convince the faculty and administration that all students should be taught information literacy in a consistent, coherent, and in-depth manner across the curriculum and that all instruction would be assessed would find themselves in the position of not being able to meet demand. The standard course integrated model does not provide the institution with a mechanism to fund the increased number of librarians necessary to build and maintain a collaborative integrated instructional model across the curriculum.

## What Is Needed to Build a Sustainable, Comprehensive Information Literacy Program?

To be effective, information literacy instruction must be integrated into our institutions in the same way that all instruction is integrated. We cannot offer information literacy instruction in a manner that goes against the economic or instructional culture of our institutions. Therefore, we should approach the integration of information literacy at the curriculum level rather than at the individual course level. Stable, comprehensive and sustainable information literacy programs must be developed at the curriculum level, and they must become official components of the curriculum. Information literacy programs that result from agreements between individual faculty members and librarians, or individual academic departments and the library, are not officially recognized at the curriculum level—as a result they are not stable or sustainable in the long term. Because traditional course integrated information literacy programs have not been approved by the official academic body of the institution, they have no official standing in the curriculum, and are unable to be developed in a coherent and comprehensive manner. These programs remain ad hoc efforts that are only capable of reaching a small fraction of the students that graduate from our institutions.

Since librarians at many colleges and universities are not in the position to develop or propose curriculum, they may think these proposals unhelpful. However, rather than arguing against such proposals, librarians should take them as challenges to develop long range plans to transform their situation into one where it is possible to develop and propose an information literacy curriculum. This may not require librarians to achieve faculty status. Librarians might be able to propose curriculum through allies in various faculty departments. But for any of this to happen, librarians must first re-conceptualize their role in higher education, and reconsider what is necessary to make an information literacy program an official part of the college curriculum. What is required is a paradigm shift on the part of academic librarians.

## Criteria For an Effective Information Literacy Program

To be effective, information literacy instruction and assessment must be comprehensive in scope and reach all the students who graduate from our institutions. There will be different levels of information literacy instruction for different types of students. Undergraduates in technical fields will require a different type of information literacy instruction from undergraduates in the liberal arts.

Freshman and sophomores will need to be taught the basics of information literacy and receive instruction from a multi- or cross-disciplinary perspective. Juniors, seniors and graduate students will need more specialized instruction related to their majors and fields of research.

Information literacy instruction and assessment must also have clear learner objectives and outcomes that are assessed consistently across the entire instructional program and curriculum. Students must be aware that what they are learning is considered an important part of their education, and is required of a college educated person. Learning is a process that requires students to have clear objectives and useful and timely feedback so that they can learn from what they have done and apply what they have learned in new situations. An information literacy curriculum must be structured to give students the opportunity to learn and apply the knowledge, concepts and skills taught at multiple places throughout the curriculum.

To be effective, information literacy instruction and assessment must build on the introductory foundational knowledge taught in the freshman and sophomore years and be infused throughout the rest of the curriculum. Academic librarians must be intimately involved in this process, either as the primary instructors, or as team teachers and co-assessors, or at a minimum as consultants to teaching faculty. This approach to teaching information literacy provides a rationale for academic librarians holding subject masters or doctorate degrees. Teaching librarians who hold graduate degrees in other subject fields can offer advanced information literacy instruction in their secondary area of expertise, and/or collaborate more closely with faculty in those areas to design information literacy instruction and assessment at the upper division and graduate level.

Information literacy instruction and assessment should be viewed as one of the communications disciplines, or as a key component in the assessment of critical thinking. Information literacy instruction has goals similar to writing, reading, and speech instruction. As such it should be done by faculty who are experts in the field, just as writing, reading, and speaking are taught and assessed by faculty who are experts in their fields. Librarians are the experts in knowledge organization, translating an information need into a search strategy, developing and applying appropriate search techniques, the evaluation of resources, and the social context in which information is produced, disseminated, organized and used. To be an effective researcher, a person must understand the political, economic and cultural contexts in which information is produced and organized. While librarians are not the only ones who know about the information production and distribution process, as a profession we know it better than most, and we know it in a cross-disciplinary way that most faculty do not understand. Librarians also have a broader understanding of intellectual property, and have the ability to teach students why and how information property laws affect society. Students must also understand why intellectual freedom is important for democratic systems of government, and their role and responsibilities as citizens. Librarians offer students a unique and important perspective on all these issues that other faculty and disciplines cannot duplicate.

## The Minneapolis Community & Technical College Model

No two institutions are exactly alike, and what works at one institution may not work at another. However, for those interested in developing a curriculum based information literacy program, many aspects of the Minneapolis Community & Technical College (MCTC) program will apply.

### *Conceptualizing the Program*

The first step is to conceptualize the program you ultimately want. Institutions of higher education are very political environments and they are cautious and resistant to major changes in the curriculum. You will likely need to make compromises to get an information literacy program started, but if you are clear about your ultimate goals, you should be able to strategically build a program over time to reach those goals.

At MCTC, we developed a plan to build an information literacy curriculum during the 1997-1998 academic year. Our state college and university system was moving from a quarter to a semester system beginning with the 1998-1999 academic year. As a result the entire curriculum was reviewed and revised, with all classes migrating from quarter to semester credits. For the library the switch to semesters meant a drastic change for our bibliographic instruction program. We had developed a strong bibliographic instruction program over the years in which we provided two hours of instruction for every section of English Composition 1, and four hours of instruction for every section of English Composition 2. We also provided one hour bibliographic instruction sessions for upper level ESL and developmental reading courses, and for many classes in the humanities and social sciences. However, the library faculty was never happy with the results because the instruction did not allow us to assess student learning in a meaningful or comprehensive way, and we were unable to teach anything but basic skills. The move from a quarter to semester system meant a fifty percent increase in bibliographic instruction each semester and there was no way that we could accommodate the increase.

The library faculty discussed the idea of a curriculum-based information literacy program and what it meant in terms of library faculty workload, student learning, and the consequences for discipline faculty. We decided that our ultimate goal should be a required two or three semester credit freshman information literacy class that would be housed in a newly created Information Studies department chaired by the faculty library coordinator. The library faculty also envisioned the creation of more advanced level information literacy classes, as well as liberal arts course offerings in Information Studies.

### Moving the Program Forward

Our first step was to transform an existing library skills course into a true information literacy course. Two library faculty members took the lead and redesigned the course. The library skills course was a 2 quarter lecture credit class which meant that it converted to a 1 credit lecture semester class. The library faculty realized that this would not give us enough time to teach the content that we wished to cover, but since we were recommending that the course be made a requirement for the Associate of Arts degree, we knew that taking more than one credit from the degree electives would be politically unwise. If the information literacy course proved to be a success we could go back to the curriculum committee and ask for an increase in credits.

We sought and gained the support of our Academic Vice President and the English department. Both were crucial allies whose support was necessary. The library faculty held many candid conversations with the English faculty over who was best qualified to teach information literacy. Some English faculty expressed concern over the potential negative impact on their workload if they dropped the teaching of research skills from English composition. It was finally decided that the library faculty were the ones most qualified to teach information literacy and that removing the teaching of research skills from English composition classes allowed the English faculty to spend more time teaching the writing process.

The proposed one lecture credit information literacy course was approved by the curriculum committee in January 1998, and was first offered fall semester 1998 and became a requirement for the Associate of Arts transfer degree. The first year was a transition year. Four sections of INFS 1000: Information Literacy & Research Skills were offered fall semester, with six sections in the spring. The library faculty also continued to offer a reduced number of bibliographic instruction sessions. After the transition year the library dropped all bibliographic instruction.

### Where We are Today

Three years after the introduction of INFS 1000 we went back to the curriculum committee and requested the course be increased to 1 lab credit—a lecture credit is 50 minutes per week, and a lab credit is 100 minutes. The change allowed us to double our student contact time while not taking more credits from the degree electives. The course had proven to be a success and gained widespread support of the faculty and administration. However, students complained that the course required too much work for 1 credit, so we gathered information over a two year period and used it to support a request to increase the class to 2 credits. We also held discussions with the English faculty for the need to make INFS 1000 a prerequisite to English Composition 2. The English faculty was concerned about this approach. In the end, the library and English faculty decided to request that English Composition 1 and INFS 1000 be required within the first 24 credits of the Associate of Arts degree. The English faculty also supported the library's request to increase INFS 1000 to 2 credits (1 lecture, 1 lab). The new requirements were approved and went into effect fall semester, 2004.

The Library & Information Studies faculty also developed three liberal arts courses in Information Studies, an A.S. degree and two certificates in Library Information Technology, and an additional 1 lecture credit information literacy class (INFS 1005) aimed at technical and professional degree program students. Beginning fall semester 2006, the A.S. in Business Administration program will require students to take either INFS 1000 or INFS 1005 as a program course requirement. The A.S. in Child Development requires INFS 1005, and the Information Technology and Graphic Design departments recommend INFS 1005 as a general education elective for their program students.

During the 2003-2004 academic year the college created a Communications Caucus with the intent to design and assess the communications knowledge and skills of students across the curriculum. Writing, reading speech, and information literacy were identified as communication disciplines. The Library and Information Studies faculty worked with English, Reading, and Speech faculty, academic administrators, and other disciplinary faculty to develop assessment rubrics for writing, reading, speech, and information literacy. These assessment rubrics have been used with faculty in various departments to create and assess learning in each area. The college has also performed campus wide assessment of student knowledge and skills in each of the areas.

Our curriculum-integrated model works with the economic modeled used by our college to fund instruction. Tenured Library & Information Studies faculty are able to teach six sections of INFS 1000 and two sections of INFS 1005 per semester, along with one section of our other Information Studies classes. Additional sections of INFS 1000 are taught using adjunct library faculty. This funding model has allowed the library to build its staff and faculty from an original size of one full-time ten month library technician and four tenured library faculty in 1997-1998, to four full-time twelve month library technicians, six tenured library faculty, and an additional two to four adjunct library instructors per year.

## INFS 1000 Pedagogy

From the beginning the library faculty decided that INFS 1000 would be a competency based course. We adapted the ACRL Information Literacy Standards for use in the course. Our goal was to assess individual student learning, individual class section outcomes, and overall program outcomes. As a result, we developed the course so that all sections would use a common syllabus, common in-class exercises and take home assignments, and a common mid-term and final competency examination project. This past year we also added a common true/false and multiple choice pre- and post-test. From the beginning we used a common scoring sheet with the mid-term and final examination projects, which allowed us to assess specific information literacy outcomes. We use these grading sheets to score the exams and produce an annual information literacy program assessment report. Over the years we developed a more precise assessment rubric to score the exam. The exam rubric proved so useful that we designed assessment rubrics for use with the individual homework assignments. Not only do these rubrics provide faculty with an objective set of criteria to assess student learning, they also provide students with a clear understanding of why and how they are being assessed.

To be information literate, students must understand the political, economic and social contexts in which information is produced, distributed and organized, and they must understand this before they attempt to search for and evaluate information. As a result, INFS 1000 was developed using a critical information literacy approach. The implications of this approach are described well by Michelle Holschuh Simmons in her article, "Librarians as Disciplinary Discourse Mediators: Using Genre Theory to Move Toward Critical Information Literacy." Simmons summarizes the underlying philosophy of the MCTC information literacy program well when she states that:

Critical information literacy is a deliberate movement to extend information literacy further than the acquisition of the research skills of finding and evaluating information. Instead, it is the 'refram[ing] [of] conventional notions of text, knowledge, and authority' in order to ask more reflective questions *about* information: "Who owns and sells knowledge?" "Who has access to information?" and "What counts as information (or knowledge)?" Additional questions such as "Whose voices get published?"—or more importantly—"Whose voices do not get published?" are the types of questions that can help students begin to see scholarly communication as a dialogic, political, and contested process. These types of questions encourage students to see that information is not neutral but that it reflects social, political, and economic ideologies that are situated within an historical context.[1]

INFS 1000 course material—including syllabi, assignments, examinations, grading rubrics, and annual program reports—can be found on our course web page <http://www.minneapolis.edu/library/courses/infs1000/support.htm>. The material is updated often.

## Conclusion

While the specific instructional model used by MCTC might not apply at every college or university, the development of a curriculum-integrated information literacy program is a possibility at many institutions. If information literacy instruction and assessment is going to move from the fringes of higher education to its core, and thereby reach all of our students, it must become an official part of the curriculum. A program of information literacy instruction must be offered in the same manner as other instruction is offered on our campuses, and the program must be housed in a department with the expertise and inclination to advance the curriculum and the field of study. The only people with the knowledge, interest, or desire to advance a serious information literacy program in academia are librarians. The challenge for academic librarians is to alter our traditional paradigm which sees us as supporters of the teaching and research mission, to a new paradigm that sees us as active teachers and researchers, and as "the experts" in information literacy.

## For Further Reading

Cushla Kapitzke, "Information Literacy: A Positivist Epistemology and a Politics of *Out*formation." *Educational Theory* 53, no. 1 (2003): 37-53.

Christine Pawley, "Information Literacy: A Contradictory Coupling." *Library Quarterly* 73, no. 4 (2003): 422-52.

Jeremy J. Shapiro and Shelly K. Hughes, "Information Literacy as a Liberal Art: Enlightenment Proposals for a New Curriculum." *Educom Review* 31, no. 2 (1996). Available online from http://www.educause.edu/pub/er/review/reviewArticles/31231.html. [Accessed August 21, 2006].

Michele Holschuh Simmons, "Librarians as Disciplinary Discourse Mediators: Using Genre Theory to Move toward Critical Information Literacy." *portal: Libraries and the Academy* 5, no. 3 (2005): 279-311.

## Notes

1. Simmons, Michele Holschuh. "Librarians as Disciplinary Discourse Mediators: Using Genre Theory to Move Toward Critical Information Literacy." *portal: Libraries and the Academy* 5, no. 3 (2005): 279-311.

# CHAPTER 6
## *Program Management*

Mary C. MacDonald

A review of advertisements for Information Literacy (IL) Manager or Coordinator positions presents the following list of responsibilities: plan, coordinate, manage, implement, market, recruit, staff, train, schedule, teach, evaluate, and assess. You may find yourself in the situation of having just been hired, appointed, or convinced to fill the position that will manage or coordinate the information literacy program at your library. IL program managers must have in-depth knowledge of information literacy and be skilled instruction librarians; beyond this, there is an ever-growing repertoire of skills that will enable you to reach the goals set for your program. However, outside of a possible management course in library school, many information literacy program managers are unprepared for the myriad of tasks that await them as coordinators or managers of an IL program. At the Twenty-ninth LOEX conference, Mary Jane Petrowski summarized the role of an Information Literacy Manager, stating that "IL program managers assume multiple roles, focus externally as well as internally, and understand the importance of relationship building. We all have to be able to solve problems, communicate, facilitate group process, network, nurture, market, take risks, build teams [and] exercise political savvy."[1]

Of all of the important items noted above, two abilities will become the "backbone" or anchor of any IL manager's success: the ability to imagine and the ability to effectively communicate. Imagination is more often listed in the repository of abilities expected of leaders than of managers, but to manage effectively one must be able to imagine all possible variables and options for the IL program that will satisfy and sustain your institution's IL needs. In a letter written to a fellow artist, Vincent Van Gogh wrote, "in my opinion, two things that reinforce one another and remain eternally true are: Do not quench your inspiration and your imagination, do not become the slave of your model; and, take the model and study it, otherwise your inspiration will never get plastic solidity."[2] Van Gogh encourages the reader to continually search for inspiration to feed the imagination, and to keep an open mind to new explorations and new ideas. Though Van Gogh is speaking of painting, we can easily transfer these recommendations to those responsible for designing, implementing and maintaining an IL program. Set your mind free of what is now, what must be, what cannot be, what you do not have staffing for, or do not have funding for, and think of only one thing—how your IL program can best support student learning achievement.

IL managers may have responsibility for a variety of areas. This chapter will briefly discuss areas that will help you to succeed as an IL manager or coordinator regardless of specific responsibilities, namely creative thinking; communication; planning; staffing and training; and marketing and outreach.

## Creative Thinking

How many times have you been asked or asked others to "think creatively," or to think "outside of the box?" For many of us, we have heard and read the phrase so often that it has lost its impact. Here then, are several examples that will help get you and your colleagues jump-started as you reconsider, or re-connect with the ideas of thinking creatively. Ed Bernacki reminds us that "thinking inside the box means accepting the status quo," while thinking outside of the box

> "requires different attributes that include a willingness to take new perspectives to day-to-day work, an openness to do different things and to do things differently, being able to focus on the value of finding new ideas and acting on them, striving to create value in new ways, listening to others, and supporting and respecting others when they come up with new ideas .... [it] requires openness to new ways of seeing the world and a willingness to explore. Out of the box thinkers know that new ideas need nurturing and support."[3]

Here again, we see the need for IL managers to focus on using their imagination and communication abilities. Further, he states, "they also know that having an idea is good but acting on it is more important."[4] IL managers are people who have the ideas, who listen to ideas from their colleagues, and make the ideas happen. Creative thinking can require a change of mindset from the typical work setting.

When creative thinking gets stalled, it can be difficult to get reactivated. One approach to consider is Todd Packer's "thinking *inside* the box." Packer suggests a seven-step plan for people who want or need to stay "inside the box." The seven steps are based on how children play and are intended to produce results that will unleash "innovation potential." The steps are:

1. See mud, find grid.
2. Accept your messy box.
3. Name your mess.

4. Find your crystal question.
5. Use only four words.
6. Play more.
7. Share your mess.

These steps involve finding the regular patterns within the mess of our daily work, accepting the mess, identifying the variables that impact the mess, finding the essential "crystal" question, using key words to "frame positive change" and play with these ideas, and finally, sharing the mess with each other as a means to develop change in the group, program or institution.[5]

Esther Grassian and Joan Kaplowitz have offered several methods for creative problem solving (CPS), noting that "you can help create a culture of creativity and mutual respect by focusing on defining, and solving problems that we all face by using CPS techniques …You may even recognize some of these techniques as cooperative or active-learning methods you have used in synchronous in-person or remote teaching."[6]

The chart below outlines their techniques.

| **Sample Creative Problem-Solving Techniques**[7] | |
|---|---|
| 1. "Brain Writing Pool" (VanGundy 2003, p. 153) | |
| a. | 5-8 people sit at a table and individually write down a list of up to four ideas. |
| b. | All ideas are placed in the middle of the table. |
| c. | Each person takes someone else's sheet of ideas, adds to it, and puts it back in the middle of the table. |
| d. | Participants keep exchanging sheets of paper and adding ideas for 10 to 15 minutes. |
| 2. "The Outrageous Idea" (Prather and Gundry 1995, p. 38) | |
| a. | Identify a problem. |
| b. | Get a group of staff together and ask them to come up with some outrageous suggestions to solve the problem. |
| c. | The first few suggestions may be unthinkable, but they will generate new and interesting ideas that you might want to consider. |
| 3. "Gallery Method" (Van Gundy 1992, pp. 154-155) | |
| a. | Flip chart pages are posted around a room, one for each person in the group. |
| b. | Each person silently writes her or his ideas on a page, all at the same time, for a specified period of time. |
| c. | Group members walk around, silently review other people's flip chart pages, and take notes. |
| d. | Participants add new ideas, comments, and improvements to others' flip chart pages. |

| 4. "Force Field Analysis" (Robson 1993, Chapter 9) | |
|---|---|
| a. | The facilitator states the problem and points out that here are opposing forces, some working to improve it, others working to worsen it. |
| b. | Participants identify both types of forces and rank them in importance. |
| c. | Participants then rank these forces in terms of how easily they can be influenced and by whom—"us" or "them". |
| 5. "Nominal Group Technique (NGT) (Andersen and Fagerhaug 2000, pp.49-53) | |
| a. | Individually, group or participants write down ideas, one per card. |
| b. | The facilitator assigns a letter to each idea and writes the ideas on a flip chart. |
| c. | Group members ask for clarification and combine duplicate ideas. |
| d. | Each person individually ranks the ideas on cards, assigning points (up to 5) for each idea. |
| e. | The facilitator totals the points and lists the ideas in prioritized order by number of points. |
| 6. "Brutethink" (Michalko 1991, pp. 159-171) | |
| a. | Identify a challenge. |
| b. | Select a random concept or word. |
| c. | Write down a list of related actions, concepts, and words. |
| d. | Force yourself to make some connections between the challenge and any of the other actions, concepts, or words. |
| Note: See also the Web page, "Creativity Techniques", for a very long list of links to descriptions of many different CPS approaches for individuals and groups, including references to sources of many of these techniques (Mycoted 2003). | |
| (http://www.mycoted.com/Category:Creativity_Techniques) | |

Reprinted with permission, Neal-Schuman Publishers, Inc. from *Learning to Lead and Manage Information Literacy Instruction*, copyright 2005.

## Communication

All management requires good communication skills, but success at managing an IL program is nearly impossible to do without great communication skills. In order to fulfill the responsibilities of an IL manager as outlined in the beginning of this chapter we must each build networks of communication that can flow to and from every level of the institution: with individuals, within your unit or department, throughout your library, the institution, and even beyond campus to the public arena.

Although there are many theories about how people communicate, and many methods and tools to help one improve both interpersonal and group communication style, the most important tools are an open ear, an open mind, and a fair bit of diplomacy. A familiar way to think about good communication style is through the lens of a reference librarian. Many IL managers have worked or continue to work as reference librarians and are skilled in the art of the reference interview. An IL manager who uses these same skills in communicating with administrators, colleagues and staff will encourage open lines of communications. There is virtually no act of communication that cannot benefit from the use the reference interview process: the use of active listening, open-ended questions, neutral questions, probing questions, and closure.

A manager who uses active listening acknowledges and encourages the other person's comments and ideas, showing respect and appreciation for their time and the energy spent in investing in the project or problem at hand. As you listen more closely to your colleagues you will also be able to see things from that person's point of view, which can be enlightening. Carefully listening to an individual's or group's thoughts and ideas will produce a variety of possibilities to solve the question or problem at hand, instead of falling into the trap of "my way or no way." In addition to the spoken word, be mindful of the many non-verbal cues expressed by colleagues that as reference and/or instruction librarians we are trained to observe and respond to. The facial expression, physical stance and physical space used during any communication process can be enormously informative to the astute observer.

While experience teaches us that effective communication includes much more listening than responding, as managers, it is very often our own communications that we remember best. Working to recognize and understand our individual communication style helps to reveal how we might work with and manage a group of colleagues. Knowing that there are different communication styles helps to develop recognition and respect for the differences in those with whom you work, and with those whom the IL program will serve. It is possible to identify varying communication styles by identifying psychological type or personality characteristics, such as Myers-Briggs.

Some people have a natural or innate sense when it comes to management, but for many, the skills can be developed over time and with experience. There are several models of interpersonal communication that can help us to understand and improve our own management style. Chris Argyris and Donald Schön provide several models of interpersonal communication with important implications for the success of IL managers, arguing that "individual behavior is controlled by personal theories for action—assumptions that inform and guide behavior."[8] Argyris and Schön call these "espoused theories," used by managers to "describe, explain or predict their behavior."[9] In response to this, Argyris and Schön developed two models called *Theories-in-use* that describe observable behaviors, with one clearly the more effective model. Theories-in-use, Model

I and Model II, are used to describe two opposing methods of how managers communicate within organizations. Model I describes a manager who operates under the assumption that they must always be in complete control and on the offensive or risk being done in by someone else in the organization.[10] Model II, however, describes a manager who can "express openly what they think and feel, and actively seek understanding of others' thoughts and feelings."[11] At first glance it may seem easier and simpler for you as a manager to closely control of the flow of information and to do the lion's share of decision making on your own; but this behavior weakens the fabric of collegiality and reduces the intellectual growth and development of the organization, thus hampering imagination and creative thinking—those key ingredients which will launch and sustain your IL program!

Once you have built a framework for success by employing active listening skills, understanding your individual communication style, recognizing interpersonal communication style differences, understanding personality types or differences, and developing a positive and effective organizational communication strategy, you will need to ensure that communication is flowing freely within, around and through your IL program.

To keep the IL program moving in the right direction it is important to hold both planning meetings and other less formal work-group or workshop sessions. For instance you may arrange to hold regular monthly planning meetings and quarterly workshop sessions with your group of information literacy instructors. You will also want to invite, perhaps on an occasional or as-needed basis, other IL support staff to your meetings. Information technologists or instructional designers that have a vested interest in the IL program will enrich meetings and lessen the follow up time for projects that include them.

When scheduling meetings and work sessions for your group be sure to consider the impact of the academic calendar on your plans. Prepare an agenda and send it to all involved in time for them to use the information to prepare for the meeting. Whenever possible, it is useful to meet briefly with those who are on the upcoming agenda to discuss their ideas, proposals or reports before the actual meeting to encourage a productive and efficient meeting. Share expectations with the group about how the meeting will proceed, how a record of the meeting will be prepared and when the report will be shared with a larger group. You will also want to be certain that the results of your meetings are sent beyond your group to inform others in the library, such as your boss, other project groups, library administration, as well as other college deans and program administrators, and even, if possible, the provost and president.

Careful meeting minutes are a must, and these may become part of your annual report, along with serving as the basis for other important documents such as executive summaries and accreditation reports. For example, at the University of Rhode Island, we hold monthly meetings for our IL credit-course instructors. I report the results of this meeting at the monthly Public Service Unit Heads Meeting and at the Public Services General Meeting, and in turn, the Chair of Public Services reports all of our activities at the monthly Library Faculty Meeting. This chain of communication keeps everyone informed and provides various feedback and decision making mechanisms. Our meetings cover a wide variety of issues such as pedagogy, classroom management, assignment design, current projects, future projects, logistics and long term planning.

You may want to create an instruction department or team page for your library's web site, a listserv for your IL instructors and perhaps even a blog or wiki depending on the projects at hand and the time allotted for maintaining each communication tool. Will you be able to maintain all of these communication tools? Perhaps not, but test a few and find out which work best for your group. Perhaps you will use a blog or wiki for a particular project, but run a permanent listserv for ongoing discussion. Set meetings at regular intervals for various groups that will be involved directly in the planning and teaching of your information literacy program. Create open lines of communication using phone trees, e-mail mailing lists, chat, blogs, wikis, and the old fashioned open door with a cup of coffee. At the University of Rhode Island, many of us work near each other, and when a mini-crisis or a great idea happens, people generally cluster in the hallway to get feedback on it. We have often mused about our very productive and informal hallway conversations, but by identifying the fact that, indeed, these conversations are useful, we have almost institutionalized them for our group. Formally, we hold monthly meetings to discuss our work and we maintain a listserv that is open to anyone who currently teaches or has taught in the past. In sum, you should try out a variety of communication tools and settle on the ones that will create the bridges that you need to keep the program moving along in a positive direction.

## Institutional Knowledge

Managing an information literacy program of any size requires operating on multiple levels at one time. You will want to simultaneously be able to review the past with 20/20 hindsight, keep the current program operating with clear sight lines and keep your eyes to the future for both challenges and rewards that are on their way. To do this, you will need to be knowledgeable not only about the library, but the entire institution. Discovering the mother lode of institutional knowledge will help you to understand the underpinnings of what makes your institution work, and how the library fits into the institution's organization and plans.

You need to know how best to obtain and transfer information on your campus. In order to do this, identify both the movers and the shakers of curriculum reform as well as the solid, but quiet supporters of the library. You will find people in both camps that may become long-term stewards and supporters of your IL plans and programs. All of this investigating and identifying takes time to accomplish. Discovering the history and background of the administration, faculty, staffing, students, programs, projects, and curriculum of the institution will require you to dig beyond what is easily available on the surface. Institutional knowledge can be found in many places. You'll need to meet and talk with people from the right combination of schools, programs and departments that can provide background information and history that will enable your keen insights to give way to creative foresight. Scout out and become familiar with various institutional organizational charts so that you can learn the chain of command and who reports to whom. Along the way, you might also learn that someone you are already friendly with is in a prime position to support your IL plans.

All institutions of higher education have a document outlining important policies. At the University of Rhode Island (URI) it is the University Manual.[12] The University Manual's table of contents includes the following sections: administration, schools and program divisions, rights and responsibilities, faculty and staff, academic regulations, student activities and administrative procedures. This document provides information on URI's general education curriculum, as well as programs and departments that the IL program plans to, or may be able to, serve or collaborate with. Your institution has a similar document that you may mine for valuable information, ideas, and leads in the hunt for the crucial information that will help you manage an IL program. Further your research by reading any and all documents available to you such as meeting minutes, web pages, annual and special reports, and white papers that will provide the official word on what has happened, is happening or might happen in the areas that you are interested in. Further, make it a point to get to know the movers and shakers on your campus that will have impact on your plans and programs. Colleagues, faculty and staff from various campus units can provide the inside scoop—the practice and the policy—that can provide meaningful information for your program's success. It is also wise to become knowledgeable about any possible detractors of your IL program. Often they are not so much against your efforts, but competing for the same attention, funding and students that you both need and want. If you have created an exciting narrative to describe your IL program, you may well convince detractors that your program will in turn support part of their own goal and is worth an investment of their time.

Within the library, meet with all those who are involved in information literacy and library instruction. Find out their history, programs they have run and been involved in, and what they see as their own and the various programs' successes and challenges. You will learn the underpinnings of the library, the curriculum, and the campus culture as your involvement in various committees and activities grows and deepens. If you are able to be appointed to library-wide and campus committees, do so, and listen carefully to find links that can be made between IL and programs outside the library. If you are new to the institution, or need to learn about your, it will take a bit of sleuthing until you discover where the "holy grail" of information is actually stored. Persistence typically pays off in the long run. Finally, armed with institutional knowledge and memory, you'll soon see the institution's strengths and weaknesses, and how these can help direct your program goals and plans.

## Planning

Your role as IL manager or coordinator will put you at the forefront of any planning initiatives for the IL plan and program. Planning may be done with a small group of librarians in the reference or instruction unit of your library. It may be done by a broad cross-section of interested and vested faculty and staff from the institution's community. Have a game plan for the initial planning meetings. Knowing the expected time line for the development of the IL Plan/Program will inform you of several key items. Can you build the program in baby steps, one idea at a time, or are you expected to come out of the gates with an entire program all ready for prime time? As IL manager, you may be handed an already developed IL plan to implement or you may be asked to gather the information, the staff, and the brain power to both develop a long range IL plan and to then implement the ideas created for an IL program for your institution.

Whether you are reviewing a program already established or starting from scratch, most IL managers will find that there comes a time when planning on a broad scale is necessary. The size and shape of the institution will determine the level of information required for the planning that is to be done. Before you attack the task of creating an IL program it is necessary to "plan to plan."[13] Planning to plan includes establishing a planning group, creating or accepting a charge for the group, determining a timeline for various stages of the project, conducting a needs assessment and gathering background information. Deciding who will be invited to join the planning group is as important as the first day you begin your new program. Consider the institutional knowledge that you have gathered and select group members who can assist you in productive and powerful ways. The group could include a variety of librarians, faculty, administrators, students and support staff. Each of the members should represent a different audience or voice on your campus. Who are the "friendly faculty," those already identified and known library instruction supporters who will be interested in collaborating with you? Administrators of various colleges, schools or special programs that will benefit from your information literacy program will be able to provide valuable information about their program goals and needs.

Inviting students, both graduate and undergraduate, to be part of the planning group will provide a powerful voice that can advocate for preferred learning styles of students and may have the inside scoop about what level of student information literacy needs exist at your institution. Students can answer questions for the group, such as do students at your institution prefer small face-to-face instruction in a workshop or seminar setting? Or is twenty-four/seven online instruction a more appealing and reasonable method for your student body? Invite as many different constituencies as possible to be part of the planning group. If that proves unwieldy, you may invite stakeholder investment by creating a smaller planning group and inviting the wider circle of interested people to a series of hearings or focus group style review of your initial plans.

The first order of business for the planning group is to receive and review their charge. Developing a clear understanding of the responsibilities assigned to the group will go a long way to streamlining the agenda. Whether you are receiving or creating the charge for the planning group, be sure it is clear to the group what is expected, that the goals are manageable, and that they are set within a time frame that can be accomplished. Discovering what the institution needs or requires for its IL program is essential. Be prepared to plan your program based on a common understanding of what student learning outcomes you want to achieve. As librarians we often assume from our day-to-day experiences that we know what a good IL program would look like at our institution. The information gathered by an interested and diverse planning group along with the results of a campus-wide needs assessment will insure that all institutional IL needs will be addressed.

At the broadest level you may want to investigate widely and implement an overall environmental scan and needs assessment that will provide a birds-eye view of the institution's entire educational scene and how it relates to the institution's need for information literacy. Or you may create a smaller, more local, needs assessment project, perhaps only involving the first year experience program or a particular college or population of students. Environmental scans are effective in higher education as a means to survey multiple areas of interest, described as "a method that enables decision makers both to understand the external environment and the interconnections of its various sectors and to translate this understanding into the institution's planning and decision-making processes."[14] The Association of College and Research Libraries' (ACRL) 2003 Environmental Scan is an example of a large scale environmental scan that can also be used by IL managers as a support in building an institutional rationale for planning an IL program. The ACRL Environmental Scan was done to "identify trends and emerging issues that may affect the future of higher education, academic libraries and the association."[15] ACRL reviewed many different publications and sources in an attempt to predict the impact of current societal trends on academic libraries. Of particular note, are two related sections in the ACRL environmental scan, *Internet as Information Provider* and the *Increased Educational Role for Librarian,* that address the current state of affairs for academic information literacy librarians.

Although most IL managers will not be in a position to direct a large scale environmental scanning project due to the amount of time, staff and funding that is required, it is very possible that your institution or consortium has produced either an ad- hoc, periodic or continuous program of environmental scanning that you may consult for a broad overview of the institution.[16] Conduct a needs assessment using either passive or active methods. Passive methods include gathering anecdotal and/or observational evidence. The danger in relying only on passive assessment is that you may not gather information from a diverse cross-section of your institutional population. For example, if you base your assessment on observations done at the reference desk, you are only observing the behavior of students who actually seek assistance from library staff. Effective active methods for needs assessment include paper and online surveys, individual interviews, and focus groups for both faculty and students.

Along with the results of the environmental scan and/or needs assessment the planning group should gather documents of the institution, such as the mission statement, vision statement and strategic planning documents. You will want the IL program to support the mission, vision and strategic plans of the institution. Keep these documents close by as you create the proposed IL plan and program. Refer to them often as the planning group develops ideas to see how your ideas mesh or support the ideas held within the documents. The mission statement, vision statement and strategic plan are also part of the institutional knowledge you have already gathered as part of your research about the institution; in this situation you will use them to ensure that the planning group is developing a group understanding of the institutional overall picture.

If the planning group includes members who are unfamiliar with information literacy concepts, provide a list of readings and point them to organizations and associations involved in furthering the cause of information literacy education. Just such a list may be found on the ACRL Information Literacy web site, particularly "Information Literacy for Faculty and Administrators."[17] The LOEX Clearinghouse for Library Instruction[18] has an extensive list of links to information literacy oriented organizations that includes the following: the National Forum on Information Literacy, EDUCAUSE, and the International Federation of Library Associations' (IFLA) Information Literacy Section. Books that will surely inform the planning group include Ilene Rockman's *Integrating Information Literacy into the Higher Education Curriculum: Practical models for Transformation,*[19] Craig Gibson's *Student Engagement and Information Literacy,*[20] and Patricia Senn Breivik's *Student Learning in the Information Age.*[21] These materials will provide wide-ranging and useful understanding of how information literacy is viewed by higher education and beyond that by various organizations and corporate entities.

Many of these associations, organizations and books provide useful examples of IL programs at their own and other institutions. While looking at various IL plans and programs, focus on what your peer institutions, "generally determined by criteria that include type of institution, size of student population, degrees offered, location, and/or funding levels," are doing to provide information literacy instruction.[22] Your planning group may identify model programs or facets of programs that will work at your institution.

Many higher education accrediting agencies are requiring some degree of responsibility from institutions of higher education to ensure that students graduate proficient with information literacy. Review the standards of your institution's accrediting body and identify the level to which you will be held accountable. Consult the ACRL Information Literacy web page titled "Information Literacy and Accrediting Agencies"[23] for information about the higher education accreditation standards in regards to information literacy expectations in your geographic area. This information may impact your institution's understanding of IL and in turn, help to provide the level of administrative support necessary to fulfill meaningful student learning outcomes regarding information literacy. Accrediting body information could also help to direct the structure and design of the IL program that you ultimately offer your institution.

To aid in both developing and implementing a new program or revising a current model, your planning group should begin with the Association of College and Research Libraries' (ACRL) Information Literacy web site.[24] The ACRL Information Literacy Standards Toolkit is an essential source of information literacy standards, objectives and guidelines for your use. A first stop should be the ACRL Instruction Section's Guidelines for Instruction Programs in Academic Libraries[25] which provides guidelines for developing a statement of purpose or mission statement, program design, content and modes of instruction, classroom and technology supports, evaluation and assessment, financial support, instructor support, continued professional education and training. Following that, examine the *Information Literacy Competencies for Higher Education*[26] which describe the five information literacy competencies that have been determined to support student achievement of information literacy in higher education. Each competency is further explained by a number of performance indicators and learning outcomes. In order to implement the Competency Standards, refer to the *Objectives for Information Literacy Instruction: A Model Statement for Academic Librarians.*[27] "The Competency Standards are the basis for the IS [ACRL Instruction Section] Objectives and it is recommended that the two documents be used together. The IS Objectives flesh out and make more specific the Standards, Performance Indicators, and Outcomes of the Competency Standards."[28]

Your planning group may also avail themselves of the *Characteristics of Programs of Information Literacy that Illustrate Best Practices: A Guideline,*[29] a document that will be of enormous assistance in both pre-planning and for assessing the program once it has been in use for a period of time. Further along in this handbook, Chapter Ten will address evaluation and assessment in great detail.

Based on data and other information collected and gathered from surveys, interviews and observations, and in concert with the Association of College and Research Libraries (ACRL) documents listed above, your planning group can now create a locally developed IL mission statement, and an information literacy plan, complete with specific goals and objectives. With these in hand, and the all important institutional knowledge, you will be ready to employ creative thinking methods to define and build an IL program that will work on your campus. While planning is an enormous job, particularly if you are starting from square one, you can break the tasks down into manageable blocks of time. Ask yourself what can be accomplished in the short term, the long term and what can wait for the future. It may be best to organize the work of developing the program into chunks of time that fit the academic calendar. Short term planning and projects may fit into a month, a semester or an academic year, longer term projects may take several years before the fruits of your labor can be seen. Planning for the future often means looking two or more years out and can include projects such as developing more complex pieces of the IL program and addressing future technological, staffing and space needs.

Remember that many IL managers find that the well developed and established plans that were made must change due to a variety of possibilities, such as a new administration, a budget crises or staffing changes. A happy, albeit challenging, benefit of overflowing success is the unexpected but fabulous opportunity that arrives on the library's doorstep. All of these variables are certain reminders to stay flexible! Plans should always be considered living documents, and not carved in stone without room for adjustments. In the end, program success will be achieved through your use of creative thinking, institutional knowledge and good communication on all levels—across, around, up and down.

## Information Literacy Program Models
What will your actual IL program look like? During the early planning sessions you may feel like you are overburdened with the myriad of ideas out on the table

for discussion. This is the reason that determined and creative planning takes time and is so valuable; you *want* to have all those exciting ideas and options! Will you offer credit-bearing courses for all freshmen, a series of course-integrated instruction for upperclassmen, drop-in library workshops, or an online tutorial designed to meet all your information literacy needs? Does all the instruction need to be completely online or can you also offer face-to-face instruction? Can you offer IL instruction to all campus populations? These are difficult decisions that must be made in concert with staffing, resources and funding in mind.

However, once suggestions have been offered by the planning group, it becomes the IL manager's responsibility to take the plan generated by the group and discuss them all with the instructors, or the group who will ultimately be involved in delivering the program. This group can review all of the ideas offered by the planning group and match them with the resources that are, or will be, available to make an effective and viable program. At this point, it can be very useful to do a curriculum mapping project in advance of the final program model design.[30]

Curriculum mapping is a method often used in education fields to assess curricular strengths and weaknesses. Gather and review a year's worth of instruction statistics and analyze what schools and programs are receiving the most and the least instruction. Next, have each library liaison review their subject area in the course catalog to see where IL could be a support for student learning. There are several important questions you will want to answer with the results of a curriculum mapping project: Who is receiving instruction? How much or how often is instruction is happening? What type of instruction is most often used? What is the content of the instruction? What IL concepts and skills are being learned? For those who receive multiple IL sessions, are all competencies being addressed over a reasonable period of time? You may discover that some students attend multiple library instruction sessions over the course of their program of studies while others receive little or no information literacy instruction at all.

For all of the information gathered, ask the all important questions of who, what, when, where and why. Use the results of the curriculum mapping project to get a bird's eye view of what is currently happening in your instruction program and what is not happening. The unspoken question, of course, is the one inquiring minds really want to know—Who *isn't* receiving instruction and *why*? Is it lack of library liaison activity or perhaps a lack of interest or time on the part of the academic department faculty? Does the library lack space and/or technology to offer enough instruction opportunities? What departments and programs offer prime opportunities for introducing IL concepts and skills to large groups of students? Use the information from the curriculum mapping project to meet with faculty in those areas identified as under-served and discuss what IL instruction would be useful and how it can best be implemented. The results gathered from the curriculum mapping project will also provide you with opportunities for improving the current instruction program. If the information literacy instruction provides uneven service, how will you correct the balance? Are certain departments more inclined to receive instruction for some of the previously discussed reasons? Holding an instruction retreat following the mapping project may offer you and your colleagues a prime opportunity for considering these sometimes difficult questions in order to retool the IL plan and program.

At this point, you should have enough information to see some obvious patterns of instruction delivery emerging. Now you are ready to utilize the plan to build the new (or revise an existing) IL program as a whole. Where will your energy be directed? It is unlikely that you will meet all of your program goals in the first attempts; thus, it is wise to build a comprehensive, incremental program model that can be launched and delivered in stages. A comprehensive program will include the program ideas that have the optimum potential for meeting the information literacy needs you have identified on your campus. An incremental program sets the stage by allowing you to begin with the most effective piece of that program. During this process continue to refer to the reports and work of the original planning group to help you design a new program or to retool an existing program. Perhaps you can build the program by focusing around one of the following attributes or categories: student levels (freshmen to graduate level), discipline or program, type of instruction, location of instruction, or by the delivery style of the program. Perhaps you hope to begin at the beginning, with freshmen and work up to the senior or graduate levels over time? Or, is it more plausible that you will be able to build and deliver online information literacy learning modules before you can offer a reasonable number of face–to-face sessions? Consider the strengths and numbers of your staff, the funding, the space, and the time available to you. The content and quality of the instruction is paramount, but the delivery variables that will propel your program to success are equally as important.

**Program Content Elements:**
- IL Competencies: Know, Access, Evaluate, Use, Ethical/Legal

**Program Delivery Variables:**
- Student levels: Freshman to graduate student
- Type of Instruction: Problem-based learning, active learning, resource based learning
- Method of delivery: Online vs. Face-to-Face, Tutorial, credit course, drop-in workshops, course-integrated sessions, learning communities, freshman seminar
- Audience: by discipline, college or program

- Time of Delivery: year round, specific semesters, intersession/winter break

For example, you may decide to offer a fall semester, first year experience program utilizing an online information literacy tutorial in conjunction with face-to-face library tours. You may also want to offer subject-specific, course-integrated information literacy sessions to all junior year introduction-to-research courses as part of the comprehensive program. If you are beginning your program from ground zero, you must consider which program will consume the most time, staffing and funding, as well as which program will be the most advantageous to the most people. These programs may be the same one, or there be an array of programs in the equation. You may need to address how the goals can be achieved for all without detracting from the others. What will help to identify the IL program as a success? Where is your time and energy best spent? What can be accomplished sooner rather than later? These are not simple questions to answer, but you must make hard decisions in order to launch and sustain a quality information literacy program. Making the decision to work on various parts of the program in stages allows you to tackle what is most important to your instruction team, or to your institution, first, and leave other program plans to future semesters or academic years.

Once you determine the size, shape and content of the program that you want to offer, consider who will administer each aspect of the program. Often, program administration falls completely to the IL manager, but at some institutions various IL program responsibilities are assigned to several instruction librarians. For example, the IL manager may be responsible for oversight of staffing, program content, classrooms and technology, and assessment while others take responsibility for the specific content and scheduling of separate programs such as information literacy instruction for the college writing, first year experience, or summer pre-matriculation programs. This model creates a shared knowledge of the IL program within the library and builds a deeper understanding of the program's successes and challenges.

## Staffing and Training

Before a staff can be prepared to deliver the new IL program, they must be identified, recruited and trained. Where will you find people interested in serving this great endeavor? Will you find the best and the brightest? Will they be willing and excited? In many cases, you may be a new manager of an established library instruction or IL program. This requires taking time to observe how the staff works and how they work together. Don't rush to make immediate staffing changes, but instead, visit with each instruction librarian in their office or at lunch to discover their thoughts and ideas about information literacy at the institution. Ask to observe or team-teach a library instruction session with each instructor to get a sense of the rich talent that is already available to the program. Think broadly and take note of individual strengths to see how and where those strengths can be utilized.

You may have the opportunity to observe or work with different staff members at the reference desk. You will also begin to know each staff member better through work in committees and at library staff meetings. As a manager you may not have as many opportunities as you would like to work alongside your colleagues, but it is important to find time to observe and discover each librarian's teaching and learning style. Knowing this information can provide solid information about who might be best in what position within the IL program. There are many roles to fill in a large program, ranging from face-to-face instructors to instructional designers, classroom technology specialists, online instruction adventurers and many other primary and supporting positions. If your program is large or complex you may need additional instructors. Who then, to recruit? If you are working under an IL mandate, a request to administration may be all that is necessary. If you are working in a grassroots environment, you will need to present a more powerful and convincing case for additional staff. In either case, however, encouraging or convincing staff to devote more of their professional life to information literacy can be notably the more complex part of developing an IL staff. They will certainly have questions and it will be your job to provide answers. How will a new IL responsibility impact staff workloads or expectations? What work will the library "give up" or relinquish or re-assign so that staff become available to serve in their new IL capacities? Where will the money come from to support this new program? Will they have to learn new methods of teaching? How many students will they have to teach?

Many IL programs are comprised of both complex and simpler program pieces. It is possible to recruit staff to teach in the IL program if you can provide training and support at an appropriate level to develop the instructors' comfort level and effectiveness as a teacher. For example, you may offer a program such as an online tutorial that is used in conjunction with face-to-face instruction or a toolkit of problem-based-learning problems or case-study examples that are used for instruction with a large curriculum. If these program pieces have a reasonable learning curve and can be delivered easily then you may be able to recruit a wider variety of staff to the instruction team. Consider inviting librarians who have not taught before, library administrators, adjunct faculty, paraprofessionals and library school or other graduate students to help in delivering the program. Each institution has its own particular situations and needs that may preclude this from happening easily, but do be open minded. Often the most exciting staffing opportunity is the one that we overlook on first glance.

Program pieces such as credit-bearing courses and multiple session course-integrated sessions need staff who are more experienced and who have time that can be devoted to developing their subject content and teaching style. However, even a comprehensive IL program that includes a three-credit course may reduce some staff stress by creating a generic syllabus and a programmed menu of learning opportunities, thereby alleviating each IL staff member from having to reinvent the wheel.

## Training and Support

In advance of the new or revised IL program's activities, plan and provide workshops or training sessions for all staff that will be affected or involved in the program. IL instructors should receive thorough training in information literacy concepts and skills as well as training in teaching. The ACRL Institute of Information Literacy's Immersion Program[31] is a very effective and exciting program for both new and experienced IL teachers and program coordinators. Other national, regional and local opportunities may include information literacy and/or teaching workshops and training sessions at American Library Association or Association of College and Research Libraries national conferences or at other libraries within a consortium or from the local or regional professional association chapters of ACRL or ALA. Look to your own institution's Center for Teaching Excellence or Instructional Design Program for on- campus seminars and training on teaching. As IL manager you may create in-house training sessions, hold brown-bag lunch discussion groups and invite guest lecturers to speak on relevant topics of interest. All of these opportunities will enrich the staff and ultimately the program. Following are some examples of successful staff training and support programs:

### In-House Retreats

Holding a retreat for teaching librarians is a refreshing, invigorating opportunity for all involved. Following are comments from two instruction coordinators who have held successful retreats that may pique your interest in holding one for your own staff. At Emerson College, Anna Litten planned and organized a retreat to engage the instruction staff in thinking more broadly about how to further develop their information literacy program. Litten notes that "our small retreat had a big impact. Members of the teaching team, often excluded from discussion of changes in the program, were involved in charting our future."[32] Doreen Simonsen, of Loyola University New Orleans, writes about the rationale for offering library retreats for her instruction staff, noting that "a retreat can offer library instruction coordinators and their librarian colleagues, who teach, a chance to step back for the daily rush of desk hours, meeting and instruction sessions and look at their whole instruction program. It can also offer librarians the opportunity to share the latest teaching ideas with their colleagues."[33]

## Workshops

Offering a series of regularly scheduled workshops for IL instructors will keep the instruction staff up to date on pedagogy and technology. Traditionally, the most active instruction season occurs in the first half of each semester, which means that you will want to carefully consider when to offer workshops. Depending on the tempo of your IL program, you may find it best to plan workshops of any extended length in the breaks between semesters or during the summer. An example of a comprehensive and very successful model for in house workshops is the University of Michigan's Instructor College.[34] Instructor College offers teaching librarians a curriculum of four foundational sessions including orientation, marketing, working with faculty and planning a session. Additionally, the program offers various thematic sessions covering such topics as presentation skills, working with content, technology, assessment and learning theory/instructional design.

Alternately, at the University of Rhode Island, librarians attend monthly instructor group meetings. Very often, due to limited time available to us, information literacy staff meetings are task oriented and used to create or review policy, logistics or a program that has just passed or is forthcoming. If it is difficult to find time to hold more relaxed or creative gatherings for your staff, try to incorporate a period of time at each meeting for group or individual reflection and sharing, for imagining, and for brainstorming. At the University of Rhode Island, task oriented meetings are held once a month with more creative gatherings held at the end of each semester and generally once in the summer.

About once a semester, we also invite speakers to present talks on topics of current interest. Recent sessions have included a presentation by a URI-Graduate School of Library and Information Studies student on how to teach students to develop higher order questions in their research plans, a session on using problem based learning by the information literacy librarian from Roger Williams University in Bristol, RI and a session that included a lesson on teaching students the graphic display of information by one of our own instruction team members.

## Conferences

Other avenues of providing training and support for your IL team include the many national, regional and local conferences that address all aspects of information literacy. These include the ACRL and ACRL Instruction Section (IS) pre-conference programs, IL programs held during the ALA Midwinter Meeting and Annual Conference, LOEX (Library Orientation Exchange) annual conference and LOEX of the West's bi-annual conference. In Canada, two conferences of note are WILU (Workshop on Instruction in Library Use) and the Augustana Information Literacy in Academic Libraries Workshop. Other conferences that are focused more generally on libraries, teaching and technology issues include: EDUCAUSE, the Distance Teaching and Learning Conference and Computers in Libraries, and regional groups such as the North East Regional Computing Program (NERCOMP), which is an affiliate of EDUCAUSE.

### Mentoring and Coaching

Generally, mentoring is understood to be a general support and training opportunity for the purposes of encouraging and providing insight from a more experienced person to a less experienced person. If your institution offers formal mentoring programs for new staff, does it address the particular needs of instruction librarians? Or is it more focused on the institutional policies and processes that the new staff member needs to understand and navigate? Formal in-house mentoring for instruction librarians is not very common, but as IL manager you should develop at minimum a casual program for you instructors. Be sure to meet individually with instruction staff initially to introduce them to your program's mission, goals and objectives and to introduce the communication systems your group uses, such as listservs, web sites, blogs or wikis that other instruction staff are using to share information and materials with each other. Next, you will want to be sure to introduce them to their peers, this could be anyone in the library who provides instruction services, and with luck, the new person will develop a natural mentoring relationship with one of the staff members. If you feel that you need to make formal connections, pair a new instruction librarian with an experienced librarian who is able and willing to mentor. Identify people who will balance each other's ideas, match their personalities, or nurture each other's talents. Mentoring is productive when the mentor fosters intellectual growth and development and encourages professional development in the mentee. Mentors can take note of the intellectual interests of their mentee and be sure to share possible contacts and share suggestions for further growth in those areas. The mentor to an instruction librarian might provide broad information such as career development ideas and opportunities or simply be available to listen and provide support when the mentee in learning new pedagogies.

### Awards and Rewards

As a rule, academic librarians do not enter into their profession with the goal of winning awards or earning specific rewards other than the glory achieved in helping patrons find, evaluate and use information. However, all workers appreciate being identified and rewarded for a job well done. Supporting IL instructors can be as easy as providing a listening ear for their challenges and offering public acknowledgement of work well done in a newsletter or other library or campus publication. Other ideas that will show support for the instruction staff is to arrange for a relaxing lunch meeting away from the office, or to create an annual in-house instruction award or to nominate your program or staff for campus or national awards. Perhaps you will be able to provide extra financial support for the instruction librarians so that they may attend programs normally beyond the library's budget capabilities. However you choose to publicly notice your staff's good work, be sure to develop equal and fair criteria for all awards and rewards—it is not a productive idea if the awards and rewards cause competition, animosity or dysfunction within the instruction staff. Support for IL instructors can come in the form of intellectual acknowledgement, emotional or financial reward; the important thing is to do it.

## Stress and Burn Out

A gentle reminder about staff stress and burn out is in order here. It is often difficult to decide how much one person or even a small committed group should accomplish. Margaret Mead famously stated, "Never doubt that a small group of thoughtful, committed people can change the world. Indeed, it is the only thing that ever has." Information literacy librarians are a passionate and committed group of people, who, given all the necessary support, may well change the world! And, while it is not unreasonable to strive to produce a bit more than you expect is possible for the growth or delivery of your program, there is, however, a breaking point—the burn-out point—where staff will develop symptoms of stress and burn-out from over work. In your eagerness to propel your program to excellence be wary of producing too much too fast, thereby frustrating your colleagues and perhaps promising more than is possible to deliver in a given time period. When burn-out hits, consider if it is possible for instructors to trade responsibilities for a change of pace, or if necessary, adjust individual librarian's workload assignments. A fast track to a successful program will surely please the library and the institution; however, keep in mind that for continued positive growth to occur, all the supports for keeping momentum moving at an even pace must be securely in place. These supports include all of the items covered in the "Characteristics of Programs of Information Literacy that Illustrate Best Practices: A Guideline" document but most important to consider are the administrative and institutional support and staffing sections.[35]

Take a deep breath, look out the window, and consider the possible on-the-job stress and burn out factors that IL managers might experience. Beyond the immediate concerns of the every day rush to get things done, to plan, to oversee, to be creative, concerned, and to do great work—there is the added challenge of being the person who will keep the IL flame steadily burning at your institution. For many IL librarians, there is more than the expectation that you will keep the IL program running and growing smoothly; there is also the knowledge that many eyes are on us to convince or perhaps prove to our campus community that IL is necessary and really does add a main ingredient to the rich content of higher education. How will you cope with this stress? Your first successes will sustain you mightily, your next few projects will be a joy, yet at some point—a staffing, budget or other crisis, or when you hit the wall and lose your motivation, it is time to remember the recommendations of our mothers. Everything in moderation! Rest, exercise, eat well, sleep well, play with your friends and get some fresh air! Do your work the best way that you can, and then rest well in knowing it is done.

## Marketing and Outreach

Any new program or product needs to be identified and marketed to its audience. Branding is getting a lot of air play these days, but it is not new. Consider branding your IL program with a catchy name and a snappy and memorable icon. Your first challenge towards marketing your new or revised IL program is to find a branding image that will become such a positive icon that it will stick in the students' minds and at the same time appeal to administrators, staff, students' parents and alumni. For this task, you may want to go back to your original planning group or approach the campus news bureau or publicity group to help you devise a marketing campaign for the program. If these resources are not available to you, find an up and coming marketing guru by approaching marketing, creative writing or journalism professors and ask them if a group of their students would like to help the library develop an information literacy campaign.

When the time comes to market the new, or new and improved, IL program to your institution strive to reach far and wide with the exciting news. You will want to reach students on every level, administrators, supervisors and coordinators from across the institution, all continuing and temporary faculty, and the clerical, custodial, and building and grounds staff. The campus population will resonate with the excitement that you can generate. It may be hard to envision, but close your eyes and try to match the energy that the athletic department exudes for their teams.

There are many ways to spread the word that *help is on the way!* Perhaps you can use the first day of a new semester, or the week that is traditionally, but unofficially, "term paper or project research week" in your library and use it as a launch event. From holding a launch day for your program in the library, student union, or on the campus quadrangle, to using traditional print, media, and a web 2.0 publicity blitz, you can create a buzz on your campus about the new Information Literacy program at your institution. You may also create some noise about your IL program by sharing information about student success that comes out of the information literacy efforts that you've begun. Find out if a local, regional or state-wide newspaper publishes an occasional education section or assigns an education reporter to follow up on new campus initiatives. Spread the good word about your great efforts.

Examples of the types of products and projects that will create a buzz on your campus include a thirty-minute film titled, "It Changed the Way I do Research—Period: Augustana Talks Information Literacy"[36] created at the University of Alberta, Augustana Campus, by Nancy Goebel and her creative staff of librarians, and Ross LaBaugh's Info-Radio[37] program at California State University—Fresno, a series of radio spots on the campus radio station that offer students short informative pieces that explain how to use library resources. At the University of Rhode Island, the information literacy instructor group offers a series of forums titled "Issues of the Information Age."[38] While these projects each illustrate only one aspect of a larger information literacy program, they all serve to point out the good work being accomplished by the librarians on their campuses.

You might also consider using a professional organization package to help you with marketing, particularly if information literacy is going to be a major initiative at your library or across your institution. ACRL's Marketing @Your Library[39] campaign offers an Advocacy Toolkit complete with guides, tips and suggested practices that you may adapt to address your marketing needs. Perhaps your efforts will entice the entire library to take part in promoting the libraries' services to your institution!

## Information Literacy across the Campus

Finding the best way to utilize contemporary instructional tools is the information literacy coordinator's challenge. While electronic classroom settings are the traditional space for many IL instruction programs, this setting may not be the only, nor the most effective location for delivery at every institution. A careful review of your IL program goals may reveal that a broad-based program that plans to reach every student can work well if you consider reaching beyond the traditional classroom setting. Many information literacy programs offer online tutorials, and research and assignment guides in modular self-paced formats that can be delivered beyond classroom walls via the library's information or learning commons, campus course-management systems, student computing labs, and/ or remotely to any student of the institution with an Internet connection.

Librarians and libraries are creating instructional support services for their users via various social networking tools such as wikis, blogs, RSS feeds, podcasts and most recently, a library presence in Second Life, Info Island. Second Life is an "online society within a 3D world, where users can explore, build, socialize and participate in their own economy."[40] These technology tools should be considered as part of the toolkit of options for the provision and outreach of information literacy programs. The Teaching, Learning, Technology Group (TLT) web page, "Exploration Guide: Educational Uses of Blogs, Wikis, RSS Feeds, etc."[41] is an excellent source of information for those looking to begin using various Web 2.0 tools for information literacy instruction. Information literacy education and technology are hand-in-glove partners that weave a close and strong support structure for students, faculty and staff who are teaching and learning in higher education.

## Conclusion

The chapter began with encouragement to use your imagination in order to keep your IL program ever-growing in both vision and reach. Emphasis on effective and open communication is meant to support the flow of ideas in your information literacy community. I have attempted to cover basic tasks and responsibilities involved in managing an information literacy program with a few suggestions for ideas that have worked at other libraries. In closing, remember that as we are careful to review and revise the information literacy program plan on a regular basis, it is equally important to review your own position description on occasion in order to revive and refresh your perspective and vision. The position of Information Literacy Manager or Coordinator is an exciting one that will provide rich and varied opportunities for personal and professional growth. As you work closely with your colleagues and the campus community to develop and further the information literacy plan and program on your campus, you will be contributing to the development of an information literate community and individual life long learning on a day to day, and year to year basis. Your role will be not only manager or coordinator, but ambassador and visionary.

## Notes

1. Mary Jane Petrowski, "Managing Information Literacy Programs: Building Repertoire," in *Managing Library Instruction Programs in Academic Libraries. Library Orientation Series. Selected Papers Presented at the Twenty-Ninth National LOEX Library Instruction Conference, held in Ypsilanti, Michigan, 4 to 6 May 2001* (Ann Arbor: Pierian Press, 2003).

2. Vincent van Gogh, Letter to Theo van Gogh, in *The Complete Letters of Vincent Van Gogh* (Boston: Little, Brown, 2000), p. 479. Also available online from http://webexhibits.org/vangogh/letter/11/241.htm [Accessed 18 November 2006].

3. Ed Bernacki, "Exactly what is "Thinking Outside the Box?" *CANADAONE,* April 2002. Available online from http://www.canadaone.com/exoine/april02/out_of_the_box_thinking.

html [Accessed November 18, 2006).

4. Ibid.

5. Todd Packer, "Think Inside the Box," *Leadership Excellence,* August 2006, 16.

6. Esther S. Grassian and Joan R. Kaplowitz, *Learning to Lead and Manage Information Literacy Instruction.* (Neal-Schuman: New York. 2005), 74-75.

7. Ibid., p. 80-81. Reprinted with permission of Neal-Schuman, Inc.

8. Lee G. Bolman and Terrence E. Deal, *Reframing Organizations: Artistry, Choice and Leadership,* 3rd ed. (San Francisco: Jossey-Bass, 2003). p. 163.

9. Ibid., p. 163.

10. Ibid., p. 163-164.

11. Ibid., p. 166.

12. University of Rhode Island. Faculty Senate. *University Manual,* 11th edition. Updated 6 September 2006. Available online from http://www.uri.edu/facsen/MANUAL_05.html [Accessed February 4, 2007].

13. Joanna M. Burkhardt, Mary C. MacDonald and Andrée J. Rathemacher, *Creating a Comprehensive Information Literacy Plan* (New York: Neal Schuman, 2005). p. 13.

14. Shannon Cary, Margot Sutton Conahan, Stephanie Orphan, Mary Jane Petrowski, Irving Rockwood and Hugh Thompson, "ACRL Environmental Scan 2003," Association of College and Research Libraries. Available online from http://www.ala.org//ACRLtemplate.cfm?Section=whitepapers&Template=/MembersOnly.cfm&ContentFileID=16234 [Accessed February 5, 2007].

15. Ibid.

16. James L. Morrison, "Environmental Scanning" in M. A. Whitely, J. D. Porter and R. H. Fenske, eds., *A Primer for New Institutional Researchers* (Tallahassee, Florida: The Association for Institutional Research, 1992). p. 86-99.

17. Information Literacy Advisory Committee. "Information Literacy for Faculty and Administrators," Association of College and Research Libraries. Available online from http://www.ala.org/ala/acrl/acrlissues/acrlinfolit/infolitoverview/infolitforfac/infolitfaculty.htm [Accessed 5 February 2007].

18. LOEX Clearinghouse for Library Instruction, "Organizations and Programs," Available online from http://www.emich.edu/public/loex/organization_prog.html [Accessed 5 February 2007].

19. Ilene Rockman, *Integrating Information Literacy into the Higher Education Curriculum: Practical Models for Transformation* (San Francisco: Jossey-Bass, 2004).

20. Craig Gibson, *Student Engagement and Information Literacy* (Chicago: Association of College and Research Libraries, 2006).

21. Patricia Senn Breivik, *Student Learning in the Information Age* (Phoenix: American Council on Education, Oryx Press, 1998).

22. Joanna M. Burkhardt, Mary C. MacDonald and Andrée J. Rathemacher, *Creating a Comprehensive Information Literacy Plan: A How-To-Do It Manual,* (New York: Neal Schuman, 2005), 13.

23. Association of College and Research Libraries, "Information Literacy and Accrediting Agencies," Available online from http://www.ala.org/ala/acrl/acrlissues/acrlinfolit/infolitstandards/infolitaccred/accreditation.htm [Accessed 4 February 2007].

24. Association of College and Research Libraries, "Information Literacy," Available online from http://www.ala.org/ala/acrl/acrlissues/acrlinfolit/informationliteracy.htm [Accessed 4 February 2007].

25. Association of College and Research Libraries, "Information Literacy Instruction, Objectives for: A Model Statement for Academic Librarians," http://www.ala.org/ala/acrl/acrlstandards/standardsguidelines.htm [Accessed 25 May 2007].

26. Association of College and Research Libraries," Information Literacy Competency Standards for Higher Education," 2006. Available online from http://www.ala.org/acrl/ilcomstan.html [Accessed 4 February 2007].

27. Association of College and Research Libraries, "Objectives for Information Literacy Instruction: A Model Statement for Academic Librarians," 2006. Available online from http://www.ala.org/ala/acrl/acrlstandards/objectivesinformation.htm [Accessed 4 February 2007)

28. Ibid.

29. Association of College and Research Libraries, "Characteristics of Programs of Information Literacy that Illustrate Best Practices: A Guideline," 2006. Available online from http://www.ala.org/ala/acrl/acrlstandards/characteristics.htm [Accessed 4 February, 2007).

30. Lisa Janicke Hinchliffe, Beth L. Mark and Laurie H. Merz, "Bridging the Gap Between Information Literacy and Campus Curricula: Using Curriculum Mapping to Achieve a Holistic Information Literacy Program." Available online from http://wilu2003.uwindsor.ca/ENGLISH/pres/hinchliffeetal/CM_files/frame.htm [Accessed 10 December 2006].

31. "Immersion Program," ACRL Institute for Information Literacy. Available online from http://www.ala.org/ala/acrl/acrlissues/acrlinfolit/professactivity/iil/immersion/immersion-programs.htm (accessed February 4, 2007).

32. Anna Litten, "We're All in This Together: Planning and Leading a Retreat for Teaching Librarians" in Patricia Durisin, ed., *Information Literacy Programs: Successes and Challenges* (New York: Haworth, 2002), 59-60. p. 67.

33. Doreen Simonsen, "Planning and Playdough: Designing a Retreat that Will Revise Your Instruction Program and Rejuvenate Your Colleagues," in *Managing Library Instruction Programs in Academic Libraries.* Library Orientation Series. Selected Papers Presented at the Twenty-Ninth National LOEX Library Instruction Conference, held in Ypsilanti, Michigan, 4 to 6 May 2001. (Ann Arbor: Pierian Press, 2003), p. 155.

34. University of Michigan Libraries, "Instructor College," http://www.lib.umich.edu/icollege/program (accessed December 10, 2006).

35. Association of College and Research Libraries, "Characteristics of Programs of Information Literacy that Illustrate Best Practices: A Guideline," American Library Association, 2006. Available online from http://www.ala.org/ala/acrl/acrlstandards/characteristics.htm [Accessed 4 February 2007].

36. University of Alberta, Augustana Campus, "It Changed the Way I Do Research–Period. Augustana Talks Information Literacy," (Camrose, Alberta: University of Alberta, Augustana Campus, 2006).

37. Ross LaBaugh, "InfoRadio," California State University Fresno. Henry Madden Library. Available online form http://www.csuinforadio.org [Accessed 4 February, 2007).

38. University of Rhode Island Libraries, LIB 120 Instructor Group, "Issues of the Information Age forum series," Available online from http://www.uri.edu/news/releases/?id=3499 [Accessed 4 February, 2007].

39. Association of College and Research Libraries, "ACRL's Marketing @ Your Library Page," American Library Association, 2006. Available online from http://www.ala.org/marketing [Accessed 4 February 2007].

40. Second Life, Available online from http://www.secondlife.com [Accessed 4 February 2007].

41. Teaching Learning and Technology Group (TLT), Available online from http://www.tltgroup.org/blogs.htm [Accessed 4 February 2007].

# CHAPTER 7

# *Leadership*

Karen Williams

*Never doubt that a small group of thoughtful, committed people
can change the world. Indeed, it is the only thing that ever has.*
*~Margaret Mead*

*"The basket is tyranny!"*
*~IDEO employee*

## Every Librarian a Leader

Information literacy programs need both good management and strong leadership. Good management skills are generally more concrete and thus may be more easily understood and developed. However, over the past several decades there has been much research into what makes good leaders effective. This chapter will take a quick look at leadership in general and then discuss what is most needed now to strengthen and advance information literacy programs.

A concise framing definition of leadership is: "a relationship of mutual influence leading to collective effort in the service of shared or compatible purposes and values, in a context of uncertainty or conflict."[1] To make a distinction, management is a set of processes that keeps a system running smoothly including such things as planning, budgeting, staffing, organizing, and problem solving. Management is more closely tied to the position an individual holds. While it is not uncommon for individuals to be both leaders and managers, it is useful to understand the differences.

While the Gallos definition above captures the commonly expressed elements of leadership, there are many conceptions or theories of leadership, and little in the way of empirical evidence. It can be tempting to compare leadership with love: it is hard to define, but we know it when we see it, and we cannot live without it. My professional experience and observations have led to a passionate belief that leadership is critical to the future of higher education, libraries, and information literacy programs. This strong personal investment in the topic necessitated some study, reflection, and an attempt to articulate what influences my own commitment and behaviors. For my own personal practice I have found that no single leadership theory is sufficient and drawing from a variety of approaches has proven most useful and inspiring.

A significant amount of the leadership literature from the last two decades has focused on qualities or characteristics of successful leaders. It is interesting to note that studies asking people what they value in leaders yield strikingly similar results, whether conducted by management theorists or librarians looking at our profession. Qualities of successful leaders include vision, passion, courage, integrity, focus, and self-confidence.[2]

These characteristics appear in slightly different form in works by transformational theorists such as Kouzes and Posner[3] who articulate positive leadership behaviors or actions, which include challenging the status quo, inspiring a shared vision, enabling others to act, modeling the way, and encouraging the heart. Senge[4] adds acting as a change agent, managing interrelationships, and building a learning organization. Gallos observes that leadership is more than the accumulation of knowledge, experience, and skills. It is also desire, conviction and will; mustering strength in the face of unpopular reactions. Real leadership is courage and passion in action.[5]

Karin Wittenborg offers the following reflection from her essay on leadership:

> The leaders I most admire are visionaries, risk takers, good collaborators and communicators, mentors, and people with uncommon passion and persistence. They have personal integrity, they are assertive and ambitious for their organizations, they are optimists even in bad times, they think broadly and keep learning, and they build relationships and communities. They bring energy and a sense of fun to their work, they are opportunistic and flexible, and they are not easily deterred.[6]

These qualities are both inspirational and aspirational, but we must recognize that few individuals will possess all of these characteristics, and that personal qualities are not the only factor at play. Context is important and success in a given situation will depend on a number of variables such as the prevailing environment, specialized knowledge or skills, the attitudes and characteristics of other people involved, and experience.

The most successful institutions today are those that recognize an expanded view of leadership, unrelated to role or position. Leadership is a process, offering opportunities for everyone in the organization. This new view of leadership has implications for everyone, requiring a shift in perception for both those with positional power and those accustomed to thinking of leadership as vested only in administrators. Positional power is not unimportant in the equation, as will be discussed below, but successful programs will require much more. We face rapid and constant change in higher education evidenced through a variety of factors including the information explosion, emerging technologies, the presence of multiple distinct generations on our campuses, and an increasing public call for accountability. Rapid change requires that everyone, at all levels of an organization, develop a greater capacity for innovation, self-management, and personal responsibility.[7]

A particularly empowering view of the capacity for leadership in education comes from constructivist educator, Linda Lambert. Constructivism posits that learning is a process of shared inquiry through which learners construct new knowledge from the context of their experiences, knowledge, and beliefs. In the classroom, the focus has shifted from teacher to learner; in considering leadership, from administrators to all staff in an organization. Where most ideas of leadership imply distinct differences between followers and leaders, constructivism supports collaboration and shared knowledge, with the interrelationships among all the parts providing constant feedback and continuous improvement. At any given time, roles and behaviors will shift among participants based on interest, expertise, experience, and responsibility. Individuals will move in and out of leadership, depending on the needs of a particular project, initiative, or situation. These acts of leadership require basically the same qualities and skills identified by other management theorists:

- a sense of purpose and ethics
- facilitation skills, as framing, deepening, and moving the conversations about teaching and learning are fundamental to constructed meaning
- an understanding of constructivist learning for all humans
- a deep understanding of change and transitions
- an understanding of context so that communities of memories can be continually drawn and enriched
- a personal sense of identity that allows for courage and risk.[8]

A popular teaching tool for showcasing basic elements of creativity, innovation, team work, and leadership is an episode of the television show *Nightline* entitled "The Deep Dive."[9] This segment features a company called IDEO (www.ideo.com) whose mission is to help organizations innovate through design. At IDEO, an individual's contributions are judged not by who has the highest title or the biggest office, but by who has the best ideas and is able to engage others in putting them into action. In "The Deep Dive," IDEO staff are given the assignment of reinventing the traditional grocery shopping cart. Using a rapid prototyping process described as "organized chaos," the engineers, psychologists, mathematicians and other professionals on the team gather information, conduct interviews, and brainstorm a variety of possible new designs. The company executives are an integral part of the process, but the hierarchy is unrecognized in this creative, idea generating stage. Leadership is the key.

Why is it important for us to talk about leadership in the context of information literacy? We are proposing significant change on our campuses at the programmatic level, and the scale of the intended outcome requires vast participation. We cannot do it alone. We cannot order it done—even positional leaders cannot order it done. We do not control the teaching and learning environments on our campuses, but we do have expertise and influence. We must work as advocates on behalf of students for faculty action that integrates information literacy into the curriculum.

## A Bold Vision for Information Literacy Programs

A powerful vision should be vivid, compelling, shared, and bold; perhaps even a bit out of reach. In my vision for information literacy programs, every student who graduates from our institutions is information literate, possesses lifelong learning skills; is able to stay current in a chosen profession, and participates in communities as a well-informed citizen. Information literacy programs are deeply integrated into the regular curriculum and also provide strong resources for independent and self-directed learners. Using undergraduate education as an example, students encounter and practice information literacy concepts and skills throughout a four-year curriculum, at just the right moments, as part of course assignments or research activities. They gain assistance when needed through faculty, peers, digital tools, and librarians. Because these concepts are so deeply integrated, students do not think of them as separate or even as particularly related to libraries. Information literacy is an integral part of the learning continuum, as are writing, critical thinking, numeracy, ethics, and other components of a liberal education.

I have another favorite quote from the Wittenborg reflection:

> Leaders want to change the status quo. They do not seek change for its own sake, but rather to improve or create something. Leaders continually evaluate and assess their organizations with an eye toward improving them. While many administrators advance their organizations by tweaking a few things here and there, leaders aim for substantive change that introduces something entirely new or vastly improves a service or product. In short, leaders are dissatisfied with the current situation and are motivated to change it. What differentiates a leader from a malcontent is that the leader has learned and honed skills that allow him or her to move from dissatisfaction to effective action.[10]

The teaching and learning function has been a key role for academic librarians for the better part of three decades. Many librarians have become excellent teachers, all the more notable since our professional school programs rarely prepare us for this role. We have gained some understanding of learning theory, learning styles, curriculum design and assessment but at most institutions have not fully employed this knowledge in the design and implementation of programs, as opposed to individual course sessions. On many campuses, librarians may have been the first ones to articulate the importance of information literacy. Creating awareness is a critical first step, but in order for students to benefit fully, we must form new kinds of partnerships with faculty and other campus professionals.

Librarian perspectives on and engagement with teaching and learning has been evolving since we first began working with orientation and bibliographic instruction (BI) in the 1970s. Information literacy is part of a larger reform movement in education that seeks major changes in the way institutions educate. In a nutshell,

> A paradigm shift is taking hold in American higher education. In its briefest form, the paradigm that has governed our colleges is this: A college is an institution that exists to provide instruction. Subtly but profoundly we are shifting to a new paradigm: A college is an institution that exists to produce learning. This shift changes everything.[11]

A familiar popularization of this concept describes the shifting role of teachers from that of "stage on the stage" to "guide on the side."

The application of a learning paradigm to librarians' educational efforts can be illustrated with the chart on the following page, which situates orientation, bibliographic/library instruction and information literacy instruction along a continuum.

Movement from one end of the continuum to the other represents a natural progression, or an evolutionary process. Orientation and bibliographic or library instruction are components of information literacy and, as such, are valuable. But traditional library instruction is a pale shadow of what of what information literacy promises to be. Our potential mistake would be in stopping here rather than accepting the admittedly difficult, challenging, and time consuming goal of integration.

We cannot realize a bold vision without making some changes to our current practice. In the IDEO example mentioned previously, the shopping cart team grapples with how to redesign the cart to address issues of convenience, maneuverability, child safety, and theft. One of the proposed new designs results in a cart with several modular baskets instead of a large central basket. At

| From Bibliographic Instruction to Information Literacy | | |
|---|---|---|
| | **BI or Teaching Paradigm** | **Information Literacy or Learning Paradigm** |
| Responsibility / Control | Librarian controlled; focus on instruction & teachers | Collaborative responsibility among librarians, faculty, assessment experts, instructional designers, & others; focus on student learning and performance |
| Relationship to Curriculum | External or tangential to curriculum | Integrated into the curriculum |
| Placement in Curriculum | Isolated learning episodes ("one-shots"; stand-alone credit courses) | Pervasive throughout the curriculum; integrated into courses |
| Content Focus | Focus primarily on tools, search interfaces, navigating a physical library | Focus on concepts, critical thinking, evaluation, ethics |
| Teaching Methods | Librarian control; didactic methods; "50-minute stand" | Methods consider a variety of learning styles; librarians and others as guides / coaches; methods are scalable |
| Learning Transfer | Limited learning transfer | Increased learning transfer due to multiple learning opportunities |
| Assessment | Often non-existent or formative | Focus on competencies and standards as yardsticks for outcomes-based approaches |
| Relationship to Place | Focus on specific libraries / library resources | Focus on unbounded universe of information |
| Role of Technology | Limited or inflexible use of technology | Technology used in transformational ways; technology used to scale up efforts |

## The Continuum

| Orientation | Bibliographic Instruction Library Instruction | Information Literacy | |
|---|---|---|---|
| 1 | 2 | 3 | 4 | 5 |

*Chart originally developed by Craig Gibson, modified by Karen Williams.*

checkout, groceries are placed in plastic bags, which are suspended from the cart's structure for travel through the parking lot. This design is more convenient for some shoppers and prevents theft. An interviewer asks how a cart can be a cart without a central basket. One passionate designer cries out, "The basket is tyranny!"[12]

As courageous leaders, it is time to ask ourselves what are the tyrannies of our present educational models and practices? (Note that being courageous does not mean being unafraid but, rather, persisting in the face of fears, doubts, and ambiguity.) An examination of current practice shows that we tend to work with a small percentage of individual faculty, often by making our availability known and waiting to be invited into classes. Our standard model is a 50-minute guest session. We know that one of the biggest reasons we do not get invited into every appropriate class is because faculty believe the subject content to be important and the term already too short to cover everything. We frequently make a similar mistake by cramming too much into a single session because we think what we are teaching is valuable, and we do not know if the students will have other learning opportunities with this material.

We also typically see shallow horizontal integration of our information literacy efforts, front loaded in the first year with scattershot sessions elsewhere. We have been successful on many campuses in working with freshman composition programs. Many institutions have a few areas reflecting more depth, but these are often dependent on relationships between individual librarians and faculty members rather than being anchored in the curriculum. If a key player leaves, years of effort can quickly be lost.

We should give ourselves some credit, though. One early sign of a paradigm shift is an attempt to use the tools and ideas of a new paradigm within the framework provided by the old. While we still use the 50-minute session as our primary delivery mechanism, most librarians have moved beyond the standard lecture-demonstration technique to include a variety of creative active learning components. We are adding to our toolkit of teaching techniques, acknowledging that lecture as one tool available for use in particular situations is fine, but not enough.

Learning is an iterative process. Students will most likely master information literacy knowledge and skills through repeated exposure and practice. If, for example, we want them to acquire something as simple as the habit of asking "do I need more information?", or the more complex skill of assessing the value of particular sources to the question at hand, they need multiple opportunities to practice these skills in context. The contexts will change and become increasingly complex and sophisticated as students progress through programs of study. Our present model of a librarian presenting a 50-minute session will not scale to accommodate the needed number of learning opportunities. This model also does not address the variety of learning styles and preferences among learners, nor does it meet just-in-time needs.

When we were engaged mostly in bibliographic instruction efforts, individual librarians could work mostly alone. As we move toward creating information literacy programs, it becomes impossible for us to work alone—or even just within the library. Information literacy needs to be deeply integrated into the curriculum and for this to happen we must be thinking programmatically, not about our libraries' information literacy programs but about our campus information literacy programs. As Barr and Tagg note:

> In the Learning Paradigm, learning environments and activities are learner-centered and learner-controlled. They may even be "teacherless." While teachers will have designed the learning experiences and environments students use—often through teamwork with each other and other staff—they need not be present for or participate in every structured learning activity.[13]

In my bold vision, librarians are strong and important members of these learning design teams. We bring tremendous knowledge of how information is produced, organized and disseminated; we are familiar with typical information-seeking behaviors and know what often challenges students. We may still conduct 50-minute guest sessions when this is the most appropriate technique to help achieve desired learning outcomes, but this will not be the only tool in our repertoire. I often invite librarians to close their eyes and imagine information literacy learning taking place, *without a librarian in sight*. This does not mean that librarians are out of the equation. Imagine a scenario where students are writing papers for a course. As each student recognizes the need for more information, s/he consults one or more online tools, designed by librarians collaborating with others. These tools appear to students as regular course components, listed on the syllabus or available through the course learning management system. As a part of the paper, students are required to show their thinking around the selection of resources. Instead of producing just a regular bibliography, they include information about which databases they chose to search and why; they might include their successful search strategies. They give specific reasons for why they chose at least some of their cited sources. They might also list some sources that were examined and not selected, giving their reasons for rejection. The faculty member evaluating the papers gives feedback on this enhanced bibliography, assisted by a rubric developed with a librarian.

## Moving Toward a Learning Paradigm

As noted above, librarians were often the first to articulate the importance of information literacy. We still have critical roles as advocates for its integration and as designers of new learning environments. It is important to have some picture of what the future will look like if we are successfully graduating information literate students. However, bold visions are by definition a bit fuzzy, and it is particularly important in partnership efforts not to get locked into specific ideas about the journey. To create a shared vision, we must remind ourselves to focus on interests, not positions. It will be important to set some goals in order to focus energies and measure progress. Setting specific goals within a broader context that we do not completely control is a balancing act, requiring flexibility, openness, a passion for and belief in the potential outcome, and a dash of political acuity. Having a vision and goals helps with evaluating the myriad opportunities and gauging whether or not they advance the program. In order to achieve the vision, we will undoubtedly need to change some of our current practice and turn down some requests and opportunities along the way.

Creating campus information literacy programs will require the efforts of both grassroots and positional leaders. Grassroots leaders can conduct opportunity assessments to identify likely campus partners; focusing on articulated campus, college, and department priorities where what we have to offer can be seen as part of a solution. Good advocates know their audiences, their turf and their issues. Designing and tailoring a core message is key. Focus on change makers and enlist them as early adopters and carriers of the message.

Library administrators are sometimes able to influence who gets invited to the table and we should take advantage of that. While not all library administrators have backgrounds in information literacy, they all have limited time and may need help from teaching librarians. Doing the necessary work to prepare positional leaders will be much appreciated. This can include everything from developing "sound bites" or an "elevator talk" with an intriguing hook; to drafting nomination letters that library administrators could use to recommend librarians for curriculum committees; to writing an aspirational white paper.

This shift from a BI, or teaching, paradigm to a learning, or information literacy, paradigm will not occur quickly or easily. We will need to be patient and persistent, celebrating milestones along the way. I will close with one last thought from Barr and Tagg: "In our experience, people will suffer the turbulence and uncertainty of change if it promises a better way to accomplish work they value. The shift to the Learning Paradigm represents such an opportunity."[14]

## Notes

1. Joan V Gallos, "On Creating Leaders: A Pedagogy of Courage and Passion," *Journal of Man-*

*agement Education* (February 21, 1997): 6-7.

2.  See Warren G. Bennis and Ben Nanus, *Leaders: The Strategies for Taking Charge.* (New York: Harper and Row, 1985), and Brooke E. Sheldon, *Leaders in Libraries* (Chicago: American Library Association, 1991).

3.  James M. Kouzes and Barry Z. Posner, *The Leadership Challenge.* San Francisco: Jossey-Bass, 2002.

4.  Peter M. Senge, *The Fifth Discipline Fieldbook : Strategies and Tools for Building a Learning Organization* (New York: Doubleday, 1994).

5.  Gallos, p. 6-7.

6.  Karin Wittenborg, "Rocking the Boat." In Karin Wittenborg, Chris Ferguson, and Michael A. Keller, *Reflecting on Leadership,* pp 1-15. Washington, D.C.: Council on Library and Information Resources, 2003. p. 2. Available online from http://www.clir.org/pubs/abstract/pub123abst.html [Accessed August 27, 2007.]

7.  Esther S. Grassian and Joan R. Kaplowitz, *Learning to Lead and Manage Information Literacy Instruction* (New York: Neal-Schuman Publishers, 2005).

8.  Linda Lambert, *Constructivist Leadership* (New York: Teachers College Press, Columbia University, 1995).

9.  *Nightline.* "The Deep Dive." July 13, 1999. [videorecording]. New York: ABC News Home Video.

10.  Karin Wittenborg, "Rocking the Boat." In Karin Wittenborg, Chris Ferguson, and Michael A. Keller, *Reflecting on Leadership* (Washington, D.C.: Council on Library and Information Resources, 2003), p. 2. Available online from http://www.clir.org/pubs/abstract/pub123abst.html. [Accessed August 27, 2007].

11.  Robert B. Barr and John Tagg, "From Teaching to Learning—A New Paradigm for Undergraduate Education." *Change Magazine* 27 (November/December 1995): 12-25. p. 12.

12.  *The Deep Dive,*" July 13, 1999. [videorecording]. New York: ABC News Home Video.

13.  Barr and Tagg, p. 21-22.

14.  Barr and Tagg, p. 25.

# CHAPTER 8
## *Student Academic Integrity*

Lynn D. Lampert

Academic librarians involved in library instruction have historically encountered issues of student academic integrity in limited measures. Prior to the growth of information literacy programming, opportunities to formally develop educational strategies to prevent students' unethical usage of information typically only surfaced through committee work or collaboration with concerned faculty. Today however, librarians are becoming both increasingly more relied upon and proactive in educating students about plagiarism and other issues of academic integrity through information literacy instruction and educational programming. It is important for instruction librarians, both new and seasoned, to keep abreast of the latest pedagogical approaches being employed to introduce students to issues involving academic integrity. There are many important roles that librarians and libraries can play in raising awareness about the ethical usages of information.

With the recent rise in detected incidents of student plagiarism, collusion and cheating, many college campuses are renewing their commitments to bolster academic honor codes and enforce policies that punish students found guilty of academic misconduct. Some campuses are utilizing resources like Turnitin.com and other electronic plagiarism detection services to identify student plagiarism. Currently there are two commonplace approaches employed by colleges and universities working to deal with occurrences of student academic misconduct. The prevalent institutional response is to detect and punish students found guilty of academic misconduct. The other emergent method is to actively engage as an institution in both a program of detection and educational prevention to raise awareness. The latter kind of multi-faceted campus response to the problem of declining academic integrity aims to ensure that students are educated about the standards of academic integrity that they are expected to demonstrate from the time of admission to the university. In addition to dealing with plagiarism, many campuses are also developing policies and educational programming to cover related information ethics issues such as copyright and fair use with both faculty and students. As Marta Mestrovic Dewyrup notes, campuses like the University of Maryland are creating centers for intellectual property whose programmatic efforts address issues such as the, "TEACH Act, the Digital Millennium Copyright Act (DCMA), peer-to-peer file sharing, and scholarly communication."[1]

149

In response to all of these above mentioned concerns, information literacy librarians are often requested to devise instructional solutions to improve student awareness about information ethics and academic integrity standards through information literacy instructional interventions. Many libraries are utilizing on-line tutorials and/or in-class instructional techniques to help students to better understand what constitutes legitimate usage of texts and data retrieved via both print and Internet resources. Some libraries have also developed collaborative programs and partnerships to extend their information literacy instruction efforts into these areas across their campus. This chapter will discuss how academic integrity is currently viewed within the circles of higher education, including academic librarianship. Particular attention will be placed on educational solutions that are currently in practice. The chapter also will offer librarians and libraries involved in information literacy instruction insight into ways to approach the issues involved in educating students about academic integrity by offering examples of working programmatic solutions and collaborative partnerships. Best practices in establishing anti-plagiarism and academic integrity curricula in order to foster a culture of education that replaces over reliance on a reactive culture that only polices academic misconduct will be discussed.

## Academic Integrity & Information Literacy

Since librarians typically do not teach semester long discipline courses that require grading research papers or projects, their exposure to examples of student academic dishonesty, unintended or intentional, largely occurs during their service on campus committees that deal with academic grievances or the unethical behavior of students. Colleges and universities across the United States typically establish campus committees charged with reviewing academic grievances in order to determine whether or not the student is indeed guilty or not guilty of academic dishonesty. Student misconduct cases typically involve instances of student cheating, plagiarism or other forms of academic dishonesty. Gail Wood acknowledges that many librarians serving on these committees often find themselves repeatedly asked to track down sources in reviewed plagiarism cases. According to Wood, librarians often find themselves acting as a sort of "antiplagiarism enforcer".[2] The benefit of having librarians placed on these kinds of academic conduct committees certainly outweighs the likelihood of librarians being singled out as plagiarism detection experts. These committees tend to introduce librarians to other pivotal campus partners committed to increasing student and faculty awareness about the common problems associated with a lack of knowledge about academic integrity practices. In addition, for a librarian and the library, the inherent value of working on a committee that deals with issues of academic integrity is having the platform to discuss how issues of academic integrity often correlate to students' lack of information literacy. Active participation on an academic conduct committee, by a member of the library staff, is often a critical component to creating a culture of academic integrity education solutions that includes the library and information literacy programming.

Why is creating a holistic culture of academic integrity critical to increasing student awareness about the dangers of plagiarism and other acts of academic misconduct? While the answer may seem basic enough it is clear that there are many factors that influence a student's propensity to engage in academic misconduct. Research has shown that the existence of honor codes and clear policies have a partial impact on thwarting instances of academic misconduct. However, there is also ample evidence that students need to be introduced to the ethical standards of academic life, and their chose discipline, in a number of different situations outside the faculty-student lecture setting. As Ranald Macdonald and Jude Carroll note, plagiarism is a complex issue requiring a holistic institutional approach. According to their study, a holistic institutional approach "recognises the need for a shared responsibility between the student, staff and institution, supported by external quality agencies."[3] Certainly the library and librarians, like other academic support faculty and staff can aid in such a collective endeavor.

In fact, as recent research argues, "by developing an anthropologist's sensitivity to culture, academic librarians can learn the characteristics of the academic disciplines and then help students learn these characteristics as a way for them to understand the rhetorical practices in these fields. In making tacit practices visible, librarians can facilitate students' transitions into the cultures of their chosen disciplines."[4] Clearly, assisting with students' indoctrination into a discipline's culture of academic integrity is an area where librarians can both assist and provide formal instruction to complement information literacy programming. This is particularly true in approaches that use examples of notable acts of plagiarism to raise students' awareness of the existing ramifications plagiarists encounter both within and outside of academe.

Once an institution chooses to integrate information literacy curricula into academic integrity educational programming it is imperative that academic integrity policies and information literacy standards are unequivocally defined. Standard Five of the *ACRL Information Literacy Competency Standards for Higher Education* is a critical component of any information literacy instructional approach that aims to introduce the ethical usage of information in both legal and social contexts. This standard states that an information literate student

• Accurately and appropriately documents sources, and uses paraphrases and direct quotes in order to avoid plagiarism.

• Understands issues related to privacy and security, censorship, intellectual property and copyright in order to use information responsibly.

- Legally obtains, stores, and disseminates text, data, images and sound.[5]

Librarians working to integrate academic integrity curriculum into information literacy sessions should be aware of the wide spectrum of instructional issues that can be covered by establishing lecture goals around ACRL Standard #5. Beyond identifying published university policies and standards on academic conduct, librarians should also investigate whether or not the related discipline they are working with has related published statements on academic integrity standards from bodies outside the university such as professional associations or accreditation bodies. Students' understanding of proper attribution standards and the overall reduction in student cheating behaviors are important to future employers. For many working outside academe, the current state of student beliefs and practices in regards to issues pertaining to information ethics is both appalling and unacceptable.

As the 2003 *National Survey of Student Engagement* (NSSE) revealed, "87% of college students surveyed reported that their peers sometimes "copy and paste" information from the Web for reports and papers—without citing sources."[6] While other forms of cheating certainly still persist, with the rise of the Internet and full text resources plagiarism has become the number one complaint registered by faculty questioned about student academic integrity. The rise in the popularity of downloading media has also caused many university officials to express concern over students' apparent lack of understanding or disregard for the legal ramifications involved in illegally downloading, copying or pirating music or video related media. Both subject faculty and librarians also report that students struggle with the concept of attribution when it comes to documenting external sources utilized in term paper preparation. All of these areas of concern, regardless of whether or not they involve students' improper usages of materials in or outside the college curriculum, signify a looming ethical crisis within higher education and beyond. As it has been shown educating college students about the ethics involved in these academic integrity areas addresses the concerns of faculty, potential employers and professional associations affiliated with certain disciplines and majors.[7]

What do experts within higher education mean when they use terms like academic misconduct or academic integrity? Certainly, there are many differing views about what acts constitute academic misconduct. Over the past two decades considerable research has also been conducted to explore what infringements should be classified under the rather broad heading of academic dishonesty.[8] While plagiarism has taken the spotlight within recent reports of academic misconduct infractions, cases of unethical scientific research and conduct, cheating and other forms of information piracy abound academe today. According to a 2005 study conducted by Donald McCabe, the director of the Center for Academic Integrity (CAI) at Duke University, 70% of the near 50,000 undergraduate students surveyed admitted to some form of cheating. Close to one-quarter of the participating students admitted to serious test cheating in the past year and half admitted to one or more instances of serious cheating on written assignments."[9] CAI's 2005 research goes on to show that issues involving students lack of academic integrity are growing more disconcerting. Plagiarism is on the rise and many students are not sure what all the fuss is about. The results of the 2005 research report claim that,

> Internet plagiarism is a growing concern on all campuses as students struggle to understand what constitutes acceptable use of the Internet. In the absence of clear direction from faculty, most students have concluded that 'cut & paste' plagiarism—using a sentence or two (or more) from different sources on the Internet and weaving this information together into a paper without appropriate citation—is not a serious issue. While 10% of students admitted to engaging in such behavior in 1999, almost 40% admit to doing so in the Assessment Project surveys.[10]

As Elaine Whitaker notes in her discussion of pedagogical approaches to introducing anti-plagiarism instruction, when asked to define plagiarism,

> undergraduates in my classes choose "copying" and "stealing" as synonyms. Pressed to distinguish between plagiarism and legitimate forms of imitation, they become confused. Asked about accepted conventions for acknowledging the use of the words or ideas of others within their writing, first year students are flustered…ignored in the concepts students bring to my classes are the ideas of achieving personal mastery of information, having one's own carefully considered opinion, and analyzing where one's own position falls with respect to the positions of others.[11]

Most studies on plagiarism and academic integrity issues with higher education are quick to point out that too many educators have ignored the evidence that undergraduates need to be introduced to acceptable standards of academic behavior on a continual basis throughout their academic careers.

## Literature Review

Within the literature of library and information science, research on library instruction, academic integrity and plagiarism is a somewhat recent phenomenon. Lorna

Peterson's 1988 research represents one of the first arguments supporting the notion that librarians should integrate discussions of academic integrity standards into library instruction. Peterson urges librarians to move into this area of instruction keeping in mind a particular focus on how academic integrity issues are present throughout the research process—from the retrieval of external information to its synthesis in both the writing of a paper and its bibliography. In her view, the predominant misconception that discipline faculty already introduce students to acceptable ethical academic behavior standards is one of the largest factors leading to the rise of academic dishonesty infractions. Therefore instruction on academic integrity should no longer be viewed as the sole instructional domain of discipline faculty. Peterson writes that while it, "is evident that faculty must participate actively in imparting the concept of academic integrity… librarians in their role as teachers must participate as well. There should be no fear of treading on someone else's territory. Academic integrity is the soul of the college and university."[12] Peterson goes on to chastise academic librarians' lack of involvement in issues of academic integrity within library instruction in the following statement.

> As participants in the scholarly process, librarians traditionally have seen their role as one of the teaching the mechanics of identifying and locating books and articles; only occasionally does a BI program include the evaluation of such materials or how-to of proper documentation. And, like the teaching faculty, librarians generally fail to address questions of academic integrity.[13]

The results of Peterson's study indicated that instruction librarians felt that they needed to work with students on concepts such as documentation and independent scholarship.

Since Peterson's article, which was written before the height of the information literacy movement, other researchers have also examined the need for librarians to actively approach issues of academic integrity in information literacy sessions. Studies by both Nicole J. Auer and Ellen M. Krupar and D. Scott Brandt realize the unique role that librarians can play in working on issues of academic integrity by discussing issues of plagiarism with students.[14] Both studies rightly contend that librarians' in-depth knowledge of issues such as copyright, intellectual property and research documentation styles make them ideal experts who should contribute to their university's education response to issues of academic integrity. D. Scott Brandt notes that,

> Issues related to copyright apply in a similar vein to plagiarism. In fact, copyright abuse and plagiarism are like two sides of a

permission coin—on the one side, people take without asking, and on the other side, people take without telling…. Librarians have a special perspective on plagiarism. Some teachers will talk about it from an intellectual writing viewpoint, but we can address it from an applied and technological perspective. It's not enough to say "don't do it." You must emphasize how and why it takes place, and what needs to be done to prevent it. Librarians have done a great job championing copyright, and we can do likewise condemning plagiarism.[15]

Recent examples of other studies that reflect on librarians' experiences in integrating anti-plagiarism instruction into information literacy programming include the author's own 2004 study examining how discipline based librarian approaches to combating plagiarism and academic integrity issues better engage students.[16] Other works that deserve notable attention include Jeff Liles and Michael Rozalski's analysis of how attention to instructional approach improves the delivery academic integrity issues within library instructional sessions, and the work Pamela Jackson who examines the efficacy of anti-plagiarism instruction through the development and usage of online learning modules. Jackson's study assesses undergraduate students' understandings of proper paraphrasing techniques through the usage of an interactive, web-based tutorial, *Plagiarism: The Crime of Intellectual Kidnapping.*[17]

Other studies evaluating the use of tutorials and other virtual learning modules to introduce students to issues of academic integrity include Laura Guertin's 2005 article, and the work of Fricker, Armstrong and Carty, researchers at the University of California San Diego, who introduced an online tutorial to help encourage academic integrity.[18] A review of many of the online tutorials currently employed by colleges and universities across the United States reveals a propensity for anti-plagiarism tutorials that focus on the introduction of proper citation methods using either the MLA or APA documentation styles. A review of ACRL's Peer-Reviewed Instructional Materials Online PRIMO database reveals that even fewer tutorials adequately discuss issues of intellectual property or copyright. The University of California Los Angeles's tutorial *Carlos and Eddie's Guide Bruin Success with Less Stress* is a model exception to this pattern. This tutorial, which contains multiple modules, provides students with information on various issues that fall into frequent summarizations of common academic integrity violations. In the tutorial directions for faculty the creators write that,

> *Carlos and Eddie's Guide to Bruin Success with Less Stress* was created as an interactive student-centered learning experience.

The tone is informal and the "quizzes" are constructed as pedagogical tools to engage users rather than scientific tools to assess users. If you choose to require your students to complete
any of the five major sections, printable certificates of completion are available for each section except "Citing and Documenting Sources," which instead enables students to e-mail
their quiz results to whomever they wish.[19]

Issues such as intellectual property, file sharing ethics, cheating, fabrication
and academic misrepresentation in addition to coverage on citation documentation styles are provided for both faculty and student usage in this UCLA tutorial. All of these areas are covered with examples from taken popular culture.
Detailed attention is paid to the information seeking behavior of undergraduates
who fall into the millennial generation.

## Definitions of Academic Integrity

There have been countless studies examining issues involving academic integrity
and academic misconduct. Donald McCabe who is perhaps the most notable
researcher on academic integrity in higher education and secondary schools
has authored several important studies analyzing the factors leading to student
breaches of academic integrity. McCabe's research has consistently pointed to
the need for well established and enforced honor codes which both define what
constitutes academic dishonesty and work to deter a proportion of students who
might otherwise knowingly cheat.

Researchers Donald Gehring and Gary Pavela point to the critical importance of clearly defining what an institution considers to be a breech of academic
integrity. Gehring and Pavela write that, "Reducing the amount of academic dishonesty also requires developing a clearly written statement of how academic
dishonesty is defined. Well-defined expectations and standards reduce uncertainty and arbitrary decision making, and help to discourage litigation."[20] They
propose that following four categories of unwanted behavior represent the most
critical threats to sustaining academic integrity:

> • *Cheating*: Intentionally using or attempting to use unauthorized
> materials, information, or study aids in any academic exercise.
> • *Fabrication*: Intentional and unauthorized falsification or in-
> vention of any information or citation in an academic exercise.
> • *Facilitating academic dishonesty*: Intentionally or knowingly
> helping or attempting to help another to commit an act of aca-
> demic dishonesty.

- *Plagiarism*: Intentionally or knowingly representing the words of another as one's own in any academic exercise.[21]

Another respected definition of academic integrity that can be relied upon originated from CAI in 1999. Their defining document interprets academic integrity from a value-based perspective. This explanation differs from previous definitions within the literature of higher education which characterized academic integrity by enumerating various prohibited behaviors in published higher education policies and codes. CAI identifies five fundamental values that encompass academic integrity. These five values are honesty, trust, fairness, respect and responsibility. As Hinman, one of the drafters of the CAI statement on academic integrity notes, these values call for the recognition that "academic life encompasses several principal activities—learning, teaching, and researching—and that to engage in these activities we must often participate in a community. This is a departure from conceptions of academic integrity that see it as applicable only to the activity of learning engaged in by students."[22]

By expanding the circle of those involved in educating students about issues of academic integrity, educators with higher education are more likely to reach a greater number of students. Whether collaboration partnerships arise between faculty and librarians or writing centers or writing programs it is clear that repeated exposure to standards of academic integrity are critical components to educating students about proper and ethical academic practices. A collaborative pedagogical approach to addressing student understanding of academic integrity is becoming increasingly more important due to the changing undergraduate conceptions of what constitutes the ethical usage of information.

## Collaborative Partners & Best Practices for Working on Academic Integrity

Many recent works have examined the benefits that collaborative partnerships between librarians and faculty bring to information literacy programming. The strongest examples of works that offer powerful examples of practical collaborations that work to better embed information literacy programming into curricular offerings include Raspa and Ward's *The Collaborative Imperative: Librarians and Faculty Working Together in the Information Universe* , Susan Kraat's *Relationships between teaching faculty and teaching librarians*. Recently, additional research has also concentrated on creating awareness about the benefits of collaboration between librarians and students affairs professionals.[23] These partnerships can benefit student development in areas such as academic integrity and student academic preparation from a co-curricular standpoint. Academic integrity is a natural area where collaboration can blossom between librarians, faculty and other academic support units within a university. When one reviews much of the literature on collaborative information literacy partnerships the focus is typically on the integration of information literacy into curriculum through course redesign or assignment restructuring. While examples that highlight how collaborations bring academic integrity awareness to the forefront of campus initiatives exist, few publications have focused on these kinds of programs.

A good example of a strong campus collaborative project working to address issues of academic integrity can be seen in the work of the University of Maryland Libraries Academic Integrity Initiative committee. This committee coordinates the Libraries' informational and instructional response to the issues of plagiarism and academic integrity. Through the work of this committee librarians have partnered with the following academic units to raise awareness about issues of academic integrity: The Center for Teaching Excellence, The Professional Writing Program, The Freshman Writing Program, the Project NEThics Graduate School, the Student Honor Council, the Office of Student Conduct and the campus Writing Center. The mission of this library's Academic Integrity Committee reads as follows:

In order to respond to the heightened incidence of academic dishonesty, particularly plagiarism, on campus, the University Libraries have launched an academic integrity initiative. Working with campus partners, the Libraries intend to raise awareness of academic integrity issues and provide information to students and educators on how to use research resources in a responsible and ethical manner.[24]

After holding an inaugural Summit on Academic Integrity, that invited officials from across the university, librarians at the University of Maryland were able to accomplish many goals in the following academic year. Some of the highlights of their collaborative efforts include: the development of web pages that teach students about academic integrity and provide information for faculty; workshops for new English 101 instructors and Writing Center tutors on citing information from electronic databases; a presentation to the Council of Deans; the mounting of an exhibit to mark Academic Integrity Week in April 2006; and finally the library's weeding and the withdrawal of outdated editions of style manuals from the circulating collection, so that students will not use incorrect citation styles.[25]

According to Diane Harvey, in the 2006-2007 academic year, the Academic Integrity Committee plans to work more closely with the Graduate School to provide information on academic integrity that meets the particular needs of graduate students, especially international students; continue collaborative efforts with K12 educators; collaborate with the Office of Student Conduct on projects such as Academic Integrity Week; expand the Libraries collaboration with the Writing Center by having Writing Center tutors available one afternoon and one evening each week at the Reference/Information desk; identify and highlight the work of campus faculty who model 'best practices' in teaching about academic integrity. This project's collaborative work serves as a model of an approach that seeks to work in tandem with individual Colleges and academic units who have indicated their desire to work with the Committee to promote issues of academic integrity across the campus.[26]

Through collaborative partnerships and collective programming efforts, the curriculum needed to raise awareness about integrity in information literacy sessions emerges. Sometimes the mere discussion of what constitutes plagiarism or a copyright violation opens up a frank and enlightening discussion between students, librarians and faculty within a classroom setting. For successful online learning module approaches, tying academic integrity curriculum to real-life or discipline based examples tends to make a larger imprint on students searching for meaning in new practices and academic standards. In short introducing real-life explanations that exist behind issues such as plagiarism, academic honesty, copyright and intellectual property in a frank, clear and relevant manner tends to lead to successful student comprehension and awareness.

As this author has noted before, some of the best techniques that librarians can implement when working to integrate anti-plagiarism or academic integrity discussions into information literacy sessions include:

- Reinvestigating what plagiarism and the unethical use of information mean in the context of a particular discipline.
- Familiarizing oneself with the discipline's preferred style of formatting and code of ethics.
- Examining the curricular standards required for disciplinary accreditation.
- Identifying discipline/professional associations that have a focus on ethics.
- Demonstrating a willingness to make resources available to aid in the study of the ethics of information in every discipline where it is appropriate.[27]

In order to effectively introduce academic integrity into information literacy instructional settings it is also important that teaching approaches and exercises adopt a process based approach. In this area of developing pedagogy researchers of note include Hulbert, Savidge and Laudenslager and Walden and Peacock's who have developed the *i-Map* approach at the University of Hertfordshire Centre for the Enhancement of Learning and Teaching in the United Kingdom.[28] Hulbert, Savidge and Laudenslager emphasize that information literacy exercises about academic integrity and more specifically plagiarism need to link course content to the research process and/or introduce ethical issues by constructing a problem-based scenario. The authors also stress the importance of utilizing classroom assignments that ask students to document their research steps by creating a research log or account that can be evaluated by instructors and librarians. When effectively crafted by faculty, process-based assignments give librarians a chance to work with students on the preparation of their search, information retrieval strategies, their evaluative techniques for selecting information and their understanding of documentation standards used to correctly cite synthesized information sources. A process-based assignment, "teaches the value of the question and the process, and builds a respect for the integrity of information sources and the research process."[29]

Building upon the same principles of the above research, Walden and Peacock, developed the *i-Map* approach at the University of Hertfordshire's Centre for the Enhancement of Learning and Teaching. The *i-Map*, which is also called an information handling map, allows students to develop flowchart drawings and other forms of "visual communication to represent the research process, including layout, color, typeface and line to communicate effectively." The *i-Map* is similar to the research log approach that asks students to keep a research journal. However, as the authors explain that the hallmark of their *i-Map* approach is that it is a visual and portable,

> working record of the way ideas have been developed and information gathered. The *i-Map* can record brain storming activities, intuitive jumps between subjects and ideas, and order logical thought processes. It can document potential sources, actual sources and references. It shows the interconnection of ideas and information, the strategies used to gather, evaluate and synthesize information and the structure and planning for the final text.[30]

The *i-Map* approach is similar to the new visual search technology developed by Grokker that is now being absorbed into database interfaces like EBSCOHost's Visual Search. EbscoHost's Visual Search allows students search efficiently across broad subjects, and then returns a visual map of results, organized by topic with visual depictions of results broken down by sub-categorizations and links to articles. The value of Walden and Peacock's *i-Map* exercise approach, in comparison, is that it goes beyond the search and retrieval process to ask students to connect and document their key words, search terms, URL's, authors and the titles of retrieved books, periodical articles, and web resources in their own creative way. The *i-Map* process, which is a seven step process, also requires students to begin by thinking about their assignment and their unique information need and then move into topic exploration, information retrieval and evaluation and finally the drafting and revisions of the text. In addition to emphasizing the pre-planning and evaluative process that is needed to gather and utilize information in writing, the *i-Map* also provides instructors, like faculty and librarians, with a documented and sequential road map to assess where a student is in terms of the research process and academic integrity.

Through either discussions or implementation of exercises and assignments like the *i-Map* it is imperative that academic ask students to think about the process in which they have gathered and utilized outside information. Pedagogical tools like the *i-Map* can be used to enhance an instructor's ability to raise student awareness about academic integrity issues such as plagiarism, copyright infringement and cheating. These techniques also move us away from the trap of thinking that academic integrity issues like plagiarism only surface in the realm of writing research papers. The growth of search technologies has now made information retrieval a more solitary process that often can be haphazardly carried out by fledgling students who are unaware of the need to evaluate and document where the retrieved information originated. As Walden and Peacock rightly note, "plagiarism of the written word is only one of the many issues connected with proper acknowledgement of sources for image and sound as much as print, and an understanding of issues that include intellectual property rights, the inter-connections of the network of learning, the reception and ownership of ideas, information and knowledge."[31] As educators working within higher education, librarians must take advantage of our unique positioning within the academy. We are often witnesses to our students' indoctrinations into the world of research. Therefore librarians should take an active role in guiding students through the new challenges involved in becoming information literate student by developing their awareness of our universities' academic integrity standards.

## Notes

1. Marta Mestrovic Dewyrup, "Intellectual Property and the University: An Interview with Kim Bonner, Director, Center for Intellectual Property, University of Maryland, University College," *Library Administration & Management* 19, no.1 (2005):4-6.

2. Gail Wood, "Academic Original Sin: Plagiarism, the Internet, and Librarians," *Journal of Academic Librarianship* 30, no.3 (2004): 237-242.

3. Ranald Macdonald and Jude Carroll. "Plagiarism—a complex issue requiring a holistic institutional approach." *Assessment & Evaluation in Higher Education* 31, no. 2 (2006): 233-245.

4. Michelle Holschuh Simmons. "Librarians as disciplinary discourse mediators: using genre theory to move toward critical information literacy." *portal: Libraries and the Academy* 5, no.3 (2005): 297.

5. Association of College and Research Libraries. "Information Literacy Competency Standards for Higher Education," 2000. Available online from: http://www.ala.org/ala/acrl/acrlstandards/standards.pdf [Accessed 10 August, 2006].

6. Indiana University. "NSSE: Vast majority of undergrads using IT, but 'cut-and-paste' a typical academic 'strategy',"2003. Available online from: http://www.indiana.edu/~ocmhp/121203/text/technology.shtml [Accessed 10 August, 2006].

7. See Allen Hall and Lisa Berardino. "Teaching Professional Behaviors: Differences in the Perceptions of Faculty, Students, and Employers." *Journal of Business Ethics* 63, no.4 (2006): 407-

415; Denise Nitterhouse. "Plagiarism—Not Just an "Academic" Problem." *Teaching Business Ethics* 7, no. 3 (2003):215-227.

8. See B.E Whitley, Jr..and P. Keith-Spiegel. *Academic Dishonesty: An educator's guide.* (2002) Mahwah, NJ: Lawrence Erlbaum Associates; H.S. Pincus and L.P. Schmelkin. "Faculty perceptions of academic dishonesty: A multidimensional scaling analysis." *Journal of Higher Education* 74, no.2 (2003): 196-209.

9. Center for Academic Integrity. "In New CAI Research Conducted By Don McCabe."(2005). Available online from http://www.academicintegrity.org/cai_research.asp [Accessed 10 August, 2006].

10. Ibid.

11. Elaine Whitaker, "A Pedagogy to Address Plagiarism," *College Composition and Communication* 44, no.4 (1993): 509-514.

12. Peterson, Lorna. "Teaching Academic Integrity: Opportunities in Bibliographic Instruction." *Research Strategies* 6, no.1 (Fall 1988): 168-76.

13. Ibid.

14. Nicole J. Auer and Ellen M. Krupar, "Mouse Click Plagiarism: The Role of Technology in Plagiarism and the Librarian's Role in Combating It," *Library Trends* 49, no. 3 (2001): 415-432; See D. Scott Brandt, "Copyright's (Not So) Little Cousin, Plagiarism," *Computers in Libraries* 22, no. 5 (2002): 39-41.

15. D. Scott Brandt, "Copyright's (Not So) Little Cousin, Plagiarism," *Computers in Libraries* 22, no. 5 (2002): 39-41.

16. Lynn D. Lampert. "Integrating Discipline based anti-plagiarism instruction into the information literacy curriculum," *Reference Services Review* 32, no. 4 (2004), 347-355.

17. Jeffrey A.Liles and Michael E. Rozalski. "It's a Matter of Style: A Style Manual Workshops for Preventing Plagiarism." *College & Undergraduate Libraries*, 11, no.2, (2004): 91-101; Pamela Jackson, "Plagiarism Instruction Online: Assessing Undergraduate Students' Ability to Avoid Plagiarism," *College & Research Libraries*, 67, no.5 (2006):418-428.

18. Laura Guertin. "Using virtual lectures to educate students on plagiarism," *First Monday* 10, no.9 (August 2005) Available online from http://firstmonday.org/issues/issue10_9/guertin/ [Accessed 10 August, 2006]; Beth Ann Fricker, William Armstrong and Heidi Carty "The Proposed UCSD Academic Integrity Tutorial Pilot Project: A Formative Evaluation" ERIC Document ED479133 Available online from http://eric.ed.gov/ERICDocs/data/ericdocs2/content_storage_01/0000000b/80/28/44/ad.pdf

19. University of California Los Angeles, "What is this site? *Carlos and Eddie's Guide to Bruin Success with Less Stress.*" Available online from http://unitproj1.library.ucla.edu/col/bruinsuccess/about/index.cfm [Accessed 10 August, 2006].

20. Donald Gehring and Gary Pavela, "Issues and Perspectives on Academic Integrity." Available online from http://www.uri.edu/univcol/URI101/Module_VI/issues_and_perspectives.htm. Please note that the Web site contains excerpts from Gehring, D., & Pavela, G. P. (1994). Issues and perspectives on academic integrity (2nd ed.). Washington DC: National Association of Student Personnel Administrators.

21. Ibid.

22. Lawrence M. Hinman, "Academic Integrity and the World Wide Web," Computers and Society 32, no. 1 (2002): 33-42.

23. Dick Raspa and Dane Ward (Eds.) *The Collaborative Imperative: Librarians and Faculty Working Together in the Information Universe.* Chicago: ACRL, 2000; Susan B. Kraat (Ed.) Relationships Between Teaching Faculty and Teaching Librarians Binghamton, N.Y.: Haworth Information Press, 2005. Published simultaneously as The Reference Librarian, 43, no. 89/90. For re-

cent research on academic librarians and student affairs partnerships see Scott Walter & Michelle Eodice. (Eds.). *Meeting the student learning imperative: Exploring collaborations between academic libraries and student services programs* [Special issue]. *Research Strategies* 20, no.4 (2006).

24. University Libraries, University of Maryland. "Academic Integrity Committee." Available online from http://www.lib.umd.edu/UES/integrity.html. [Accessed 10 August, 2006].

25. Diane Harvey. Email correspondence with author August 10, 2006.

26. Diane Harvey. Email correspondence with author August 10, 2006 with attachment of unpublished "Report to campus partners (August 2006)" sent to the author from Ms. Harvey.

27. Lynn Lampert. "Integrating Discipline based anti-plagiarism instruction into the information literacy curriculum," *Reference Services Review* 32, no. 4 (2004), 347-355.

28. Kim Walden and Alan Peacock. "The i-Map: a process-centered response to plagiarism." *Assessment & Evaluation in Higher Education* 31, no. 2 (2006): 201-214.

29. Janet McNeil Hurlbert, Cathleen R. Savidge & Georgia R. Laudenslager. "Process-Based Assignments: How promoting information literacy prevents plagiarism," *College & Undergraduate Libraries* 10, no.1 (2003): 47-48.

30. Kim Walden and Alan Peacock. "The i-Map: a process-centered response to plagiarism." *Assessment & Evaluation in Higher Education* 31, no. 2 (2006): 201-214.

31. Ibid., p.203.

# CHAPTER 9

# Instruction & Program Design through Assessment

Debra Gilchrist and Anne Zald

True to the intention of this chapter, we begin with learning outcomes and use them as the chapter's organizational structure. Learning outcomes represent what we want you to be able to do as a result of active engagement with this material. Within each outcome we include a short discussion of each topic along with many examples and practical applications of the concept under discussion. We hope that this format illustrates the concepts in a holistic manner and facilitates your understanding and learning.

*Readers of this chapter will be able to:*
I.   *Use the established philosophies, principles, and concepts of assessment in order to build a framework in which to value, experiment with, and apply assessment for the improvement of learning, teaching, and information literacy programs.*
II.  *Design assessments of student learning for the library classroom and as an integrated component of faculty assignments in order to affirm students' learning of information literacy concepts.*
III. *Apply assessment of student learning and principles of good instruction in order to change and improve as a teacher.*
IV.  *Holistically examine an information literacy program through the lenses of the ACRL Best Practices in order to evolve and shape it based on evidence and to demonstrate its value to student success.*

## Outcome I
*Use the established philosophies, principles, and concepts of assessment in order to build a framework in which to value, experiment with, and apply assessment for the improvement of learning, teaching, and information literacy programs.*

The main purpose of academic assessment is to provide us with a collection of evidence on which we can base decisions that are designed to improve student learning. This evidence helps us determine how students are doing relative to collaboratively defined learning outcomes, and the process of determining those outcomes assists librarians in building a shared understanding of essential learning and expectations for our students. In terms of library instruction and information literacy, the authors consider academic assessment to include assessment of student learning, assessment of the value and contributions of the information literacy program, and assessment of the teaching contributions and growth of individual librarians. Combining all three of these components forms a holistic assessment plan and a complete picture of how the library strengthens the campus community.

The discipline of teaching has historically incorporated a component of assessment to determine what students have learned, most often in the form of grades. More recent movement toward assessment of learning uses similar principles and practices but differs in several essential philosophies. Grading focuses on diagnosis while assessment is formative; grading is considered final while assessment is considered summative; grading is usually content driven and assessment is usually goal/outcome driven.

For librarians, evaluations have been a common way to elicit feedback about instruction. Evaluations generally focused on student or faculty opinion regarding the qualities of the librarian or usefulness of the session. This approach developed within an assessment context associated with accountability; one that considered administrative needs more than those of the learning enterprise. The emphasis has now shifted to focus on student learning outcomes, and the real value of assessment in this context is the clarity it provides for students, librarians, and faculty. For students, information literacy outcomes are clearly defined and consistently taught. For librarians and faculty, assessment's significance is as a tool for change since it invites us into conversations with the goal of making good decisions: What can we discover about student learning and achievement of the outcomes that will inform our individual and collective future practice? Assessment helps us clarify and match what we believe is happening in our classrooms and reference areas with student reality. Since it is first and foremost about student experience and not librarian performance or experience, our teaching progress can be measured through the most important factor—student work and actions. The goal of assessment is not to achieve a particular score from student assignments, but instead to determine what we can learn in order to increase our effectiveness as teachers.

### *Philosophical and Conceptual Foundations*

Several philosophical models ground this chapter and illustrate our approach to assessment. These include the Assessment Cycle and the concept of Assessment-as-Learning.

The overall purpose of assessment is to understand in order to take action. An *assessment cycle* illustrates how discovery and new information is used to foster growth and demonstrates the role of assessment in continuous improvement.[1] The goal is not to merely perform assessments, but to learn, re-engage

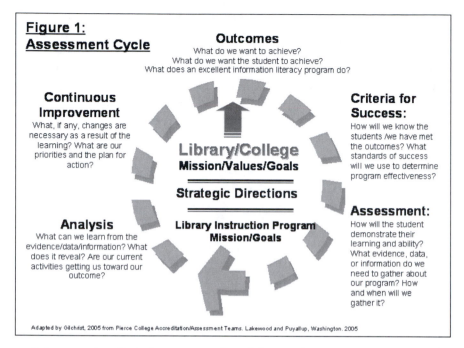

**Figure 1: Assessment Cycle**

**Outcomes**
What do we want to achieve?
What do we want the student to achieve?
What does an excellent information literacy program do?

**Continuous Improvement**
What, if any, changes are necessary as a result of the learning? What are our priorities and the plan for action?

**Library/College Mission/Values/Goals**

**Strategic Directions**

**Library Instruction Program Mission/Goals**

**Criteria for Success:**
How will we know the students /we have met the outcomes? What standards of success will we use to determine program effectiveness?

**Assessment:**
How will the student demonstrate their learning and ability? What evidence, data, or information do we need to gather about our program? How and when will we gather it?

**Analysis**
What can we learn from the evidence/data/information? What does it reveal? Are our current activities getting us toward our outcome?

Adapted by Gilchrist, 2005 from Pierce College Accreditation/Assessment Teams. Lakewood and Puyallup, Washington. 2005

and change using the information gathered during the assessment process. The majority of this chapter will be devoted to the first three steps of this assessment cycle as they pertain to assessment of student learning and assessment of information literacy programs

Educational leaders in assessment from Alverno College (Milwaukee, Wisconsin) have used the phrase *assessment-as-learning* to affirm that the true value and purpose of assessment is in the learning for the student. Through "diagnostic feedback as well as the reflective practice of self assessment by each student [they] create a continuous process that improves learning and integrates it with assessment."[2] *Assessment-as-learning* is rooted in instructional design in that it is a process that begins with a teacher clearly defining what s/he intends for the student to be able to do following an instructional session, selecting an instructional approach that directly correlates with that intention, and determining how successfully the student can demonstrate the learning. While the subject of assessment is generally treated as a separate concept (such as a separate chapter in this book), in practice it is a highly integrated element of good classroom planning.

We extend Alverno's assessment-as-learning concept one step further by affirming that assessment is also a reflective process that affords deep learning opportunities for the instructor. Librarians who adopt the assessment-as-learning philosophy can attribute a much more important and complex purpose for assessment than mere accountability. Active engagement with the assessment process in this framework also becomes an intentional process of improving teaching by continually asking the question: What can we discover about student learning that will impact our pedagogical decisions and move students toward even deeper learning?

Yet a third way to learn from assessment is through program assessment. Ruth Stiehl wisely advised, "Curriculum is a conversation not a document…"[3] Program assessment sets the stage for important discussions and invites us to come together to establish philosophy, draw connections, and design plans for nurturing what works in order to change for increased effectiveness.

Educational assessment is a very broad concept encompassing a disparate array of activities. The approach to assessment in library instruction sessions for many years has tended to emphasize practices related to resource accountability by measuring inputs that can be counted, e.g. number of sessions, number of students, etc. Statistics such as these which measure our instruction efforts do have an important function, providing useful information about effort expended on instruction programs; however they do not address the deeper questions of the library's contribution to the overarching mission of higher education which is student learning. Assessment practices built upon the philosophical foundation of assessment-as-learning shift our effort to focus on these larger questions and, in doing so, provide a powerful and meaningful context for librarians to contribute to larger institutional goals and outcomes.

## Outcome II
*Design assessments of student learning for the library classroom and as an integrated component of faculty assignments in order to affirm students' learning of information literacy concepts.*

Assessment received a professional emphasis and boost with the development of the *Information Literacy Competency Standards for Higher Education.*[4] These standards provided a framework for the assessment of information literacy and a guideline for developing local definitions, outcomes, and assessments. The Standards now serve as an excellent starting point for campus-based discussions between librarians and faculty members about what information literacy means when viewed through the lens of an institution's unique curriculum, philosophies, and values. Critical to the information literacy assessment process is that it is aligned with the institutional assessment plan; librarians should be familiar with their institution's approach to assessment.

Colleges and universities can use the Standards as inspiration to hone their own information literacy student learning outcomes in order to provide an instructional focus for librarians and faculty. Outcomes set the stage for students as well by providing them, "with a framework for gaining control over how they interact with information in their environment… making them conscious of the explicit actions required for gathering, analyzing, and using information."[5] Information literacy outcomes may take the form of an institutional core ability or a set of standards that all faculty agree to teach and assess (similar to writing or critical thinking across the curriculum), become a specific general education requirement, or be imbedded into the course or program outcomes of the various disciplines to capitalize on the unique nature of information literacy as it is understood and applied in different fields.

Assessment follows an instructional design approach that is facilitated with the following questions:[6]

| 1. Outcome: | What do you want the student to be able to do? |
|---|---|
| 2. Information Literacy Curriculum: | What does the student need to know in order to do this well? |
| 3. Pedagogy: | What type of instruction will best enable the learning? |
| 4. Assessment: | How will the student demonstrate the learning? |
| 5. Criteria for Evaluation: | How will I know the student has done this well? |

These five questions create a template for the design of an instructional session that consciously aligns the information literacy concepts, teaching strategies, and evaluation techniques with the outcome. While not always a strictly linear process as may be indicated by this presentation of these "steps", each question has a unique role in the design of a quality class session in which assessment will be incorporated. The next section presents each question individually along with examples of the application of each question, and is summarized by a comprehensive example which demonstrates use of all of the questions.

**Effective Assessment Design Question #1 Outcome: What do you want the student to be able to do?**

Learning outcomes are specific statements that express our hopes for our students' learning.[7] Focusing the outcome on what you want the student to be able to do establishes the groundwork for an active, observable assessment. Outcomes can be designed at the individual session level, at the course level or at the institutional level as illustrated in the three boxed examples which follow.

*Examples of Individual Session Outcomes. You will notice that these outcomes are focused and are able to be accomplished within 1 or 2 class periods.*
**Reference Sources:**
1) Incorporate reference sources into a search strategy in order to gather background information and facts on sociology topics.
2) Articulate the unique features of ref sources in order to demonstrate their application in the research process.

**Boolean Logic:** Construct search statements using Boolean logic in order to search databases effectively and maximize relevant hits.

**Catalog:** Utilize common search conventions and features of the library's catalog in order to increase efficiency and effectiveness of locating materials.

**Language:** Develop search language using controlled vocabulary lists, thesauri and specialized dictionaries in order to achieve breadth, depth, specificity and alternatives in catalog, web and database searches

---

*Examples of Outcomes for a Five-credit Information Literacy Course Focused on the Humanities. In contrast to the session outcomes, these outcomes take on a broader context.*
1) Navigate information structures, manipulate technological tools, & create & refine effective search strategies in order to access scholarly information in the Humanities.
2) Synthesize personal impressions of a work in the Humanities with external information and other perspectives in order to produce an informed analysis.
3) Identify scholarly information resources in the Humanities in order to a) increase understanding, interpretation, or appreciation of specific works and b) comprehend the social, political, or historical contexts of works.
4) Develop individual criteria and apply traditional criteria in order to critically evaluate information sources in the Humanities.
5) Apply research methods and information management skills in order to complete an educational research project (including a short paper, annotated bibliography, and PowerPoint presentation) about an artist from a culture outside one's own.
6) Properly citing sources and using correct bibliographic formats in order to demonstrate responsible information use.

> **Examples of Institutional Outcomes. At each of these sites, note the broad scope of the outcomes, allowing adaptation to multiple programs and disciplines.**
>
> **North Carolina State University: Information Competencies and Assignments for Undergraduates**
> http://www.lib.ncsu.edu/textiles/instruction
>
> **Concordia University, Oregon:**
> http://celt.cu-portland.edu/murdock/projects/cuoutcomes/incomes.cfm
>
> **University of Rhode Island: concepts that need to be covered throughout the program/curriculum.**
> http://www.uri.edu/library/instruction_services/infolitplan.html
>
> **Florida Gulf Coast University: Objectives clustered under four areas of abilities, each with two tiers of competencies.**
> http://library.fgcu.edu/Policies/infolit.htm
>
> **Pierce College, Washington: Outcomes and sub-outcomes for 7 concepts**
> http://www.pierce.ctc.edu/Library/information/ICdefinition2001.doc
>
> **Reed College, Oregon: Library Research Competencies for first year level, sophomore/junior level, and senior/thesis level**[8]

## Designing Outcomes

To start the process of designing learning outcomes we suggest this helpful formula:

| Verb phrase | + in order to | + why |
|---|---|---|
| Develop topic relevant vocabulary IN ORDER TO search databases with maximum flexibility | | |
| Verbs set the stage for the outcome; selecting the right verb is a critical first step. Know, understand and describe are a different level of skill than develop, interpret, analyze or evaluate. | The phrase "in order to" serves as a bridge between the ability and the rationale or application | Answering the question "why?" describes the way the student will apply the ability and brings depth and clarity to the outcome. You can also use this portion of the outcome to connect it to what is going on in the classroom so it has relevance and connection for the student.[9] |

Writing outcomes is a complex activity and the same outcome can be written in a variety of different ways. Therefore, we offer these criteria as guidance for determining whether your outcomes are workable.

> A. *Quality Outcomes are Clear to the Student:* The outcome not only sets the stage for the teacher's activities, but also conveys to the student the direction of the session or course, what is expected of them, and what is important to the teacher. Use language that is accessible. Students should view outcomes as an integrated part of their educational experience.

> B. *Quality Outcomes are Intentionally Designed:* An outcome defines what you want the student to be able to do. Good outcomes use clear verbs that set the direction for the learning that is useful and meaningful. The most effective outcomes not only include the ability the student is to do, but also place it in context by answering why it is important.

> C. *Quality Outcomes are Collaboratively Developed:* In an assessment-as-learning framework the emphasis is on the student. Effective planning for instructional sessions involves focusing on student learning outcomes collaboratively with our faculty colleagues. A strategy for this collaboration is to focus the discussion on "what *we* want the students to be able to do" after this session, instead of what content the librarian might cover during instruction. Strong and viable institutional or discipline based information literacy outcomes will emerge when we help our faculty colleagues envision the common ground we are building, demonstrate models of assessment and instruction of information literacy concepts, share where students have knowledge gaps, and articulate how we can then work together to educate. Outcomes should be based on library and institutional philosophy more than a master list of what skills or abilities students should possess.

> D. *Quality Outcomes are Assessable or "Judge-able"*: Most often we think of outcomes as being measurable. Our perspective is influenced by theorists who believe that what is assessable or judge-able are better criteria for a strong outcome. "The spectre that measurement raises is one of over-simplification of the

assessment process so that what is assessed can easily be quan-tified."[10] Can we, using our professional judgment, determine if the outcome has been achieved? If so, it usually works as an outcome. Incorporating professional judgment, in addition to measurement, expands our strategies for conducting assessment.

*E. Quality Outcomes are Developmental:* Outcomes should se-quence and integrate competencies throughout a student's academic career, all the while progressing in sophistication. Articulation of the information literacy outcomes within the curriculum identifies the scope (i.e., depth and complexity) of competencies to be acquired on a disciplinary level as well as at the course level. Selecting the appropriate verb for the outcome helps to set development on the right track, i.e. ask-ing students to *distinguish between* is a more sophisticated skill than asking them to *identify*. Taxonomies (such as Bloom's taxonomy[11]) are good resources for this activity since they categorize the development of intellectual skills and help you focus your attention on diversifying the cognitive levels at which you challenge your students in any class session, course, or program.

**Effective Assessment Design Question #2. Determining Information Literacy Curriculum: What does the student need to know in order to do this well? AND Effective Assessment Design Question #3. Selecting Pedagogy: What type of instruction will best enable the learning?**
These two questions challenge us to align our curriculum and teaching meth-ods with the outcomes. Assessment-as-learning and the five-question design process are strongly supportive of active learning pedagogies. While other sec-tions of this handbook directly address these topics, we ask you to reflect on them through the lens of assessment since "the quality of student learning is directly, although not exclusively, related to the quality of teaching. Therefore, one of the most promising ways to improve learning is to improve teaching."[12]

**Effective Assessment Design Question #4. Designing an Assessment: How will the student demonstrate the learning?**
Assessments are a measure of progress that can assist both the student and the librarian. While authentic assessments yield the most opportunity for students to have experience with the outcome and for faculty and librarians to most fully

develop the learning experience, assessments can also be incorporated into fifty-minute or individual library instruction sessions. The following set of example boxes illustrate different types of assessments.

Assessment can be *Designed by the Librarian* and included in the instruction session or presented as part of the pedagogy:

---

*Examples of Assessments in the fifty-minute Library Session:*
**You can do a lot with 5 minutes and a 3x5 card. Consider the value of informal assessments and how they might be incorporated into individual library instruction sessions. A small amount of class time can yield a significant amount of information.**

1) Students develop one Boolean search statement on their research topic at the beginning of class. At the end of class they write an improved statement and provide one sentence on why it was better.

2) After in-class discussion of search statements, students develop a topic sentence and a search statement for a database that addresses the topic in their paper/project. They are turned in before leaving the class and are returned to the students with librarian comments and suggestions.

3) Students write "one-minute papers" that describe to another student the best research hint they learned during the class and how they plan to use it in their paper/project, and one question that they wish they could ask about their own research paper.

4) Students develop a list of the 3 most important databases on their topic or the 3 most important criteria for evaluating sources, or the first 3 steps they will take in developing their research topic.

5) Students list, from their perspective, the 3 most important concepts or skills that the librarian taught.

---

Assessment can be *Formal:* Where the instructor designs a specific in-class or take-home exercise that is evaluated and returned to the student:

---

### Examples: Formal Assessment

For a research paper, students plan two different Boolean searches that would retrieve information on their topic.

As part of an assigned course paper, students include an analysis of how they have incorporated multiple voices and perspectives, and how they included viewpoints different than their own.

---

*Assessment can be Informal:* Where the instructor asks intentional questions in the classroom at a specific point in the instruction and compares student answers against a pre-determined "ideal" answer. Informal assessments often give the instructor the opportunity to immediately respond to deficiencies:

---

### Example: Informal Assessment

Following an instructional segment on scholarly/popular periodicals:

You have 8 different periodicals on each of your group tables. Sort them into categories of popular, scholarly, and trade and discuss the criteria you are using to make that decision. Each group will report out on the criteria for each category.

The instructor is listening to the group decisions to confirm the most important criteria are reported.

---

*Assessment can be Authentic:* Where the student demonstrates application of the skill or concept while performing a "real-world" task or in the context of a larger project instead of as an isolated endeavor.

---

### Examples: Authentic Assessment

At the end of an instructional session in the library, students are presented with a worksheet that steps them through a search strategy process, and asks them to reflect on how they designed their search strategy and whether or not it was successful. The librarian receives the worksheets after they are turned in and can either evaluate them on his/her own, review the results with the course instructor, or return them to the students with feedback

As part of a paper or project, students evaluate the 3 sources in their bibliography that were most significant to the development of that topic, justifying why they were the most important.

In a biology course, students are asked to determine why a particular type of algae has developed in the campus lake. As part of the lab report, each team of students describes the search strategy they used to locate information about the algae. Included in their laboratory report is an analysis and evaluation of their search strategy.

In researching a company they would like to work for, students are asked to use newspapers, journals, magazines, and annual reports and compare/contrast the unique role each of these sources have in delivering information about their company.

---

> An instructor presents a problem to a nursing class as the focus of the course. Each team of students must support their solution for a public health issue. As part of their report, they describe how they acquired and used information to solve the problem.

*Assessment can be Integrated:* Developed with the faculty and relevant to coursework. Collaboration takes place at the planning stages, delivery, assessment of student learning, and evaluation and refinement of the program. Many of the "authentic" examples also can be defined as integrated. The difference is whether they are designed and administered independently by the librarian or co-designed by the librarian and faculty and integrated into the course assignment.

> **Example: Integrated Assessment**
> As part of their history research paper, students must use both primary and secondary sources, explaining the characteristics of each type and what the use of each lends to the depth/breadth of their topic. This information is included in the assignment, and the librarian and discipline faculty member collaborative evaluate the student work. The collaboration can be formal or informal.

*Assessment can be Knowledge or Content Based:* Where a student demonstrates their knowledge of particular concepts or facts, or performs skills in an unrelated context. Traditional formats for knowledge or content assessments include multiple-choice tests, fill-in-the-blanks, true-false, matching, and short answer. These tests may be individually created or standardized.

> **Examples: Knowledge / Content Based Assessment**
> Specify True or False:
> Using the Boolean operator AND makes your set of results smaller

*Assessment can be Formative:* Assessment that is done for the purpose of immediate evidence of student learning or for immediate feedback to the student. Classroom assessment is one of the most common formative assessment techniques. The purpose of this approach is to improve quality of student learning and should not be evaluative or involve grading students.[13] We believe that formative assessment is also formative for the instructor, in that the immediate information allows the teacher to repeat, reinforce, or rejoice.

> **Examples: Formative Assessment**
> Mini-assignments inside the library instruction classroom as part of a class session.

One-minute papers at the end of a library instruction class session where the instructor asks students to respond to a specific question.

*Assessment can be Summative:* Assessment that is designed to be relatively comprehensive; it is generally used to discern the level of learning at the end of a program. A library or college's information literacy definition or information literacy learning outcomes reflect the cumulative nature of the learning that is desired. For library instruction, summative assessment can also be used to illustrate the degree of accomplishment of the library's instruction program. By summarizing the results of individual assessments that several different librarians conducted, we can get an overall picture of how students are progressing.

### Examples: Summative Assessment

A capstone course includes a component that asks students to apply a sophisticated set of information literacy skills.

Each librarian assesses the same information literacy outcome in several classes throughout the term. The results are averaged to inform them of how the library instruction program is doing with student achievement

The library administers a comprehensive information literacy exam to all graduating seniors

Portfolio: The same type of assignment in each of the 4 academic years, progressing in difficulty and with expectations of analysis and reflection. Student can choose to do the assignment with any assigned research paper in a variety of courses. The librarians provide questions to direct the student response.

Junior or Senior Theses: Within the junior or senior thesis, students are require to synthesize and evaluate the research process they used through a set of guided questions; it becomes part of the evaluation of the thesis.

*Assessment can be Self-Assessment:* Providing students an opportunity to reflect on their own learning, increases their consciousness of their own abilities, and offers the instructor insight as to the student perspective.

### Example: Prompts for Self-Assessment

What have you learned about yourself as a researcher while doing this assignment?

What is the best search tip you will pass on to other students?

*Assessment can be Progressive and/or Developmental:* Promoting deep learning that is retained over time requires not only repetition but also elaboration at varying levels of complexity and in a variety of contexts.

---

**Example: Assessment can be Progressive and/ or Developmental**
Students develop an Information Literacy or Research Portfolio where they do the same type of assignment in each of their four years, each year progressing in the level of analysis and sophistication. The student can choose to do the assignment with any research paper in any course. Integrated into the assignment are questions provided by the librarian to direct the student's responses. Librarians and faculty evaluate assignments using a rubric that is collaboratively designed.

---

## Guidelines for Development of Quality Assessments
Assessments must be thoughtfully designed if they are to yield good information. We offer the following criteria to guide the development of assessments.

A. *Quality Assessments are Collaborative:* While developing in-class assessments for instructional sessions can be successfully accomplished, developing assessments integrated with faculty assessments results in a more natural experience for students. They have the opportunity to view the research process as integrated into their role as a biologist, for example.

B. *Quality Assessments are Multidimensional:* Acknowledge differences in learning and teaching styles by using a variety of appropriate assessment techniques such as portfolio assessment, oral defense, quizzes, essays, direct observation, anecdotal, peer and self-review, and student experience. Include a variety of assessments that focus on student performance, knowledge acquisition, and attitude appraisal.

C. *Quality Assessments are Holistic:* Consider the complexity of learning by assessing its many aspects including student performance, knowledge acquisition, critical thinking, application of ability to a new context, and attitude appraisal.

D. *Quality Assessments are Assesses Thinking Process:* Assess the process that led students to make decisions about the research process and not only the final research paper or project. Assess the decision points that occur during the development of the product and the intellectual journey of the student.

*E. Quality Assessments Include Critical Thinking Elements:* This fosters student's own analysis rather than limiting them to memorization or repetition of facts. This approach increases their ability to internalize the learning.

*F. Quality Assessments Are Managed.* Not everything we teach can be assessed. Classroom assessments should focus on the most important component students need to be successful accomplishing the course assignment. At the program level, librarians can collectively choose to emphasize particular outcomes in as many sessions as possible within a given year and rotate that emphasis over the course of an accreditation cycle.

**Effective Assessment Design Question #5: Criteria—How will you know the student has done this well?**

Criteria are standards, benchmarks, or descriptions of a good response; measures of value or judgment that guide the student and the teacher toward a "good answer." It is most helpful when students are aware of criteria in advance and use them to shape their response. Developing criteria serves to communicate the often-inexplicit evaluation tenets we hold in our thoughts and to clarify our expectations for both our students and ourselves. Developing criteria means attempting to explain what sometimes might at first appear to be unexplainable. Good criteria are tied directly to the learning outcomes and work together to provide clear guidelines for the student. They provide a strong framework for an

---

***Examples of Descriptive Criteria:***

Following an instructional segment on scholarly/popular periodicals and criteria for evaluation of those periodicals, you explain to the students:

You have eight different periodicals on each of your group tables. Sort them into categories of popular, scholarly, and trade and discuss the criteria you are using to make that decision. Each group will report out on the criteria they used to sort each category of periodical.

Criteria:
- Periodicals are in correct categories (if not, students provide good rationale for their decision)
- Students report out at least one criterion for their decision from at least 4 of the following categories: audience, purpose, content, authority, language, review policy, and documentation.

---

answer but are not intended to provide or be an answer. Public criteria reduce the need for students to expend their energies on 'strategic learning', e.g. figuring out what the professor wants, and allows them to focus their energies on learning course material, exploring critical concepts, and applying critical thinking skills. Criteria can be presented in a descriptive format, or formulated as a rubric demonstrating levels of accomplishment.[14]

A *rubric* is a matrix in which descriptive criteria are organized to categorize qualitative and developmental levels of performance on any particular outcome.

*Example of a Rubric:*

| Outcome | Needs Improvement | Acceptable | Excellent |
|---|---|---|---|
| Evaluate information and its sources critically. | Student is unaware of criteria that might be used to judge information quality. Little effort is made to examine the information located. | Student examines information using criteria such as authority, credibility, relevance, timeliness, and accuracy, and is able to make judgments about what to keep and what to discard | Multiple and diverse sources and viewpoints of information are compared and evaluated according to specific criteria appropriate for the discipline. Student is able to match criteria to a specific information need, and can articulate how identified sources related to the context of the discipline. |

## Full Application of the Effective Assessment Design Questions

Our final example brings together all five of the questions to illustrate how they work together to reveal a full instructional design process. Again, we stress that the questions do not have to be engaged in the order they are presented here. Adapt them to your own personal style of teaching to fully manifest their effectiveness. For example, you may want to develop the outcome, and then the assessment, and finally return to the development of the rest of the class session. Or, the classroom assignment may fully dictate the assessment you are using, in which case writing the outcome may come second, followed by the other three questions.

> **Example of the Assessment Design Questions Applied to a 200 level Business course with one or two sessions of library instruction**
>
> **Outcome**: Locate and evaluate a local company's annual report and distinguish its qualities and application from an article in a business journal.
>
> **Curriculum:** Definition and role of an annual report; Criteria to evaluate a business journal article; Where to locate annual reports.
>
> **Pedagogy:** Small group activity, Discussion and Mini-Lecture: A team of students is presented with 2 annual reports and two journal articles. They develop lists of characteristics, similarities, and differences between the two. The instructor uses that as a basis to lead a discussion of evaluating those sources and how they might be different from each other.
>
> **Assessment**: As part of the course assignment, students will locate one annual report and one journal article on the same company and compare and contrast the type of information they find in each source.

Being explicit and intentional about student learning, whether in a fifty-minute one shot library instruction session, multiple instruction sessions, or in a full term course, is critical to the assessment-as-learning process. Outcome statements enforce clarity of intention that is fundamental to any subsequent efforts to observe and evaluate student learning success. While this section has illustrated a great deal of flexibility in the modes of assessment that can be used to gather information about student learning (informal, formal, self-assessment, integrated, etc.), assessment is most effective when it is grounded upon a clear statement of what you want the students to be able to do and why that is important for their learning.

## Outcome III
*Use assessment of student learning and principles of good instruction in order to change and improve as a teacher.*

Amongst the extensive research literature about pedagogy there are several authors who assign central importance to reframing the conception and practice of assessment as a powerful means to promote learning, improve pedagogical practice, and become a more conscious teacher. Kenneth Bain[15] derives principles of good instructional practice from extensive primary data; Maryellen Weimer[16] synthesizes significant bodies of research; while Stephen Brookfield[17] develops methodologies for critical reflection from both research literature and extensive reflective practice. This section briefly examines the contributions of each of these authors.

Kenneth Bain's cleverly titled book, *What the Best College Teachers Do* (2004), makes an impassioned case for learner-centered teaching even while drawing in those who, with the best intentions for improving their teaching, may be looking for just the opposite, i.e. a book presenting a litany of teacher-focused tips, techniques, and tricks which they can quickly apply to their own practice. Using results of a research study which interviewed, observed, and studied the practice of sixty-three college and university teachers, Bain has analyzed those practices in the context of their impact on learning in both practical and theoretical terms. In his chapter entitled, "How do they evaluate their students and themselves?" Bain finds that the best teachers challenged conventional wisdom about student assessment (e.g. grading) in order to focus on the outcomes of learning, and in the process developed ways to use assessment to promote learning.

Maryellen Weimer provides an elegant and persuasive review of a large body of research literature regarding teaching and learning in her book, *Learner-centered teaching: five key changes to practice* (2002). While Weimer's discussion of evaluation begins with a focus upon summative evaluation of student work (the societal need for grades as well as their potential to distort learning), she also identifies several alternative approaches. Pedagogical practices that incorporate self- and peer-assessment can be used to foster both student learning and improved teaching practice. As illustrated in the boxed examples previously presented, these strategies can be adapted to the many contexts in which library instruction takes place whether in a fifty-minute course-related session which may be the librarian's only formal contact with students, or in a full-term librarian-taught credit course.

Weimer explicitly points to the work on critical reflection by Stephen Brookfield as providing both an analysis of the power relations inherent in the learning enterprise and for seeking to empower teachers and learners to create equitable learning environments. His four lenses for critical reflection provide a powerful basis for questioning what he calls, "hegemonic assumptions."[18] Hegemonic assumptions are those which we as educators often hold which ultimately work against the long term interests of educators and learners. Assessment is a powerful tool for informing critical reflection through his four lenses: autobiography as teacher and learner; our students' eyes; our colleagues' experiences; and theoretical literature. Assessment-as-learning is a powerful methodology for gathering data to fuel critical reflection.

> "… we found professors who have broken with tradition to forge fundamentally different approaches to both assessment and evaluation, and in those differences to answer questions that have long plagued conversations about such matters … In their hands,

evaluation and assessment become intertwined, supporting each other in ways that deliberately benefit learning. When they assess their students, they do so in part to test their own efforts to facilitate learning. When they evaluate their teaching, they do so by looking at learning, both the objectives and the outcomes."[19]

Drawing upon the research in teaching and learning can influence assessment design and significantly advance the impact we have on students. In addition to major authors such as Bain, Weimer, and Brookfield, we recommend regular reading of the literature of many academic disciplines that focus on the scholarship of teaching and learning. The concepts and tenets these authors present could be transitioned into criteria that describe/illustrate effective instruction. Articulating these elements as criteria serves to facilitate common understandings about what effective teaching "looks like" and provides tangible goals for new teachers.

## Outcome IV
*Holistically examine an information literacy program through the lenses of the ACRL Best Practices in order to evolve and shape it based on evidence and to demonstrate its value to student success.*

The traditional mode of library instruction program assessment has been to measure the many things that can be easily counted (number of instruction sessions, number of students served, number of librarians teaching, number of hours spent preparing for or providing instruction). However useful these library-centric input/output measures may be as a measure of effort, they will not demonstrate the effectiveness of the library's instruction program, identify the library's contribution to institution's educational mission, nor provide guidance to planners as to where to direct resources to improve the library's educational impact. When communicating with current and potential participants in the library's instruction program as well as various institutional and community stakeholders in student learning success, having data and other evidence which demonstrates impact on shared learning goals will be critical to program development.

### *Process Questions for Program Assessment Design*
Program assessment is best accomplished when we are able to sustain both the learner-centered philosophy of assessment as well as the pedagogical practices. This can be accomplished by reframing the five questions we used to address instructional design and classroom assessment to now focus on what we want to accomplish in information literacy programs:[20]

| 1. Program Outcome: | What does an effective instruction program do? |
|---|---|
| 2. Program Criteria: | How do you determine if you have achieved your outcomes? What will constitute success? |
| 3. Program Assessment: | How will data or evidence be collected? |
| 4. Program Analysis and Evaluation: | How will the discussion or evaluation of the data occur? Who will be involved? |
| 5. Program Change: | What changes will be enacted? Who will take leadership? What is the timeline? What resources are required? |

These questions can be used to guide the ***process*** of program assessment. A starting point for formulating the ***content*** of programmatic outcomes and criteria has been provided by *Characteristics of Programs of Information Literacy that Illustrate Best Practices: A Guideline.*[21] As with ACRL's *Information Literacy Competency Standards for Higher Education*, the process of adapting these to local circumstances is crucial to gathering meaningful assessment data. To fully engage this section, we suggest using the *Best Practices* as a resource as we examine each question for its unique contribution to the program assessment process.

### 1. Program Outcome: What does an effective instruction program do?

The *Best Practices* document identifies elements of importance to program success. To adapt them for this purpose, we suggest recasting the categories as program-level outcome statements as we have done in the example below, adding or eliminating categories to reflect your institutional requirements. The guidelines for writing and evaluating outcome statements presented earlier in this chapter can also be guides for writing outcomes at the program level.

*Program Outcomes Inspired by the Best Practices:*

| BEST PRACTICES CATEGORY 1: MISSION | |
|---|---|
| Outcome: (What does an effective instruction program do?) | Be guided by a dynamic and learner-centered mission statement and program outcomes in order to communicate the program's contributions and align with the library and college mission and educational priorities. |

| BEST PRACTICES CATEGORY 9: OUTREACH | |
|---|---|
| Outcome: (What does an effective instruction program do?) | Engage in outreach and marketing activities using a variety of methods and modes in order to communicate the value of IL literacy learning programs to various stakeholders. |

**2. Program Criteria: How will you determine you have achieved your outcomes? What will constitute success?**

The bullet points provided under each category heading of the *Best Practices* document are illustrative and not prescriptive or comprehensive, and can be developed into **criteria** to demonstrate the extent to which you have met your program outcomes. Essentially, criteria state what is happening when a library instruction program is achieving excellence. What will satisfy you that indeed your outcome is being fulfilled? By focusing data collection efforts on these specific criteria you will document the activities and corresponding success of your program. There is no magic answer as to how many criteria you need, nor how to define the level of quality with a number or score. Each program will define that for themselves depending on size, number of librarians, campus initiatives, library priorities, and other relevant factors. Our personal opinion is that achievement is not about scores or numbers but about progress made from year to year toward that optimal end result. For example, the *Best Practices* document states:

*Category 9: Outreach*
- *communicate a clear message defining and describing the program and its value to targeted audiences*
- *use a variety of outreach channels and media, both formal and informal*

The following examples shows how these bulleted points can be reformulated as criteria identifying program activities that fulfill the stated outcome.

*Criteria Inspired by the Best Practices*

| BEST PRACTICES CATEGORY 9: OUTREACH | |
|---|---|
| Outcome | Engage in outreach and marketing activities using a variety of methods and modes in order to communicate the value of IL literacy learning programs to various stakeholders. |
| Criteria (What will constitute success?) | a) 100% of appropriate information literacy information and resources appear in relevant publications or on relevant websites, whether produced/maintained by the library, academic departments, or administrative units. |
| | b) The library (co-)sponsors 6 faculty development programs each year with appropriate groups, i.e. Teaching Center, Writing Center. |
| | c) Outreach activities reach 10% new attendees each year; grow in attendance by 15% each year; draw attendees from over 50% of academic departments, and assist the campus community in embracing information literacy as a collaborative and collective endeavor. |

Establish goals that will illustrate achievement of the various outcomes and that are meaningful to your program. For some outcomes, a percentage change over a period of time may be useful to specify in order to establish priorities, allocate resources, and evaluate progress.

### 3. Program Assessment: How will data or evidence be collected?

When choosing a data collection method it is important to match the method of data collection to the data need, e.g. what you need to know and how the data will be used. Do you need to prioritize operational activities that support your instruction program? Do you need to elicit information from faculty that will help you understand what motivates faculty to participate in instructional collaborations? Do you want feedback from library users on their satisfaction with particular services? Each of these information needs can be addressed using distinct information gathering strategies, or data collection methodologies, whether formal or informal, quantitative or qualitative.

At this point in the assessment process library staff frequently find themselves at an impasse, identifying an obligation to use rigorous research methodologies although they may be lacking expertise, or resources, or both. We propose an alternative that will encourage moving forward with assessment in order to develop an institutional culture of evidence. An institution that promulgates a ***culture of evidence*** asserts that not all assessment must have a numeric result. (See chart below.)

| *Characteristics of a Culture of Evidence* | | |
|---|---|---|
| **Absence of assessment practice** | → | **Culture of evidence** |
| Working from assumptions re:<br>  Faculty needs<br>  Faculty interest<br>  Student learning<br>  What content is important to<br>  cover, etc. | | Working from evidence |
| | | Evidence = information/data gathered from external sources to address specific questions |
| Working alone | | Working collaboratively<br>  Among library staff<br>  With faculty<br>  With administrators<br>  With academic support staff<br>  With computing professionals<br>  etc. |
| Input / Output measures, e.g.<br>  Number of sessions taught<br>  Number of students attending<br>  Prep time<br>  Instruction time | | Success measured by impact (on learning or program)<br>  What practice has changed<br>  To what degree has it changed<br>  How do you know |

When discussing a culture of evidence we identify a set of institutional practices whereby questions are asked, evidence is gathered and discussed, and changes in practices or policies are implemented on the basis of those discussions of evidence. By advocating that libraries develop a culture of evidence, or engage with the wider institutional efforts to foster a culture of evidence, we argue that there is a continuum of assessment practice that produces value in both its process and its outcome. When working to establish a culture of evidence we demonstrate that excellence does not require perfection; that doing as good a job as we are able to do within whatever constraints there may be in order to better understand our environment and other stakeholder perspectives is a valuable effort. When we work within a culture of evidence with regard to assessing student learning we are respectful towards students in our effort to reflect using the best available evidence.

Informal data collection methods are legitimate for program assessment as they are for classroom assessment. Informal methods can be used to gather data or evidence that is quantitative or qualitative in nature. Formal assessment can also be undertaken in the service of instruction program assessment and there are numerous methodologies that can be employed. A review of research methodologies is beyond the scope of this chapter,[22] however, frequently used methods include surveys (quantitative data) and focus groups (qualitative data). Surveys have become logistically easier to implement in recent years with the availability of online survey tools[23] which provide no- or low-cost options for creating, distributing, and analyzing surveys. The options for data collection are plentiful; therefore, keeping the focus on what you need to know rather than the method that is easiest to implement, is critical for making choices that will produce useful and meaningful results.

Returning to and extending the example used above of Best Practices Category 9 (Outreach), our assessment for the criteria of placing Information Literacy content in publications and Web site is an informal one; an inventory of publications/Web sites in spreadsheet format. For other criteria in the example (co-sponoring faculty development programs and conducting outreach activities) formal assessments (data collection tools) will be used to collect both quantitative and qualitative information. The various tasks and strategies identified in this example can be tackled in a sequential order over a period of months or years. The assessment effort should support and enhance your instructional program, not overwhelm it. It may be possible to develop the inventory and the focus groups of the example below in parallel during the first year of an assessment action plan. However, using the lessons learned from the focus groups can be the focus of a second annual action plan for revising publications, seeking additional placements for Web site links among departmental or administrative sites, and developing faculty development workshop content and/or partnerships. During the third year it may be appropriate to conduct the survey of stakeholder groups in order to gather evidence of the impact of the changes made using results of the focus group discussions. Alternatively, during the first year it may be in your interest to implement a survey to gather baseline data that can be used to identify areas to address in a multi-year action plan. A repeat implementation of the survey after a few years would allow for a comparison of results over time.

### Outcomes, Criteria & Assessments Inspired by the Best Practices

| BEST PRACTICES CATEGORY 9: OUTREACH | |
|---|---|
| Outcome | IL program participants will engage in outreach and marketing activities using a variety of methods and modes of communication in order to communicate program value to various stakeholders. |
| *Criteria (How will you know?)* | *Assessment (How will data be collected?)* |
| 100% of appropriate information literacy information and resources appear in relevant publications or on relevant websites, whether produced/maintained by the library, academic departments, or administrative units. | Publications/Web site inventory kept in spreadsheet format |
| The library (co-)sponsors 6 faculty development programs each year with appropriate groups, i.e. Teaching Center, Writing Center. | Survey; Session evaluation |
| Outreach activities reach 10% new attendees each year; grow in attendance by 15% each year; draw attendees from over 50% of academic departments, and assist the campus community in embracing information literacy as a collaborative and collective endeavor. | Focus Groups; Spreadsheet Analysis of activities |

### 4. Program Evaluation: How will the discussion of the data occur? Who will be involved?

The next question in the assessment planning process, evaluating whether a program is functioning well and achieving its stated outcomes, needs to be addressed very deliberately as an ongoing discussion of the evidence gathered and lessons learned. Information gathered through formal and informal assessments of the information literacy program needs to be used at the appropriate levels to fuel improvements in pedagogical practice, faculty-library collaborations, and programmatic impact. Trust surrounding the collection and use of data or evidence must be built carefully and deliberately. Ongoing conversations among peers focused on student learning provide development opportunities to practitioners who are often isolated in their pedagogical efforts (24). Teaching conversations among mixed groups of librarians and faculty members foster collaboration and widen the scope of potential impact for assessment-as-learning. Conversations about program assessment and planning among practitioners and program managers that are grounded in a shared philosophy and shared goals are vital to decision making for the library and institution as a whole. Examples of institutional outcomes were provided above in the discussion of Outcome II.

**5. Program Change: What changes need to be made? Who will accept leadership for the implementation? What timelines and resources will be required?**
The final question in this series is the simplest to understand, but often the most difficult to implement. Many assessment efforts disengage at this point because of the large number of daily tasks that already occupy our professional lives. But with this question, we get to the heart of why we do assessment , which is to change practices based on good information and increase the library's impact on student learning and success. We recommend being deliberate with this step, but also reasonable. Rather than making every change possible, plan key activities for change that will result in the greatest impact, identify the individuals who will take leadership for the change, establish timelines, and identify required resources will help to move the project from plan to reality. The results of any changes made will be assessed with the next regular assessment cycle of the program.

### *A Word about Standardized Information Literacy Tests*
Several standardized assessments of information literacy have been developed that can provide an overall assessment of students' information literacy ability. The difference between standardized assessments and locally designed assessments is their comprehensive scope. Since most information literacy programs do not teach all skills or concepts to all students, it may not be appropriate to use a standardized test as a direct measure of learning as a result of classroom in-

---

**Using aggregate scores to benchmark programs**
How well do students enrolled in programs X, Y, and Q perform on test after completing their degree? If students have higher scores after completing program X or Y, what is happening in these programs that could be a useful model for improving instruction or student learning in program Q?

[X, Y, & Q may be different programs at the same institution (chemistry, biology, political science) or the same academic program at different institutions (chemistry programs at colleges which have implemented the same standardized test).]

---

---

**Using individual scores for student placement in a degree program**
Experience of previous students shows that a score of Z or above on this test is necessary to perform well in this academic program. If your score is below Z you can take these workshops/courses to improve your knowledge/skill to the level of score Z before you will be enrolled in the program.

---

struction. Instead, aggregate results from a standardized test could either establish a baseline for entering students (placement), serve as a measure of cumulative learning for graduating students (program assessment or benchmarking), or provide information about how an individual student is performing in comparison to the group norms established by the test. The results from standardized testing can be very powerful when used as a source of insight into student learning that faculty and administrators can then use for program development.

Examples of Standardized Information Literacy Exams include:
*Project SAILS (Standardized Assessment of Information Literacy Skills)*[25]: Developed and administered by Kent State University, SAILS is a "knowledge test with multiple-choice questions targeting a variety of information skills. The test items are based on the ACRL information Literacy Competency Standards for Higher Education."

*ETS iSkills:* The Educational Testing Service (ETS) has been working to develop a standardized test of Information & Communication Technology (ICT) Literacy[26] that can be used for institutional or program benchmarking, individual summative assessment, and institutional comparisons. ETS worked with a group of higher education faculty, librarians, computing and assessment professionals to develop the assessment model, initial test items, and scoring mechanisms. The components of ICT Literacy as defined by the Higher Education Initiative and which form the basis for test development are: Define, Access, Manage, Integrate, Evaluate, Create, and Communicate. The test items of the iSkills assessment integrate cognitive and technical skills to achieve a variety of information and communication tasks in scenarios drawn from both the academic and working worlds. The ethical and legal issues which are so critical to practice in this arena are also addressed in test items and scoring.

*Bay Area Community Colleges Information Competency Assessment Project.* The project's purpose was to "develop a challenge-out or credit-by-exam instrument that might be used and/or modified at community colleges having an information competency requirement."[27] The two-part instrument incorporates multiple-choice, matching, and short answer as well as performance-based exercises and uses two publications of national information literacy standards as the basis for the assessment.

### Bringing It All Together: An Assessment Plan

Ultimately, the foundation for an assessment plan is to collect summative assessment data and this type of data can stand-alone. Formative assessment data, however, can contribute to a comprehensive assessment plan by providing the basis for annual action plans that direct effort and resources toward achieving the stated outcomes. Discussions of what has been learned from applying as-

---

**Organizations Helpful with Assessment and Creative Design**

**Carnegie Foundation for the Advancement of Teaching**
                          http://www.carnegiefoundation.org/

Several initiatives including the **Carnegie Academy for the Scholarship of Teaching and Learning (CASTL)** which offers a national program for scholars, a campus program to provide support for local efforts, and a program for Scholarly and Professional Societies to provide support and encouragement within disciplinary contexts.
        http://www.carnegiefoundation.org/programs/index.asp?key=21

**The Reinvention Center** at the University of Miami
Focuses on undergraduate education at research universities, providing publications websites, and national and regional conferences
                          http://www.reinventioncenter.miami.edu/

The **League for Innovation in the Community College**
Provides a variety of programs, publications, online forums, conferences to foster innovation in areas of learning, leadership, student success, technology, diversity & equity, workforce development, resource development, and research & practice.
                          http://www.league.org/index.cfm

**Alverno College**
Through their website and summer institutes, Alverno faculty share their theory and practice of performance-based assessment of student learning as well as their approach to program and institutional assessment of learning outcomes.
        http://www.alverno.edu/for_educators/institute.html

sessment-as-learning in various contexts, whether course-related instruction, reference service, or faculty collaborations are the fuel that will keep your program on a developmental course. Just as, "We wouldn't tolerate it if our students announced that they planned to stop studying in our disciplines and to draw all their conclusions from intuition or whim,"[28] we must acknowledge that assessment, and the learning about teaching and learning that it stimulates, is an ongoing pursuit. There is no one-shot, silver bullet, single-implementation solution for assessment when it is understood as a fundamental component of the learning enterprise. Fortunately, there are a number of professional organizations and nationwide initiatives that can provide a focal point for organizing local efforts as well as ongoing inspiration for this work. (See table on p. 190.)

## Conclusion

Assessment can be a valuable tool for individual librarians to improve both their teaching and their students' learning; for groups of librarians collaboratively designing an instruction program; for program coordinators seeking to improve the quality of instruction or to engage in planning for professional development; and for library administrators who wish to understand and further the impact of the library on student experience. Assessment is a process vital to the future of academic libraries since it so clearly demonstrates our focus on student success and provides opportunity to highlight the academic library's unique and important contributions to larger institutional goals.

## Notes

1. Adapted from: Flynn, Christie, Gilchrist, Debra, & Olson, Lynn. Using the Assessment Cycle as a Tool for Collaboration. Resource Sharing and Information Networks. Volume 17 (1), 2005.

2. Earl, Lorna Maxine. *Assessment-As-Learning: Using Classroom Assessment to Maximize Student Learning*. (Thousand Oaks, CA: Corwin Press, 2003).

3. Stiehl, Ruth and Lewchuk, Les. *Outcomes Primer*. (Corvallis, OR: Learning Organization, 2000).

4. Association of College and Research Libraries. *Information Literacy Competency Standards for Higher Education*. (Chicago: ACRL, 2000) [http://www.ala.org/ala/acrl/acrlstandards/informationliteracycompetency.htm] Accessed 20 April 2006.

5. ACRL. Standards, "Introduction"

6. Adapted from: Fenno-Smith, Kyzyl & Gilchrist, Debra. "Using an Abilities Model in Library Instruction Programs: Improving Teaching, Assignment Design, and Disciplinary Curricula". In *"LOEX" of the West: Collaboration & Instructional Design in a Virtual Environment*. K. Anderson, E. Babbitt, E. Hull, T. Mudrock, and H. Williams, Eds. (Greenwich, CT: JAI Press, 1999).

7. Stiehl, Ruth and Lewchuk, Les. *Mapping Primer*. (Corvallis, OR: Learning Organization, 2005).

8. Malone, Debbie and Videon, Carol. 2003. *First Year Student Library Instruction Programs (CLIP Note #33)*. Chicago : Association of College & Research Libraries, 44.

9. DeJardin, Judy. Personal Communication. 2000.

10. Battersby, Mark. and the Learning Outcomes Network, "*So, What's a Learning Outcome Anyway?*" Vancouver, B.C.: Centre for Curriculum, Transfer, and Technology, July 1999, ERIC Document ED430611.

11. Bloom, Benjamin Samuel. *Taxonomy of educational objectives: the classification of educational goals, by a committee of college and university examiners.* New York: Longmans, Green, 1956-64 (volume 1, cognitive domain; volume 2, affective domain)

12. Angelo, Thomas A., and Cross, K. Patricia. *Classroom assessment techniques: A handbook for college teachers.* 2nd ed. (San Francisco: Jossey-Bass, 1993).

13. Ibid.

14. California State University Information Competence Initiative. *Rubrics for Assessing Information Competence in the California State University.* http://www.calstate.edu/ls/1_rubric.doc [Accessed18 April 2006].

15. Bain, Ken. *What the best college teachers do.* Cambridge, Mass.: Harvard University Press, 2004.

16. Weimer, Maryellen. *Learner-centered teaching: five key changes to practice.* (San Francisco: Jossey-Bass, 2002).

17. Brookfield, Stephen D. *Becoming a critically reflective teacher.* (San Francisco: Jossey-Bass, 1995).

18. Brookfield, *Becoming a critically reflective teacher,* 14-21.

19. Bain, *What the best college teachers do,* 151.

20. Gilchrist, Debra. "Outcomes Assessment as Change Agent." Presentation at the IFLA/ ACRL Invitation Summit on Leadership in International Academic Librarianship. Harvard University. Boston, MA. August 2001.

21. Association of College and Research Libraries. *Characteristics of Programs of Information Literacy that Illustrate Best Practices: A Guideline.* 2003. [http://www.ala.org/ala/acrl/acrlstandards/characteristics.htm] viewed 16 April 2006.

22. See, for example, Eldredge, Jonathan D. "Inventory of research methods for librarianship and informatics," *Journal of the Medical Library Association,* 92 (Jan 2004): 83-90.

23. Examples of online survey tools include (but are not limited to) Survey Monkey, http:// www.surveymonkey.com/ and Zoomerang, http://info.zoomerang.com/,

24. Leadley, Sarah. "Teaching meetings: providing a forum for learning how to teach," *Reference Services Review,* 26 (Fall/Winter 1998): 103-8.

25. Project SAILS https://www.projectsails.org/

26. ETS iSkills http://www.ets.org

27. Bay Area Community Colleges. *Developing and Field-Testing an Instrument for Assessing Information Competency Learning Outcomes of Community College Students: Final Report of the Bay Area Community Colleges Information Competency Assessment.* http://www.topsy.org/ICAP/FinalReport.pdf [Accessed 21 April 2006].

28. Bain, p. 176.

# CHAPTER 10
## *Diversity: Cross Cultural Instruction*

Lori S. Mestre

In the past 10 years our society has experienced a rapid growth in diversity of its population. The term diversity is being used in its broadest sense, including not only race, ethnicity and religion, but also various cultural, linguistic, gender, generational, sexual orientation, ability and disability characteristics and needs of our population. Libraries have become more responsive to the needs of these diverse cultures and have recognized the importance of providing access, outreach, job opportunities, and programming targeted to these groups. Providing culturally responsive instruction to these groups is also of importance. This chapter will discuss some considerations for providing what the author would term as cross cultural instruction, including strategies for working with multiple cultural groups.

## Why Librarians Should Care about Providing Cross Cultural Instruction

The first impression created by a library and the assistance received by a patron can be long lasting. Librarians might not understand the relevance of investing time in learning how to effectively address cross cultural differences especially if they feel that the strategies they develop to help special populations are not useful for the general population. A patient and caring librarian who expresses interest in the needs of patrons can help shape their user behavior and research forays. Providing instruction that is responsive and relevant to the needs of the patron can open up an interest in the patron to continue the research exploration. Learning how to provide this type of instruction can be a challenge to the librarian who has only used teaching strategies and examples based on his or her previous experiences.

Although our urban, rural and suburban settings are more diverse than ever, the overwhelming majority of library personnel continue to come from middle class, European American backgrounds.[1] Many educators are now struggling to connect with a completely new set of learners, with cultural backgrounds distinctly different from each other and from their teachers. Across the country and throughout our region, educators are embracing the notion of cultural responsiveness as a means of helping all students reach high standards. Any acknowl-

193

edgement, inclusion or recognition of a student's cultural background in library materials or searching examples that occur in the library may help students feel better connected to the library as a place where they belong.

Because diversity within cultures varies and one cannot generalize across cultural groups, it would be impossible to provide suggestions in this chapter that work in all instances. Nevertheless, the suggestions provided in this chapter are presented with the intention that they might be applicable to a broad range of students, regardless of culture, but that they will need to be altered to best accommodate the particular student at hand. The suggestions are based on four principles that are considered the important in providing effective instruction diverse populations, namely: a) sensitivity to different learning and engagement styles, b) teaching strategies to help accommodate those styles, c) flexibility in altering techniques, and d) reflecting on what occurred in the session in order to improve future sessions.

## Role of the Library in Attracting and Retaining Students

Developing culturally responsive instruction is one way that the library can have an important role in the retention of students. Instruction not only takes place in classrooms, but also at every service area in the library. If students are hesitant to use the library resources or do not understand how to search or what to do when they find materials, they may not obtain the information needed to do well in their classes. By changing their instructional practices to accommodate the needs of diverse groups and creating comfort and enthusiasm for searching, librarians will be assisting in the academic development of these students.

Regardless of their backgrounds, students need to know that library staff care about them. Feeling ignored and disrespected will very likely adversely affect students' experience at the institution. Providing successful library experiences early on can foster the view in students that the resources (including staff resources) of the library can enhance their academic potential. A welcoming environment and instructional strategies that incorporate the diverse needs of various populations can help students learn not only that the library offers valuable resources for them but that there are trained professionals able to help them navigate the sea of resources.

## Learning about Different Cultures

It is important both to be cognizant of the differing needs of students, and to be open to implementing appropriate and relevant programs. By creating collaborations with various cultural support groups, multicultural student organizations and cultural houses on campus, a dialog can be opened for exchanges about library experiences, resources and programming. Focus groups and informal chats are two ways to learn how libraries might alter their approaches, instruction and publicity to reach more students in meaningful ways. Forging partnerships with these groups can also greatly improve the connections between the groups and the services offered. Student advisory groups may have meetings where the librarian could be invited from time to time to check in and to discuss projects. If there is no library liaison to these programs and groups, it is important that one be designated.

One role of the liaison could be to work with students to create or enhance library handouts and web pages that reflect the culture or needs of that particular group. The students can review the guides to see that instructions are clear, that examples provided are culturally relevant and that the resources suggested are appropriate; for example, students may have more relevant web pages that they would suggest.

Another role for the librarian could be to provide some training sessions for these students on relevant library databases, to show them how these databases can enhance their studies. These sessions should be informal with lots of time available for students to discuss and explain ideas to the librarian on what they would find most useful. Students may be more inclined to come to such a session if it is in their comfortable surroundings rather than in the library. Librarians can learn a lot about what students would like to see in a session, as well as approaches they might take to introduce library resources to students.

Another benefit of creating partnerships with the various cultural groups on campus is that librarians might be able to work with their Web site administrator to create a library link from their web page. This library link could have a page jointly created by the librarian and students from that cultural group that includes representative instruction guides, databases, library tips and links. Additional outcomes of these partnerships could be to work with the students on creating a presence within the library, such as student representatives for program and exhibit planning. Other resources contain more examples of multicultural outreach to student organizations.[2]

## Culturally Responsive Instruction

Recent research literature indicates the need to make learning environments culturally responsive.[3] Much of this research emphasizes the importance of an involved and caring instructor as well as a warm classroom environment for creating a positive experience in the classroom. Making instructional sessions culturally relevant to all students, rather than solely to the majority, should be a goal of all instructors. Geneva Gay discusses the importance of using the students' past experiences and knowledge, whether cultural or frames of reference, in examples used in class to help make learning more relevant and effective to them.[4]

Realistically, in a one-shot library session there may be little opportunity to explore these experiences. However, as librarians become more aware of specific examples that resonate with students, those examples could be incorporated into future sessions, handouts, and print and online instruction guides.

In instruction sessions there are many opportunities to make examples real and relevant to students, such as using authors, sources or topics with which specific cultures associate (e.g., a relevant African American, Latino, Asian American, or figure of the gay community). If the librarian is flexible enough, opportunities may arise that allow a glimpse into meaningful examples that could be used. For example, Mestre found that when asking a group what term they might use to describe Hispanics, a lengthy discussion ensued about the differences in terminology used depending upon country, areas within a country, race, and status.[5] Although this evolved into a digression from what might have seemed like a quick question, the insight gained about how Latinos view each other and the terms they use to describe each other's culture and background were very relevant to the searching experiences for these students. Additionally, their interest in the topic being discussed was sparked and resulted in comparing and contrasting terminology used in various databases and the ensuing results.

In many cases teacher involvement and flexibility can be major contributors to the motivation to succeed, especially if the instructor invests in learning of cultural and social expectations of these students. By incorporating the students' historical knowledge and analysis into classroom activities, students may feel as though they are validated and that their culture is relevant to the learning experience. They may also be more engaged and motivated to succeed if their cultural knowledge and learning styles are acknowledged.

In order to shape our curriculum to represent the diversity within our classrooms and society, librarians need to become aware of the cultures they serve. If data are available that indicate the representative cultures that the library serves, librarians can focus their efforts on learning about those cultures so that they can better serve these populations. If no data have been compiled then a needs assessment might be in order. At least being aware of the representative languages, culture and learning styles, librarians can make instruction more meaningful and relevant to their students' lives.

In order to become more aware of other peoples, librarians should first explore their own ethnic, cultural and linguistic background and learn how those perspectives guide their perceptions and attitudes and influences how they think and act. It is also important that they understand their learning and teaching styles. Because librarians encounter patrons different from themselves in regards to race, ethnicity, culture, language, generation, socioeconomic status, sexual orientation, disabilities, and learning styles, it is important to learn of the differences in their cultural strengths, norms, values and experiences. In addition to the background information, librarians should also learn about differences in verbal and non verbal communications styles and preferences of various groups.

Librarians can work with organizations on campus to institute training programs/workshops for staff that can provide, at least, a beginning knowledge base for the librarians. Inviting speakers to staff meetings is one step to hear about cultural practices, communication and learning styles, ability differences, disabilities, diverse religions, and lifestyles practiced on campus. Ongoing diversity awareness training, workshops, reading materials, attendance at conferences specific to the cognitive and social development of students from diverse ethnic, cultural, ability and language groups would be an excellent beginning. Librarians could also join local, state or national committees and discussion groups that focus on increasing diversity awareness in libraries. One such group is the Instruction for Diverse Populations Committee of the Association of College and Research Libraries, Instruction Section.[6] This committee and other groups interested in serving diverse populations are listed on the Library Outreach to Underserved Populations page.[7] In fact the American Library Association continues to identify diversity as a "key action area" with goals to improve the library services provided to members of racial and ethnic minority groups, to provide greater access to information and research relevant to the experience of diverse communities in the US, and to more effectively recruit people of color into the library and information services professions.[8]

Learning about other cultures, especially those in the region, should be a life-long process. By learning about other peoples and developing diversity consciousness, the hope is that librarians will cease to focus their teaching on a "one-size-fits-all" cultural model based on their own culture.

## Culturally Proficient Instruction

Another progression for developing diversity awareness and becoming culturally proficient is outlined in *Culturally Proficient Instruction: A Guide for People Who Teach*. Cultural proficiency is defined as "a way of being that allows individuals and organizations to interact effectively with people who differ from them."[9] The essential elements that the authors define for being culturally proficient are: Name the differences (assess culture); claim the differences (value diversity); reframe the differences (manage the dynamics of difference); train about differences (adapt to diversity); and change for differences (institutionalize cultural knowledge). These elements could serve as a good model for librarians becoming culturally proficient. The first stage (name the differences) consists of recognizing one's own culture, heritage and perspectives and then doing a study to determine which cultures are represented by the constituency served. The second stage (claim the differences) consists of accepting the differences within the classroom and developing a community of learning with them. The third stage (reframe the differences) might not always need addressing by librarians during a 50-minute session. The librarian should be aware of and responsive to any clashes that might result due to conflicts in culture. The fourth stage (train about differences) consists of ongoing training and learning about other cultures. The last stage (change for differences) consists of incorporating different teaching techniques that would reflect cultural responsiveness to other cultures. Here the librarian would design experiences that build on prior knowledge and experiences of the learner. The librarian would also look for opportunities to share the cultural knowledge gained with other individuals in the library in order broaden the cultural and instructional knowledge base of others. Culturally proficient instructors examine their own biases, expectations and views of other cultures.

Rosa Hernández Sheets points out that competent teachers acknowledge the connection between culture and learning.[10] In teaching, instructors should look for culturally inclusive resources. For example, in a library instruction session when doing sample searches, librarians can use authors from cultures represented in the class or topics of interest to students present. Librarians can provide opportunities for social interaction, selecting culturally inclusive resources or online examples, providing multiple instructional strategies, and hands-on activities. Building in cultural practices and experiences may take time, so starting with one or a few ideas at first, and then building on them in subsequent sessions might be a comfortable way to proceed.

Although many instruction librarians work with faculty prior to the session to collaborate on the goals for the session, chatting with students as they enter the classroom can build rapport and bring out additional cues about interests, providing linkages between home and school.

During and after a class session the instructor can reflect on how students responded to the classroom climate, instructional strategies used, and content. Did the students connect with the content and were they able to go to the next level or were they confused or needing clarification? Did they respond to certain examples more than others? Did particular teaching strategies resonate more than others? Were the examples or instructions too complex for them? If cultural examples were included did they inspire comments or participation? The process of reflection, and perhaps having a peer look for these characteristics during a session, can help inform future sessions. In the reflection the librarian could describe a successful or unsuccessful lesson to think about patterns that emerge, noting when students were engaged or not and then making appropriate adjustments in the lesson, content, and delivery of instruction to better achieve learning goals.

Whether conducting a one-shot instructional session or a semester-long course, librarians should incorporate a variety of assessment tools into their teaching. In addition to providing feedback on whether or not students achieved the stated goals and objectives, assessment used in a formative fashion can also help librarians improve their instruction, particularly in matters related to cross cultural sensitivity. No matter what instructional tool is used, it is important to evaluate the effectiveness of that tool. As with the general reflection of the instructional session, librarians should examine whether or not students did better when asked to respond orally, in writing, in a peer response or demonstration or in some other activity that was assessed.

To provide better services to more students, librarians must understand how culture influences cognitive and social development and know how to apply these understandings in teaching and learning situations. Students must be given multiple and consistent opportunities to practice higher-level thinking skills, if they are to develop as advanced critical thinkers. Cultural adaptations may be needed with diverse learners because students acquire and display knowledge in different ways. It is also important to remember that all students come into the classroom with some prior knowledge on which they can build. Again, making the task relevant to their everyday practical experience will help students be successful in recognizing patterns and classifying and categorizing terms and tasks. Providing opportunities for students to view reality through numerous perspectives helps them understand, evaluate, question and challenge the issues.

## Generational Diversity

While considering the teaching strategies that might be relevant to accommodate the greatest number of students, it is also important to consider generational aspects of users. Patrons who have not been exposed to online information seeking strategies, such as some of the older returning students, may need more focused, slower paced extended sessions with mastery being reached on specific steps moving on. However, the Millennials, also referred to as Generation Y, the Net Generation, Echo Boomers and Google Generation, who have grown up immersed in the digital environment, are used to multitasking and having lots of tactile experiences. They prefer to do what is of interest to them and are motivated by authentic tasks or self-selected tasks. Therefore, allowing them to choose their topics, rather than using a librarian-controlled term, may motivate and engage them more.

Frances Jacobson Harris discusses some of the searching behaviors of Millennials, which have implications for how librarians work with them, including: get something now and in as few steps as possible; cast a wide net, then discard what's not relevant; have tactile and visual experiences (the drag and drop and click features); use mobile tools (such as portable or hand-held devices where information can be loaded); decide the information to find, not have an imposed task.[11] To satisfy the above needs, librarians may need to develop more online instruction tools geared for interactive, quick access to "the source." In an instruction session, as much as librarians would like students to really think about their terms carefully and to refine them before searching, they may need to consider that students are fine with getting more resources than could possibly be useful as a result of a search and then casting off what they don't want. Librarians will need to be innovative and flexible in their teaching.

An approach that might work well with this group (and perhaps with most groups) is to have a student at the instructor station doing the keying. It can be very informative to watch the approach a novice takes to get from point A to point B, even if adept with technology. This approach can be done in a couple of ways. One way is for the librarian to provide the steps and observe while the student works the keyboard. The librarian is able to observe hesitancies, perhaps because the librarian did not provide sufficient direction or because the student is unable to find the element they were instructed to find. Another benefit of this approach is that the student (and those imitating the demonstration at their seats) is proceeding at the pace of a student, rather than a librarian. Often librarians may communicate actions they are taking (e.g., "Now I will choose the term 'search' and enter my terms…"), but it could take students a lot longer to find where "search" is, and by the time they've found it the librarian may be quite far ahead. By having a student in the driver's seat, the librarian will have to modify instructions based upon the progress of the student. Many other useful questions might be posed by a student if s/he is in charge of navigating rather than a librarian. Students also like to cheer on their classmate and get much more involved in the results since they want their classmate to succeed.

Another way to work with a student at the keyboard is for the librarian to ask questions and have the student try to figure out the answer on their own. For example, if the librarian asks "What do you think I would need to do in order to retrieve these items?" the student first might ask "What do you mean by retrieve?" Or, if the student understands that concept he or she would talk aloud and explain "Well, I've already checked the items that I want. I guess I would look for some button that says "get the articles or open…." Chances are the database will not have those terms, which then provides a great learning opportunity for the librarian to help the students construct meaning from the search. Many times students will contribute suggestions because they really want to help their classmates. The librarian could also ask the class what they would want to do with these articles or citations once they got them. Hopefully someone would provide words like "look at them, print, save, e-mail"). These types of brain-storming sessions allow the librarian to work with the students on how they might think about the way things are termed or organized. By allowing the student to do the keyboarding, librarians can get a glimpse at how novices search and try to assist them in understanding how things work and why. Students are much more engaged when they are active participants. In fact, students are quite attentive in class because they do not know when it might be their turn to be at the keyboard. In fact, although it will take longer to get through a demonstration, it will most likely engage the participants and provide a more lasting and meaningful learning experience.

## Teaching Strategies

Because not all students learn optimally with the same instructional strategy, librarians should develop a repertoire of teaching strategies and alter them as needed during a session. Although there are times when teacher-centered strategies may be appropriate, librarians should develop student-centered instructional strategies. Teacher-centered strategies include direct instruction, such as lectures, demonstrations, presentations, drills, discussions, and brainstorming. Student-centered strategies allow the student to play a more direct role in the learning process, with the librarian facilitating the lesson rather than simply dispensing it. Common in these strategies are active learning activities, cooperative and collaborative learning, peer tutoring opportunities and teaching, and guiding activities. Various ethnic groups of color prefer group learning and active/affective learning.[12] Students from cultures that have been socialized in a collective, interpersonal culture, such as African Americans, Asian Americans and Latino Americans, may regard themselves as part of a group and community that should work together to help their classmates. However, European American students who are socialized in an individualistic society may be more used to a competitive and independent learning style.

In today's schools, however, teachers are working towards providing more group and peer learning even in the early years so students often come to college already exposed to a variety of student-centered learning, are comfortable with it, and even expect it. Even if a student comes to the library with a cultural background similar to that of the librarian's, there may still be a disconnect if the librarian attempts to teach in a way that does not match the student's optimal style. By replacing teacher-centered strategies with student-centered strategies, librarians will be prepared with multiple teaching tools to help accommodate the cognitive, social, and learning styles of culturally diverse students. This, in turn, can lead to increased engagement and the development of higher-level thinking skills. Chapter three in this Handbook further addresses teaching styles.

## Questioning Techniques

As librarians attempt to engage the class by asking questions, they might do well to think about how they ask questions. Many librarians have already shifted from asking closed-ended questions to open-ended questions. By shifting to that type of inquiry librarians can allow for multiple responses, rather than expecting one correct answer. Open-ended questions also give students who prefer an inductive problem solving and reasoning approach an opportunity to focus on the whole, rather than on the details. Some students of color prefer this type of inductive process.[13] Rather than asking a question like "How many responses did you get for this search?" the librarian could ask "What can you tell me about the results you got from this search?" This phrasing of the question allows the students to reflect on what is important to them in the search process. They may mention the number of results, but more importantly for them, they may provide a bigger picture of what was retrieved, such as the focus of the information received, the types of sources, and how relevant they may be for their needs. A particular citation might trigger something for them that they might share with the class, as they work towards the detail level. Open-ended questions are good tools for developing critical thinking.

From the students' perspective, answering questions may be intimidating. They may hesitate to volunteer an answer because they may be concerned about what their peers or instructor would think of them if they provide a wrong answer. This reaction is especially true for groups that are not raised in individualistic, competitive environments. The librarian can create a safe environment for students by encouraging multiple answers and not judging negatively on any answer. For example, rather than asking "what's the correct subject heading for someone looking to find information about African Americans and achievement?" the librarian might say something like: "The library catalog doesn't always reflect current cultural terms or even provide what we would think as logical headings. Take a minute to write down a couple of ideas of what terms you would try. After a minute I'll ask you to share them while I write them on the marker board." By providing first an explanation reassuring them that if their term does not show up in the catalog it does not mean that it is incorrect, students will not feel stress and pressure about getting the "correct answer." Second, students get a chance to process their thoughts by writing them down. After this exercise, they may be more willing to share their response if they see the librarian writing down all of the answers provided, not just the ones the librarian feels are correct. This nonjudgmental approach provides an opportunity for engagement with the topic without fear of rejection.

## Learning Styles

In order for librarians to appreciate the learning styles of others, they need to be aware of their own individual learning preferences. Such an assessment will help them avoid teaching only via their own dominant and preferred style of learning. It is very easy for instructors to teach in the style with which they are most familiar. If their previous experiences were in lecture-based environments their comfort level will most likely be highest within the lecture mode of instruction. However, today's students are experiencing more collaborative, active learning environments that engage them. There is not one preferred learning style for all students or even for any one particular ethnic or cultural group.[14] Not all students from any particular group learn in the same way. In fact, different measurement models assess different dimensions of learning styles that address factors such as: instructional practices, information processing, social interaction tendencies and the influence of personality. Librarians will need to develop a repertoire of strategies to use and to alter strategies in order to tailor them to individual students. Some students, especially those whose first language is not English, may need to have material in print in front of them before a session so they can refer to it ; some may prefer more hands-on practice, rather than just being lectured at. Still other students may need visual cues, or perhaps more tactile work. In short, if instructors vary their teaching styles to accommodate different learning styles and also try different approaches to find the best fit for the user, they will be accommodating many users' learning needs. As instructors vary their teaching styles, they also help strengthen students' ability to learn in multiple ways. Additionally, more on learning theory can be found in chapter two of this Handbook.

## Cross Cultural Instruction Strategies

There are many examples of strategies that might be used to provide cross cultural instruction, including:

• Match cultural norms to classroom instruction. Some groups thrive on collaborative learning and working with peers. Provide those opportunities for problem solving or tasks in the classroom.

• Extend the wait time when asking questions so that students can process the information and formulate responses. Rephrase questions to assist students with different linguistic abilities.

• Make the environment less formal by standing by the door as students enter the classroom. Chat with them and learn something about them. Even learning three people's names as they enter could be a good tool so that you can refer to them during the session.

• Provide non-threatening environments for all students. Ways to do this can include providing opportunities for students to be involved in small groups or working in pairs, and providing index cards where they write a response to a question that they then pass down the aisle for the instructor to pick up and use. The technique known as "think, pair, share" would work well in this scenario.

Even allowing the student to collaborate in writing out an answer with their neighbor allows for reflection time and sharing. The instructor can then ask for volunteers to share responses.

• Make the material relevant to students. If the instructor can relate how the library can improve their studies, students may take more notice. Select authentic information from historical, literary, and scientific viewpoints of multiple diverse cultural groups. Incorporate music, such as using musical strands to represent different parts of the lesson. This approach can provide an environmental stimulation, as well as connection to their everyday life.

• Use searching examples that include accomplishments of diverse ethnic and cultural groups and people with disabilities relevant to our nations' past, present, and future economic, political, cultural, and social growth. In short, use meaningful instructional examples applicable to the experiential background of all students.

• Check that instructions are clear with logical sequences that can be easily duplicated. When using library jargon have students rephrase what was said in their own terminology—what meaning they make out of that term, phrase or step. Having a student rephrase what was just explained is a good check, not only on their comprehension, but on the instructions themselves.

• Use a variety of classroom discourse to provide multiple, active, repeated messages, perhaps reiterating in different ways what the main points were.

• Develop a process for mentoring, coaching, collecting ideas, and sharing instructional experiences with other colleagues. One of the most valuable resources for librarians is the successful experience of colleagues.

• Take the opportunity to have students "drive" by manipulating the keyboard as instructions or questions are given.

• Train graduate assistants of color to provide library instruction sessions. Their input on instructional design can help advance the instruction program, as well as increase the diversity seen by the public. Students may be more likely to ask peers questions than the librarian, who may be seen as an authority figure.[15]

The suggestions above that focus on including relevant cultural examples should also be applied to web pages, tutorials and user guides. Culturally relevant examples should permeate the library web pages for the thousands of users who look for their guidance there. Care also needs to be taken that the web pages provide instructions that are clear to multiple constituencies.

## Conclusion

Within today's diverse society all students need to have access not only to the information resources, but also to appropriate instruction on how to access, search, use and evaluate them. When designing projects, creating publicity, establishing evaluation, and presenting workshops, educators should keep in mind that their targeted audience extends beyond the mainstream population.

Librarians and media specialists have key roles to play in assisting students and teachers to learn computer applications and educational technology. Librarians are teachers. The librarian's influence as a teacher (the influence that they have as a type of authority figure as well as their influence in deciding what students are exposed to and how it's presented) plays an important role in whether or not a student will use the library and learn computer applications. It makes a difference in students' intentions to use those resources. Librarians need to be innovative and demonstrate to their users' alternate ways to access information. However, in doing so, they will need to keep in mind that students do not all learn in the same way and they will have to be open to varying the way they assist students from diverse cultural backgrounds in acquiring information, especially through technology.

Librarians should aspire to creating a classroom environment that affirms, respects and acknowledges differences in individuals and in groups by offering multiple teaching and learning strategies and examples responsive to students. Creating culturally inclusive teaching-learning events will not only enhance the experience of students but is one step in providing cross cultural instruction.

## Notes

1. Office of Diversity and Office of Research and Statistics, American Library Association. *Diversity Counts*. Chicago: ALA, 2007. Available online from http://www.ala.org/ala/ors/diversitycounts/DiversityCounts_rev07.pdf. [Accessed August 20, 2007.]

2. See for example: Scott Walter, "Moving Beyond Collections: Academic Library Outreach to Multicultural Student Centers." *Reference Services Review*. 33, no. 4 (2005): 438-58; Elizabeth W. Kraemer, Dana J. Keyse, and Shawn V Lombardo, "Beyond These Walls: Building a Library Outreach Program at Oakland University." *The Reference Librarian*. 82 (2003): 5-17; Teresa Y. Neely and Lee-Smeltzer, Kuang-Hwei (Janet) Eds., *Diversity Now: People, Collections, and Services in Academic Libraries*. Haworth Press, Inc., 2001; Janice Simmons-Welburn, "Designing Effective Instructional and Outreach Programs for Underrepresented Undergraduate Students: The Iowa Approach". In Dewey, Barbara I. (Ed.) *Library User Education: Powerful Learning, Powerful Partnerships*. Scarecrow Press: Lanham, MD, 2001. 222-9; Janice Simmons-Welburn and William C. Welburn, (2001), "Cultivating Partnerships/Realizing Diversity. *Journal of Library Administration* 33, nos 1/2, (2001): 5-19; Trudi E. Jacobson and Helene C. Williams (Eds). *Teaching the New Library to Today's Users: Reaching International, Minority, Senior Citizens, Gay/Lesbian, First-Generation, At-Risk,Graduate and Returning Students, and Distance Learners*. Neal-Schuman: New York, NY, 2000; Elaina Norline and Patricia J. Morris, "Developing Proactive Partnerships: Minority Cultural Centers." *The Reference Librarian* 67-68 (1999): 147-60; Karen E. Downing, Barbara MacAdam, and Darlene P. Nichols, *Reaching a Multicultural Student Community: A Handbook for Academic Librarians*. Greenwood Press: Westport, CT, 1993; and Barbara MacAdam and Darlene P Nichols,. "Peer Information Counseling: An Academic Library Program for Minority Students". *Journal of Academic Librarianship* 15, no. 4 (1989): 204-9.

3. James A. Banks, *Cultural Diversity and Education: Foundations, Curriculum, and Teaching*.

Seattle: Pearson Education, Inc., 2006; Kikanza Nuri Robins, Randall B.Lindsey, Delores B Lindsey, and Raymond D. Terrel, *Culturally Proficient Instruction: A Guide For People Who Teach.* 2nd edition. Thousand Oaks, CA: Corwin Press, 2006; Rosa Hernández Sheets, *Diversity Pedagogy: Examining the Role of Culture in the Teaching-Learning Process.* Boston: Pearson Education, Inc., 2005; Lori. S. Mestre, "Culturally Relevant Instruction for Latinos." *Academic Exchange Quarterly* 8, no 1(2004, Spring): 46-51; Jacklyn Blake Clayton, *One Classroom, Many Worlds: Teaching and Learning in the Cross-Cultural Classroom.* Portsmouth, NH: Heinemann, 2003; Geneva Gay, *Culturally Responsive Teaching. Theory, Research and Practice.* New York: Teachers College Press, 2000; Geneva Gay, "Culturally Responsive Teaching in Special Education for Ethnically Diverse Students: Setting the Stage." *International Journal of Qualitative Studies in Education (QSE),* 15, no. 6 (2002, November): 613-629; Karon N.LeCompte and Audrey Davis McCray, "Complex Conversations with Teacher Candidates: Perspectives of Whiteness and Culturally Responsive Teaching". *Curriculum & Teaching Dialogue* 4, no. 1 (2002): 25-35; Christine E.Sleeter, "Preparing Teachers for Culturally Diverse Schools: Research and the Overwhelming Presence of Whiteness." *Journal of Teacher Education* 52, no.2 (2001): 94-106; Sonia Nieto and Carmen Rolón, "Preparation and Professional Development of Teachers: A Perspective from Two Latinas." In Jacqueline .J. Irvine (Ed.), *Critical Knowledge for Diverse Teachers and Learners.* Washington, DC: AACTE Publications, 1997; and Raymond. J Wlodkowski and Margery B. Ginsberg (1995, September). "A Framework for Culturally Responsive Teaching." *Educational Leadership* 53, no.1:17-21.

4.  Geneva Gay, *Culturally Responsive Teaching. Theory, Research and Practice.* New York: Teachers College Press, 2000.

5.  Lori S. Mestre, *Latinos, Libraries and Electronic Resources.* Ph. D. thesis, University of Massachusetts, 2000.

6.  See the *Library Instruction for Diverse Populations Bibliography,* ACRL Instruction Section, Instruction to Diverse Populations Committee, 2003. Available online from http://www.ala.org/ala/acrlbucket/is/publicationsacrl/diversebib.cfm.[Accessed August 20, 2007] and the *Multilingual Glossary,* ACRL Instruction Section, Instruction to Diverse Populations Committee, 2006. Available online from http://www.ala.org/ala/acrlbucket/is/publicationsacrl/multilingualglossaryacknowledgements.cfm. [Accessed August 20, 2007.]

7.  For committees related to cultural diversity see American Library Association. Library Outreach to Underserved Populations: Resources in Cultural Diversity. 2006. Available online from http://www.ala.org/ala/olos/outreachresource/resourcescultural.htm. [Accessed April 27, 2006.]

8.  American Library Association. *ALA Ahead to 2010: Draft Strategic Plan.* 15 April 2005. Available online from http://www.ala.org/ala/ourassociation/governingdocs/aheadto2010/plan.htm. [Accessed April 27, 2006.]

9.  Kikanza Nuri Robins, Randall B.Lindsey, Delores B Lindsey, and Raymond D. Terrel, *Culturally Proficient Instruction: A Guide for People Who Teach.* 2nd edition. Thousand Oaks, CA: Corwin Press, 2006.

10.  Rosa Hernández Sheets, *Diversity Pedagogy: Examining the Role of Culture in the Teaching-Learning Process.* Boston: Pearson Education, Inc., 2005.

11.  Frances Jacobson Harris, *I Found It on the Internet: Coming of Age Online.* Chicago: American Library Association, 2005.

12.  Gay 2004; Gay, 2000; Mestre, 2000; Robert Slavin, "Cooperative Learning and Intergroup Relations." In James A. Banks and Cherrie A.M. Banks (Eds.) *Handbook Of Research On Multicultural Education.* San Francisco: Jossey-Bass 2001. 628-624.

13.  Shirley Brice Heath, "Questioning at Home and at School: A Comparative Study." In George D. Spindler (Ed.), *Doing The Ethnography Of Schooling.* New York: Holt, Reinhart & Win-

ston, 1982. 96-101; Jacqueline .J. Irvine, and D.E.York, "Learning Styles of Culturally Diverse Students: A Literature Review". In James.A. Banks and Cherry M. Banks (Eds.), *Handbook of Research on Multicultural Education.* New York: Macmillan, 1995. 484-497.

14. For more on learning styles related to students of color (with references to many others who have worked in this area) see: Downing, 1993; Rita Dunn, "Capitalizing On College Students' Learning Styles: Theory, Practice and Research". In Rita.Dunn and Shirley A. Griggs (Eds.). *Practical Approaches to Using Learning Styles in Higher Education.* Westport, CT: Bergin & Garvey, 2000.3-18; Slavin, 628-624; Harris 2000, Mestre, 2000; and Irvine, 484-497. For an interesting conversation about how multiple intelligences and cultures intersect see Thomas Armstrong, *Multiple Intelligences in the Classroom.* 2nd Edition. Alexandria, VA: Association for Supervision and Curriculum Development, 2000.

15. See, for example, Mark Winston, "Cultural Sensitivity or How to Make the Library a Better Place". *Reference Services Review* 23, no. 3 (1995): 7-12; Downing, 1989; MacAdam and Nichols, 1989.

# CHAPTER 11

## Instructional Technologies

Steven J. Bell, John D. Shank, and Greg Szczyrbak

### Learning and Technology

Chapter two of this handbook discusses learning theory. Perhaps the most important concept to grasp about instructional technology is that it is more about instruction than technology. In addition to having mastery of all types of technologies for learning, the instructional technologist understands how people learn, knows the different schools of thought about how learning takes place and recognizes the importance of assessing whether and how learning occurs. The role of the instructional technologist is to understand how technology can contribute to effective learning. This is possible when learning is the focus and we understand the role of the learner, the teacher, and the instruction. The figure below, created for this chapter, illustrates the connections between these three elements. Various techniques are used by educators to create a bridge between themselves and learners. Educational technologies are but one part of the equation, but in today's technology-driven society it is often an expectation of both educators and students that technology will play a role in the learning process. Educators also expect, rightfully so, that their institutions will provide professional development and support for integrating learning technologies into their teaching methods. That support is typically provided by an instructional technologist. Having a strong grasp of learning theory and practice allows the

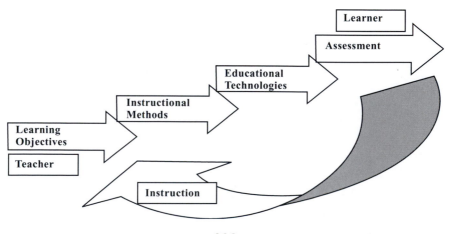

instructional technologist to advise educators in making critical decisions on the appropriate application of technology for learning. Doing so allows the educator and instructional technologist to apply technology more appropriately to the needs of specific learners and different learning situations.

It is important to consider how technology can influence the relationship between teachers and learners, and the instruction methods used to create the bridge between the teacher and learner. Think about your own instruction. You may be a great teacher. You know about learners and how they learn, and you have good mastery of different instruction methods. But how do you enhance your teaching by the integration of technology into your instruction? Could you enhance student learning by providing a web-based tutorial prior to an instruction session? What is the impact of placing a pre-test in the students' course management system (e.g., Blackboard, Angel, etc.)?

Because instructional technologies can provide many possibilities and options for facilitating learning, it is incumbent upon any information literacy instructor to experiment and explore how instructional technologies can best be integrated into the learning experience. But all librarian educators must acknowledge that technology may be the inappropriate solution in certain situations. With access to technology comes the responsibility for using it sensibly to promote learning, not simply using technology because we can. One of the roles of the instructional technologist is to assess the learning situation and determine what pedagogy most effectively fits, whether it involves a technology solution or not. In this chapter the authors explore different facets of instruction technology with the goal of assisting the reader to identify ways in which the skill set of the instructional technologist could enhance his or her own information literacy instruction. It also provides a set of examples to illustrate those ways in which emerging technologies may be adapted by library educators to build better bridges between themselves and their students.

## Technology

What exactly is technology? A preferred definition among instructional technologists is "the systematic application of scientific or other organized knowledge to practical tasks"[1] Generalizing from the previous definition, instructional technology has been defined as applying scientific knowledge about human learning to the practical tasks of teaching and learning. That is, instructional technology applies basic research on human learning to produce instructional design principles and processes including the use of hardware products that teachers and students use to increase learning effectiveness.[2] What are some of these instructional technologies?

The range of technologies being applied to learning situations is expanding rapidly. Some technologies, such as traditional audio-visual equipment, are time-tested learning tools, and are still being sensibly integrated into the teaching and learning process. But many of these long-time teaching technology standards are being replaced or supplemented by a wide range of emerging instructional technologies. The most revolutionary instructional technology of the past 25 years is, in fact, the computer, because it makes so many other types of instructional technologies possible. Consider the possibilities:

> Educational software
> Multimedia productions
> Graphics for visual learning
> Computer-based instruction and online tutorial
> Course Management Systems (discussion boards, online assessments, etc.)
> Responsive answer systems

The other significant innovation in instructional technology is the Internet. It takes the computer and adds to it the power of the network for communication and collaboration. Not only can most of the technologies above be distributed on networks, but consider some of the new possibilities the Internet offers for integrating technology into teaching and learning:

> E-mail
> Wikis
> Screencasted tutorials
> Archived Web casts and virtual conference segments
> Library databases
> Web quests
> Podcasts
> Weblogs
> Online community learning
> Collaborative writing

From this wide array of instructional technologies, the information literacy educator's task is to determine in what ways each of these technologies might be applied to help students learn to improve their research skills. If learning is a relatively persistent change in what a student knows or can do, the objective of incorporating technology into an instruction situation should be to help learning take place. But in what ways can technology make a difference when it comes to facilitating the persistent change that defines learning? It's common to have computer technology at one's disposal in most teaching settings. Many instruction sessions are only an hour long and there may be little that technology can do to improve the information literacy librarian's chances of creating some persistent change in a learner.

The question of how to most effectively create the persistent change that signifies learning is often answered with a single word—experience. The most effective method to facilitate learning is to provide authentic and varied practice. In other words, put the learner in the situation in which he or she will experience a real or simulated experience that requires the skills being learned in the classroom. That is where instructional technology can contribute to learning. There are abundant examples of the ways in which librarians use instructional technology to create a simulated learning environment. Consider the many instructional tutorials available for use. A well known example is TILT (Texas Information Literacy Tutorial) found online.[3] This tutorial resulted from the work of a team of librarians, instructional designers, and instructional technologists investing many hours into the creation of a multimedia production that allows the learner to choose his or her preferred research topic. Assessments are built into the learning environment. Understanding the importance of providing students with authentic and varied learning experience is one thing; creating real opportunities for it is a considerable challenge as the labor intensiveness of the TILT example demonstrates.

## The Tie That Binds: Instructional Design

To enhance their ability to support faculty some librarians are obtaining advanced degrees in instructional design and technology. Currently that's rare among librarians, but as their teaching role expands it is likely that more academic librarians will become "blended."[4] That is, in addition to their traditional library science skills more librarians will incorporate the skills of instructional designers into their work. Learning more about instructional design and technology also better equips academic librarians to communicate effectively with their institution's instructional designers and technologists. We can learn from our colleagues or enter into formal degree programs. Either option moves an academic librarian in the direction of becoming more blended. One of the important things that librarians will learn about instructional designers is that their approach to learning is unique, and that some of their theory and practice can influence what we know about delivering information literacy instruction.

At its root instructional design is the process of solving instructional problems through a systematic analysis of the conditions for learning. It is derived from a combination of theories from the fields of psychology, systems design, and communication. The instructional designer's perspective is that learning should not occur in a haphazard manner. Rather, it should happen as the result of an orderly process in which there are clearly stated outcomes that can be measured. What ties together nearly all forms of instructional design is a generic instructional systems design model known as ADDIE[5], an acronym for:

- **A**nalysis—the process of defining what is to be learned
- **D**esign—the process of specifying how it is to be learned
- **D**evelopment—the process of authoring and producing learning materials
- **I**mplementation—the process of installing the instruction product in a real world context
- **E**valuation—the process of determining the impact of the instruction

An instructional designer that works for a company that designs learning materials for corporations may spend hundreds of hours working as part of a larger design team to develop instructional materials. It's unlikely any academic librarian would have the necessary time to thoroughly and fully implement AD-DIE in designing information literacy instruction. Equipped with an instructional designer's mindset it is possible to develop an understanding of learning needs that is the first step on the path to the thoughtful, organized, and purposeful development and evaluation of instructional products designed for helping students achieve information literacy outcomes. These next sections provide more insight into how ADDIE is applied in educational settings.

## Analysis

When presented with a new instructional challenge, for example, trying to help students in a junior level science writing course develop better techniques for analyzing research questions and developing research strategies, the first step is to try to understand what the students already know and what they don't know. To best analyze the situation a blended librarian needs to identify the learning gap, and one method is to prepare a brief survey. For effective results the librarian then integrates it into the students' courseware site so it's efficient to conduct the assessment. This makes it possible to quickly identify that most of the students are confused by the process of articulating a research question and then identifying keywords that can be used in a search strategy. The analysis determines that is what the students need to learn.

## Design

Next the librarian enters the design phase. This requires the development of a design grid that will inform the development process. A design grid typically has three columns: objectives; assessment; instructional strategy. Here is the type of information that would be found on a typical design grid:

- Objective: After reading the faculty member's assignment the students will be able to write a single English sentence that articulates a specific question that will be answered with a research process.

- Assessment: Given the assignment students will spend 15 minutes in class developing a research question that will be written on a sheet of paper and then submitted to the instructor. The librarian and instructor will review the research questions and return them to the students with comments for revisions, if needed.

- Instructional Strategy: First, the students will watch a 5 minute video in which a librarian is shown going through a one-on-one consultation with a student in which a research question is being developed. Second, students will go through a 15 minute drill-and-practice writing a research question for a sample assignment.

Take note that a librarian equipped with a firm knowledge of pedagogy makes it a point to offer a multimedia learning material that will address the needs of different learners. The selection of drill-and-practice as a secondary instructional method fits in well with a writing class where skills are often developed through repetitive exercises. The completed design grid will feature perhaps three to five specific objectives that the librarian believes will specify how the objectives will be learned. The librarian will also share the grid with the instructor to obtain feedback to make sure the objectives, assessment, and instructional strategies appear feasible and manageable.

## Development

Now that the librarian has designed the blueprint for the instruction session and related instructional materials, it is time to move into the development phase. This will involve some work with one of the university's instructional technologists to obtain assistance in the preparation of the video for use in the session with students. Prior to recording the video, the librarian conducts another part of the ADDIE process referred to as prototyping. Prototyping allows a designer to test his or her instructional product before deciding on a final version. If the librarian is working with a new technology prototyping allows for experimentation. This involves sharing the ideas and the script with a colleague or two, and the librarian may even do a bit of role playing with them just to see if the plans sound reasonable. As a result of going through prototyping the librarian did discover some script problems.

Based on feedback, the librarian makes some changes to the text of the script. Then, using one of the library's study rooms as the location for the video, the instructional technologist uses a digital video camera to capture the librarian explaining to the student why it's important to develop a well-articulated research question before beginning the research for the assignment. The librarian is shown writing a research question on a board in the study room. Later, the instructional technologist uses digital video editing software to reduce the video to five minutes. The librarian also develops a one-page handout that takes the students through a step-by-step process to write out a research question.

### Implementation and Evaluation

Clearly, professional instructional designers would spend considerably more time on all these phases of ADDIE, but time isn't a luxury that most librarians have so they need to condense the process. In fact, there is insufficient time to test the video with a few students in a phase known as formative evaluation which serves to identify weaknesses in the instructional product before it is implemented. Instead, once the video is deemed acceptable, the librarian will implement it in the class session. At the completion of the session the librarian will distribute a brief survey to the students to obtain their feedback on the session in order to determine if the original objectives were achieved. That feedback is then used to further refine the objectives and instructional methods, or perhaps start all over again with a new approach if this one appears unsuccessful.

Did this seem like an exceptional amount of work for the librarian? It clearly takes more time to approach information literacy instruction like an instruction designer. But what is the alternative? Well, the alternative is an unsatisfactory learning experience for students. When librarians develop instructional materials without being properly informed about the students' learning gaps it is more likely they choose instructional methods that are not informed by clear objectives. When there is no plan for evaluation, the instruction appears haphazard and poorly executed. Making use of the ADDIE approach, allows librarians to maximize their time with the students, impress instructors, and increase the likelihood of being asked to further collaborate in the future to help students master outcomes for information literacy at her institution.

## Instructional Technologies: Some Tried and True, Some Experimental and New

As stated earlier in this chapter, the number and range of potential technologies that may be adopted to enhance learning are growing rapidly. In the following section we will learn how technologies can be adapted for instructional purposes, including some developed without academic teaching in mind. Selecting and utilizing a particular technology should be a teaching and pedagogy driven process. Instead of focusing on the technology, focus on the students' needs and the instructional strategy. Then select the most appropriate instructional technology to assist in enhancing the instructional process. Just as we would not select a tool to accomplish a particular task before we have identified the task, we should not select a technology before we have determined the instructional needs. Too often poor instructional design leads to poor instruction and no instructional technology can compensate for this. Likewise, the best instructional strategies can be compromised by either selecting the wrong technologies or poor implementation of the technologies.

This section uses Chickering and Ehrman's "Implementing the seven principles: technology as lever"[6] as a framework that demonstrates how various technologies can enhance instruction and, thereby, assist in selecting the most appropriate educational technologies for your instructional needs. Their article states that in order for technology to be truly effective, it should be consistent with the "Seven Principles." The Seven Principles are:

1. Good practice encourages contacts between students and faculty
2. Good practice develops reciprocity and cooperation among students
3. Good practice uses active learning techniques
4. Good practice gives prompt feedback
5. Good practice emphasizes time on task
6. Good practice communicates high expectations
7. Good practice respects diverse talents and ways of learning

## Weblogs

Most of us are familiar with personal and library weblogs (blogs). In the last two years both have expanded exponentially, and there are hundreds of library bloggers and dozens of academic libraries have created their own library blogs. While these types of blogs are useful for disseminating general and personal information, community news, opinions and commentary, a savvy librarian may find other uses for a blog. It could be used to increase the information literacy skills of everyone in the campus community. For example, a blogger could submit posts, including screenshots or video tutorials, detailing techniques to improve research using library databases. A post could also simply be used to provide links to resources that promote information literacy. These are potentially interesting uses of a blog, but since they are passive in nature it is difficult to know if any library patrons would actually find their way to these sorts of blog posts. We need to remember that our patrons have access to millions of blogs, so we need to ask what will compel them to visit our blog site. Remember that instructional technology is focused on matching the appropriate technology to enhance teaching and learning. How then might an instructional technologist find a way to use a blog to enhance the process? A library blog developed to support an information literacy assignment would need to be integrated into or developed for specific courses. That would require the cooperation of the faculty member so that the information literacy blogs created by the students would be an integral element of the course. When librarians lead the way with instructional technology for information literacy, it's wise to use it as a way to connect and collaborate with faculty. Some institutions, such as the University of Minnesota, acquire and make blogging software available to all students. Since that's far from the case at the majority of institutions, the students will have to acquire their own blogging software, but that is easy enough to do from sites such as Blogger or Word Press. One way to apply blogs for information literacy is to direct students to use their own blogs to record or reflect on a research experience for either a current or past project. This allows students to reflect on their research methods in a community where other could share their experiences. Students would also submit comments about other's blog postings, perhaps to share information about using the resources. The librarian responsible for coordinating the information literacy for the course should also be blogging along with the students, and responding to their posts.

How can a librarian do that efficiently? As instructional technologists, we also need to be well versed in technologies such as RSS and news aggregators. Web 2.0 technologies are going to become mainstream over the next decade, and librarians should be developing expertise with them now. These technologies make it possible to subscribe to various blogs and read ongoing posts conveniently with one piece of software, the aggregator. It could be that the librarian would need to visit the class to get the students started on the project, from acquiring their blogs, to learning how to post, and then learning how to subscribe to the blogs of their classmates using the aggregator. The good news is that today's college students would likely find these technologies easy to learn and adapt into their technology-driven lifestyles.

Think of the information literacy blog as a form of preemptive support for information literacy assignments. Rather than doing the standard class instruction session and then wondering if students "got it," or waiting to see if students will contact the librarian for help, an information literacy blog that allows students to write posts about their research projects could certainly reveal in what ways students are being challenged to complete the assignment, understand the library research tools, or format their citations. Then it is up to the librarian to take the lead in writing a post for the entire class or to communicate with individual students. The librarian will want to ensure students do more than just complete an information literacy-related assignment, but that they can actually achieve some real, substantive learning. If used appropriately, a library blog can promote both the 1st and 4th principles, encouraging contacts between students, faculty, and librarians as well as, facilitating prompt feedback from librarians to student's posts.

## Wikis

Wikis are also gaining popularity in higher education as a tool that can facilitate and increase communication by and among students. While a blog project could help to develop a community of learners, a wiki is perhaps even better because it is based on the concept of bringing together a community of learners to develop a single resource that benefits all members though the sharing of information. The unique capacity of a wiki is that it is a form of a community writing tool. In other words, each member of the community is able to add new content as well as edit existing content. Most librarians are likely familiar with Wikipedia, which is the best known example of a wiki, and which demonstrates how a community can develop a shared information resource.

In a number of ways, compared to having students develop individual blogs, a Wiki can be a more manageable technology for a group project. Again, it is the job of the information technologist to first work with the instructor to determine what he or she would wish to have the students learn, and then determine if a wiki would be the best technology to help students achieve the learning outcomes for the course. Likewise, when invited to participate in a course by developing an information literacy exercise or activity, the information literacy librarian must use the skills of instructional technology to assess a variety of learning technologies to determine which is most appropriate to achieve the stated learning objectives of the assignment. If, in addition to the objectives for learning how to learn to use the library resources for an assigned research project, there are objectives for achieving active and constructive learning, then a wiki may be well suited to the project.

The real issue is how the wiki would be used for information literacy instruction. The wiki could be used by the library staff to develop an information literacy clearinghouse for its institution. For example, each librarian could develop a section of the wiki. Different pages of the wiki could represent different information literacy courses, and each could serve as a resource guide for the community. A section of the wiki could be devoted to an information literacy project for first-year students. It could contain course-related information, specific assignments, rubrics for assessment, resources for faculty, and more. As new information becomes available new sections of the wiki are developed. In this application, the wiki is an information literacy resource that is available to the user community, but the user community can also add information to the wiki.

A wiki could also be applied to an information literacy assignment. A librarian could create a wiki for a specific course, and then add content appropriate to the course and its information literacy outcomes. The wiki could contain objectives for the course's information literacy component, and provides details of the assignment created for the course that will help students develop specific information literacy skills. A wiki truly lends itself to a collaborative project, so a librarian using a wiki for an information literacy assignment should develop an activity that would engage the students in gathering information that would be used to collaboratively build an information resource or a joint project. For example, students could develop a group bibliography, they could develop a resource that other students would use to evaluate web sites, or they could develop a group writing activity that would involve an information literacy component. Currently there are limited examples of wikis being used in information literacy initiatives. That may be because wikis are currently being used primarily for web-based community projects. We suspect that in time more librarians will experiment with this technology as they become more familiar with its attributes and with its capacity to promote collaborative learning. Wikis fit into the "seven principles" by the ability to use the technology to promote active learning techniques in group work as well as, facilitate contacts between students, faculty, and librarians.

### Podcasts/Vodcasts

Audio and video are powerful learning tools because they appeal to a variety of learning styles. As was discussed in previous chapters on learning and pedagogy, the wise instructional technologist seeks to make use of technologies that meet the needs of many different learners and their multiple styles. A rapidly developing technology that makes use of portable music and video devices to deliver content directly to students are the podcast and vodcast. A podcast is an audio recording of one or more individuals. A vodcast is similar but adds video or other multimedia to the transmission of information or entertainment. Both media are recorded using technologies that are available freely on the Internet, but there are some fee-based software products that facilitate the recording of podcasts and vodcasts. The ability of individuals to record their own podcasts and vodcasts with little training or technology investment has contributed to the rapid growth of this technology.

Some of the initial experimentation in education was conducted by higher education faculty recording their lectures for distribution on podcast Web sites such as iTunes. The podcast as learning tool was popularized when Duke University provided iPods to all incoming freshmen in 2004.[7] There was no certainty about how faculty would use the iPods with students, but the recording of lectures and other content became a significant application of the iPod for learning. Since then the number of faculty creating podcasts has dramatically increased. So too has the debate about the pedagogical value of podcasts. Supporters claim that podcasts help students learn by providing content that they can easily listen to on their mp3 playing devices to get additional out-of-class support. Critics claim that students use podcasts as a substitute for coming to class, and therefore are likely to miss valuable lecture content that faculty deliver in class. As with many instructional technologies, podcasts are just media for transmitting information. What impact they have, for good or bad, most likely will depend on how an instructor chooses to deploy them.

Both podcasts and vodcasts may hold some promise for disseminating information about library resources and information literacy activity. One of the challenges of a typical 50-minute instruction session is attempting to bring all the students up to the same level of knowledge before moving ahead with the coverage of specific techniques and search skills. But what if all the students had spent fifteen minutes listening in advance to a librarian discussing some of the basics of library research? Then the instruction session leader could jump quickly to more substantive content. A podcast related to a library instruction session could be produced without much difficulty and then made available to the students on the library's web site or preferably in the students own courseware site.

Recordings on specific topics, such as how to format citations, how to evaluate a Web site, or special features of unique library databases all have potential as podcasts. They could even be tailored to students conducting specific course-based research assignments. Most students have access to an mp3 player device, and those who don't can easily listen to the podcast on a home computer. Vodcasts are still relatively new, and the addition of images to the sound can make for an even more powerful learning tool. But special knowledge can also be helpful in creating content that makes the most of the available technology. Recording a lecture is one thing, but developing a creative video is entirely different. As this technology becomes more mainstream the tools and technical knowledge needed are likely to become more commonplace, and will likely contribute to the growth of podcasts and vodcasts. Podcasts/vodcasts can promote both the 5th and 7th principles by increasing the out-of-classroom time librarians have to introduce information literacy concepts to students while also meeting diverse ways that students learn.

## *Personal Response Systems*

The Personal Response System, also known as the "clicker", is a good example of a controversial instructional technology. The clicker device has been the subject of debate in the field of education over whether it contributes to or detracts from learning. As its name implies the clicker allows individual students to respond to questions from the instructor. The clicker is a small electronic device, with some physical similarities to a remote control unit, that allows students to submit answers to multiple choice, true-false, or other question types. The questions asked can be factual in nature or they may be opinion oriented. There are a number of publishers and electronics firms that sell the equipment to education institutions, and most of the products allow faculty to integrate their question slides into existing PowerPoint slide presentations. Instructors, upon giving a question, prompt their students to submit their answers via the clicker. The devices, which work on radio frequencies, transmit the student responses to the system software, which compiles the responses and summarizes the results for the class.

Those who support the use of clickers claim they are a relatively low-tech method to better engage students in the classroom. Instead of listening passively to a lecture or just taking notes, student are now asked at regular intervals to respond to specific questions about the course content. Instructors also point to the clicker's ability to help them gauge if students understand course content. For example, a chemistry professor can introduce 15 or 30 minutes of new content, and follow it with several questions that help him or her to determine if students were able to grasp new material while it was presented, or it may simply indicate where students need more time spent on course content. This may also help students to better recognize what they themselves do or do not understand. Finally, clicker supporters say they are effective for allowing students who may refrain from asking or answering questions orally to be actively involved in the course.

Clicker critics make the point that the devices are ineffective if what an instructor really wants is to have students more engaged with the course material and what is happening in the classroom. They claim that students can be completely inattentive to what is happening in class and simply click their responses without really thinking about correct answers. Some critics are more vocal about clicker use in smaller classrooms. While clickers might make sense for large lecture sections where students often have no opportunity to engage in discussions, they may be completely inappropriate for classes where real discussion should be encouraged. It would be an inappropriate use of an instructional technology if an instructor allowed the technology to create a situation in which he or she is able to evade responsibility for creating a learning environment best suited to the size and needs of the class.

Information literacy instructors should be encouraged to experiment with clicker technology if available at their institution. It can be difficult, especially within a short time frame for instruction, to engage students in a library instruction session. This is especially true when instructing outside of hands-on computing labs. For example, a librarian could ask basic questions, such as "Which of the following is the best synonymous term for...", and then present several multiple choice options. This could lead into a discussion about the importance of identifying and using synonymous terms when developing a search strategy.

This could also be directly after a discussion of synonymous terms to help the instructor determine if the students had grasped the concept. One of the advantages of clicker technology is that it is relatively easy to use. Anyone with the ability to create PowerPoint slides should be able to integrate this instructional technology into their skill set. Personal Response Systems fit into the "seven principles" by the ability to use the technology to promote prompt feedback from librarians to student's understanding of the library instruction session.

### Courseware Management Systems/Learning Management Systems
Course/learning management systems such as Blackboard, WebCT, ANGEL, eCollege (courseware) have been in existence less than a full decade, but have had a considerable impact on higher education. Initially designed to facilitate and enhance distance education courses, courseware soon became seen as beneficial for enhancing traditional face to face courses. It is quite likely that by the end of this decade more face to face courses will offer a courseware component then those that do not.

Courseware has many powerful features that can save the instructor time managing the class, but the features that have helped this technology become so readily adopted by faculty and embraced by students are it resource sharing, communication, and assessment. Librarians and libraries could and have benefited greatly from these features. While it is still not the standard to have a strong library and librarian presence in campus courseware it is slowly becoming increasingly accepted as beneficial to the institution, faculty, and students.[8]

The resources sharing components of courseware allow instructors to link to articles, Web sites, and course materials (including lecture notes, textbook supplemental materials, syllabus, and assignments). Libraries could benefit from this feature by integrating their course reserves and interlibrary loan services into courseware. This allows students easy and convenient access to their course materials, saves time on task because they do not need to physically travel to the library, and encourages the students to read the materials. Penn State University is a good example of this integration. The university libraries integrated its reserves system directly in to ANGEL (Penn State University's Learning Management System) so that students are able to directly access their course reserves right from their instructor's courseware site.

Librarians could also benefit from the resource sharing features if able to access the instructor's course site. Penn State University libraries have successfully partnered with the universities ANGEL administrator to create "librarian" status user accounts that allow instructor to add a librarian to their course. This feature allows librarians to access course syllabi and assignments so that they know first hand what the instructor is assigning and they save the faculty member time by not needing them to forward them the information outside of their course. Additionally, besides giving access to a librarian to view course materials this feature allows a librarian to post information. For example, librarians may wish to give students direct access to already existing library created web tutorials, help sheets, path finders, bibliographies, indexes, and full-text databases. This encourages students to view these materials by lowering the barriers of access because it requires little to no effort on the students part. Also, the varieties of materials that can be made available are limitless. Librarians could provide access to various digital learning materials including: interactive tutorials, videos, games, simulations, audio recordings, recorded instruction sessions, and so much more thereby, allowing students with diverse learning styles to access the materials in the format that best suits their learning.

The resource sharing feature can also enhance librarian instructional sessions because they can be tied directly to an assignment in the instructor's courseware site and any library related materials, exercises, or assignments can be deposited in the courseware site so that the librarian and instructor can access and evaluate them. Also, librarians can partner with faculty so that students would be required to review these library related materials before their library instruction session thereby, allowing the librarian to create a level playing field and provide exposure to library skills outside and prior to the instruction session. This would then allow librarians to have less lecture style instruction sessions and allow them to integrate more active learning components into the sessions.

The communication components of courseware (i.e. e-mail, chat rooms, and message boards) have allowed instructors to save time and increase communication with their students. Likewise, libraries and librarians could and have benefited from these communication features. Penn State University libraries have integrated a virtual reference desk software package into ANGEL so that students have easy access to asking a librarian online a reference question.

Additionally, because Penn State University librarians have a user account status of librarian and can be added to an instructor's course they can fully participate in the communication taking place in the course. This allows librarians unprecedented ability to develop and strengthen contacts with students and faculty. Also, it lends creditability to the librarian and facilitates their ability to identify and inform students who lack basic information literacy skills. While this increased level of communication can be time consuming it can also allow a librarian to address a student's query and post a response that the entire class can see and, therefore, save the librarian time in repetitively answering the same types of questions.

Finally, the assessment components of courseware have enabled faculty to increase the level of quizzing and providing prompt feedback while decreasing the amount of time creating and grading. This can allow student's to have a greater understanding of their own deficiencies and help guide them in their learning. Libraries and librarians can again benefit from this courseware feature. At the institutional library level, creating a tutorial such as TILT (Texas Information Literacy Tutorial) and integrating it in to courseware can allow the library to instruct and assess a large group of students (i.e. all incoming freshman) and determine where these students need further instruction.

Librarians can benefit creating pre-assessment and post-assessment surveys and quizzes that will allow them to identify the needs of students prior to an instruction session as well as assess the degree to which students succeeded in learning the material presented at a session. This can also benefit the students because too often students in a library session believe they know everything the librarian has to say. They are therefore are not open to learning as students who realize they are not as knowledgeable and can use additional instruction. CMS can be utilized to promote several of the "seven principles." It can be used to encourage increased contacts between students, faculty, and librarians. Additionally, librarians can utilize the courseware features to assess and respond to students learning needs. The CMS also allows librarians to share resources and information that can increase the "time on task" students spend with library instruction topics.

## *Digital Leaning Materials*

Digital learning materials (DLMs) are part of a new generation of digital informational formats that are increasingly being used by faculty and librarians to enhance instruction. There are a multitude of stake holders besides faculty and staff at educational institutions that realize how useful DLMs can be in enhancing the instructional process. These include: nonprofit educational & professional organizations, governmental organizations, entertainment providers, and for profit publishers.

A DLM is any interactive web-based digital resource that can be utilized for instructional purposes. There are characteristics common to all DLMs. DLMs can include "learning objects," "instructional objects," "education objects," and "knowledge objects." The informational elements that make up digital learning materials can include text, graphics, animations, audio, and video. DLMs can come in many formats such as HTML Script, Flash, Java Script, AVI, WMV, MP3, WAV, JPEG, TIFF, and the list goes on. They also come in many forms, including but not limited to the following: tutorials, simulations, demonstrations, exercises, online modules, games, experiments, and case studies. However, the biggest difference between traditional formats such as monographs, periodicals, and traditional media (i.e. TV, overhead projectors) is that digital learning materials included active learning components that promote student learning.

DLMs allow students to better match their ideal style of learning through interaction with the content in various modes. For example, digital learning materials often incorporate audio and visual content. For some student learners this may be one of the primary ways they enjoy and can be most successful at learning. Additionally, students can practice with DLMs multiple times and at their own pace while testing their knowledge and receiving immediate feedback that helps provide the students with guidance in learning new concepts and skills. Although they may designed primarily for online use librarians can utilize these DLMs to enhance face-to-face instruction. Because these materials promote active learning, are geared for multiple learning styles and provide feedback and assessment librarians who utilize these DLMs in their instructional sessions are better equipped to assist students in experiencing with and ultimately learning library skills and concepts.

Some wonderful examples of library created digital learning materials are:
• Texas Information Literacy Tutorial (TILT—http://tilt.lib.utsystem.edu/),
• Plagiarism and Academic Integrity Simulation (http://www.scc.rutgers.edu/douglass/sal/plagiarism/intro.html), and the
• Boolean Operators Tutorial (http://library.nyu.edu/research/tutorials/boolean/tutorial.html).

The above examples demonstrate that librarians have been creating DLMs to enhance library instruction programs, however, there is less evidence that librarians have been assisting our faculty, staff, and students in locating this form of materials. Librarians should be actively involved in aiding faculty in locating these materials. This would help librarians become even more relevant to the teaching and learning process as well as assist faculty who are often information overloaded in their attempts to locate DLMs that can enhance student learning. Librarians could point faculty too and assist them in searching the repositories, referatories, and digital libraries that have been and are being created to house these materials. Since many DLMs are meant to be shared and/or reused it is best to first determine if an appropriate one has already been created elsewhere. The discovery process is not always easy and the most effective way to locate existing DLMs is to use existing repositories. Several good sites are found at:
• MERLOT—http://www.merlot.org/Home.po
• PRIMO—http://www.ala.org/CFApps/Primo/public/search.cfm
• Wisconsin Online Resource Center—http://www.wisc-online.com/
DLMs are important because they can be used to promote a number of the "seven principles" including the 3rd, 4th, 5th and 7th principles.

## Chat

Many of us are familiar with library use of chat services as a type of online reference. While some libraries have purchased software explicitly designed for reference interactions, others have used the freely available AOL Instant Messenger, or Yahoo Messenger. Unlike other tools such as bulletin boards or e-mail, chat happens live and thus facilitates synchronous interaction between librarian and student. If you consider reference activities an authentic teaching and learning experience, then those interactions can indeed be excellent learning experiences. In fact, teaching via reference encounters may be one of the most effective learning experiences provided by libraries. That is, it is learning at the time of need, with an authentic experience with high probability of effecting a persistent change in behavior. Even simple reference questions, such as, "Do you have this book?" can be turned into a transformative learning experience. If the librarian demonstrates or describes a search in the library catalog, the student may be more likely to try it on their own the next time. Additionally, if the student is satisfied with the reference interaction, they may also learn that 'librarians are helpful people.' Chat makes all of these learning experiences more convenient. Instead of coming away with the feeling that the library is hard to use and no one is available to help, students will observe that the people at the library are helpful and make themselves available at convenient places and times.

Chat can also be used as an alternative means of communication with classes of specific students. An instruction librarian could schedule specific chat times as a follow-up to an instruction session, or simply provide the students with her IM screen name. Teen-agers' perceptions of e-mail are not the same as ours. They consider it overly formal and inconvenient. They have a strong preference for chat and SMS text-messaging. Chat promotes the 1$^{st}$ principle by facilitating increased communication between students, faculty, and librarians.

## WebQuests

WebQuests emphasize time on task. The model, pioneered by Dodge and March, is an inquiry based activity.[9] Students use resources on the internet to learn about some topic. The goal of a WebQuest is the integration of some new knowledge. In a WebQuest, the students are guided by a instructor created Web site including the task, process, hints or links, and a conclusion. Very often, WebQuests are group activities thus enhancing "reciprocity and cooperation among students ". Additionally, the students are usually required to create a Web site based on the information analyzed during their quest. WebQuests are quite common activities in primary and secondary settings, yet unfortunately have been overlooked to some degree in higher education. WebQuests offer lots of good practice possibilities and if designed well can include all of the seven principles.

Of course, good web design skills are a prerequisite, yet the graphic design plays only one part. Motivation is the real key to a successful WebQuest and a skilled instructional designer will know how to go about incorporating this. Information literacy skills seem ready made for WebQuests. In fact, every WebQuest is really a lesson in information literacy whether by design or not. WebQuests can promote both the 5$^{st}$ and 7$^{th}$ principles by increasing the "time on task" spent on information literacy concepts as well as, developing reciprocity and cooperation among students as they work on the assignments together.

### Video

Video is an early instructional technology, however, it was initially expensive to use and produce. Now, even amateur videographers can produce and publish their own short movies. The tremendous popularity of YouTube, with 35 million streams daily, is evidence of this. Filmstrips, then VHS, and now DVD's put prerecorded video into the hands of the masses. Then analog and now digital camcorders gave video production capabilities to amateurs. Cellphone cameras and camcorders have made the devices ubiquitous. Relatively inexpensive software (Adobe Premier, Windows Movie Maker, ) include sophisticated production tools such as editing, dissolves, fades and transitions. Whether it be prerecorded or home-grown, video is now an extremely accessible instructional technology.

We won't belabor the obvious appeal of video to a generation of students who have grown up with multiple televisions, and computers as well. The benefits of using pre-recorded video in the classroom, also seem obvious. If a picture is worth a thousand words, how many is a moving picture worth? A million? Of course there are detractors, yet video is here to stay and the appeal is tremendous. Most appealing though, is the more recent access to video production for amateurs. Lectures, presentations, or demonstrations can be recorded and broadcast synchronously or asynchronously with very little effort. Edited broadcasts can be produced with a little more effort and some extra time. Video quality over the web depends largely on connections speeds of the user, so often it is useful to offer varying download speeds with corresponding video quality. However, if the purpose of using video is to recreate the classroom lecture experience, it seems a wasted effort. Video offers such tremendous possibilities: recordings of 40 minute lectures shouldn't be high on the priority list. Instead imagine short skits demonstrating a reference interaction, or an orientation to the library building. Like podcasts/vodcasts, video can promote both the 5$^{st}$ and 7$^{th}$ principles by increasing the out-of-classroom time librarians have to introduce information literacy concepts to students while also meeting diverse ways that students learn.

## Electronic White Boards

The chalkboard may be one of the first instructional technologies in history after paper and pen or pencil. Chalkboards are just a larger version of paper and pen so that more students can see the instructor's writing. Today's electronic white boards take the concept much further. They can display anything that a PC monitor can display, but they do more than an LCD projector, as they also offer interactive possibilities for the displayed information. One of the most intriguing possibilities of this technology is that of a more sophisticated student interaction. We are all familiar with the nightmares of having to complete a math problem at the blackboard. Instead imagine building a puzzle, completing a crossword, or interacting with a chart. Electronic white boards are important because they can be used to promote several of the "seven principles" including the 3rd, 4th, 5th, 6th, and 7th principles. A newer innovation that provides a similar technology boost to a course is the tablet computer. When coupled with a projector it can capture notes as the instructor types them, and allow students to engage in collaborative writing projects.

## Library Aggregator Databases and E-Journals

An overlooked instructional technology that the library profession must do more to promote is the library's own electronic database resources. By some definitions an instructional technology is the hardware, the software, and the systems created for or adapted to an educational purpose. Library aggregator databases and e-journals are certainly systems, their interfaces are a form of software, and they can quite naturally be adapted to education. Almost any library database system, from the big aggregators such as ProQuest, EBSCO, Gale Group, Lexis/Nexis, and Wilson, to many niche products, has the potential to help students learn more about specific discipline- based assignments. If information literacy is generally recognized as a valuable skill to learn, for both its ability to help students succeed in college and beyond, then offering library databases as tools in learning should certainly qualify them as instructional technologies. As resources for helping students complete coursework library databases offer multiple functionalities. First, there is their obvious role as a source of bibliographic and full-text news, information, magazines, and scholarly content. Second, with the availability of persistent links, they can be integrated into a faculty member's courseware site, which provides the students with direct links to library content. Third, as their technology advances the databases have added value features such as the ability to format citations that can be used to teach specific information literacy skills. These are just some examples of the ways in which our library resources can be used as instructional technologies to support teaching and learning. As part of the information literacy initiative, there needs to be ongoing faculty development about using library research databases so that our faculty feel comfortable with these instructional technologies. We should also make sure that our colleagues in the academic technology support areas of the institution are also aware of our databases and their features. Given their regular contact with faculty looking for ways to integrate technology into their courses, those colleagues can be our best sales representatives.

## Conclusion

While it is critical for information literacy librarians to have a firm understanding in the theory and practice of pedagogy, it may be equally important in our rich technology environment to be adept at identifying those technologies that can be best integrated into the learning process in a way that advances, not detracts, from helping students to achieve information literacy learning outcomes. In addition, it is essential that academic librarians collaborate with those academic support professionals, such as instructional designers and technologists, who can support our efforts in these areas as well as help us to further our own knowledge of instructional technology.

In this chapter our goal was to communicate both how instructional technology supports the academic librarian's teaching of information literacy skills, and provide some practical examples of what types of instructional technologies, both traditional and cutting edge, that we believe can support information literacy instruction. But we conclude by acknowledging that those technologies will change. Some will become obsolete; they will be replaced by new technologies. In this chapter they are simply examples of the many ways in which an information literacy librarian, armed with some practical knowledge of instructional design and technology, can accomplish.

We advocate that information literacy librarians should always focus their use of technology on determining what available methods best further the goal of achieving student learning outcomes. We must determine what technology best works to communicate these messages and skills to our students. And in fact, in some cases, the answer may be that a technology solution is the least appropriate response. As we indicated early in the chapter, our vision is one where academic librarians grow more "blended" in their knowledge of both theory and practice in instructional design and technology. We believe it is the blended librarian who will best adopt all types of instructional technologies to their instruction methods, and will do so through the thoughtful and purposeful integration of technology into their teaching and learning process.

## Notes

1. J.K Galbraith, *The New industrial state*. Boston: Houghton-Mifflin, 1967.

2. T. J. Newby, James Lehman, James Russell, and Donald A. Stepich., eds. *Instructional technology for teaching and learning: Designing instruction, integrating computers, and using media.* New Jersey : Prentice-Hall. , 2000

3. University of Texas. 2004. Texas Information Literacy Tutorial. <http://tilt.lib.utsystem.edu/> (accessed July 2, 2006).

4. Stephen Bell and John Shank. "The Blended Librarian," *College & Research Libraries* 65 (2004): 372.

5. Barbara Seels and Zita Glasgow. *Making instructional design decisions.* 2nd edition. Columbus: Prentice- Hall, 1998.

6. Arthur Chickering and Stephen C. Ehrmann, 1996. Implementing the Seven Principles: Technology as Lever. <http://www.tltgroup.org/programs/seven.html>. (accessed July 2, 2006).

7. Scott Carlson, Duke University will give iPod music players. *Chronicle of Higher Education* 50 (2004): A21.

8. John Shank and Stephen Bell. A_FLIP to courseware: a strategic alliance for improving student learning outcomes. *Innovate: Journal of Online Education* 2 (2006). <http://www.innovateonline.info/index.php?view=article&ID=46> (accessed July 3, 2004).

9. Bernie Dodge. 1997. Some thoughts about WebQuests. <http://webquest.sdsu.edu/about_webquests.html> (accessed July 2, 2006).

# CHAPTER 12
# The Future of Information Literacy

Lisa Janicke Hinchliffe

Predicting the future of information literacy requires close examination of trends in information literacy, academic libraries, and higher education as well as inferences about where those trends will lead in a context of rapid technological innovation, democratization of authorship, changing notions of authority and expertise, pressures for less hierarchical organizational structures in libraries, and political demands for accountability through standardized testing. Any one of these factors is complex in and of itself and the potential interplay among all of them leads to a multiplicity of possibilities for the future. What does emerge from such factors, however, is the conviction that information literacy will continue to develop as a cornerstone of academic librarianship in the twenty-first century. Following is an attempt to suggest some broad parameters of information literacy development over the next five to ten years.

## Information Literacy as a Conceptual Framework

While the concept of information literacy is now widespread in higher education and pervasive in academic libraries, the conceptual framework for understanding information literacy is still very tied to the defining elements presented in 1989 in the *Final Report* of the American Library Association's Presidential Committee on Information Literacy:

> information literate people know how to find, evaluate, and use information effectively to solve a particular problem or make a decision.[1]

Though expanded somewhat in the *Information Literacy Competency Standards for Higher Education*:

An information literate individual is able to:

- Determine the extent of information needed
- Access the needed information effectively and efficiently
- Evaluate information and its sources critically
- Incorporate selected information into one's knowledge base

230

- Use information effectively to accomplish a specific purpose
- Understand the economic, legal, and social issues surrounding the use of information, and access and use information ethically and legally.[2]

The fundamental framework is markedly similar and is a normative approach to defining information literacy. In contrast, conceptions of information literacy based on findings from phenomenographical research methods, developed primarily in the United Kingdom and Australia, which present information literacy as experienced by people rather than defined by experts, offer intriguing opportunities for re-thinking, re-forming, and re-defining the conception of information literacy pursued in academic libraries in the United States.

Dissatisfaction with over-arching and discipline-neutral information literacy standards is evidenced by the move to develop discipline-specific standards (e.g., Information Literacy Standards for Science and Engineering/Technology[3] and Information Literacy Standards for Anthropology and Sociology Students[4]) that reflect disciplinary conceptions of information and a movement towards understanding information literacy in the context of a community. Initiatives to develop information literacy in a community context will continue and will gain momentum in the coming years. Such activity will challenge normative conceptions of information literacy as well as the authority of organizations such as the Association of College and Research Libraries to capture information literacy as a "brand."

## Content of Instructional Programs

While the emphasis on "information" rather than "books" or "library resources" in current information literacy frameworks mentioned above allows for an expansive consideration of the potential medium for any needed information, in practice, academic librarians have developed information literacy programs that closely align with traditional library materials (e.g., books, journals, and indexes/abstracts) with the primary emphasis on new media (e.g., Web sites, zines, and electronic discussion archives) being the deficiencies of the new media relative to the reliability of traditional library resources.

With the pace of development of information media likely to be unfettered for the foreseeable future, conceptions of information literacy will be too anemic to be of use if librarians do not begin to explicitly consider the multitude of inscription technologies available and widely used to present and re-present information. This presents the largest challenge to academic libraries that have not collected and made accessible formally published media (e.g., films, audiocassettes, and video games) in widespread fashion, much less addressed the admittedly complex and thorny issues related to informal media (e.g., discussion forums, citizen journalism, or Web sites). Conceptions of information literacy will be stunted by the collections of academic libraries if the collections are not expanded or if information literacy librarians do not teach beyond, or even against, the confines of the collections of the libraries that employ them.

Regardless of how academic library collections change, or do not change, attention to the attitudes, beliefs, and actions of undergraduate students may in the end be more likely to drive academic librarians to pursuing instruction programs with more inclusive considerations of the information landscape and more nuanced frameworks of information access and evaluation. Understanding how students understand information will be crucial to librarians' understanding how to expand students' understandings. As students are increasingly familiar with a breadth of non-library information sources, some of which are highly authoritative, reliable, and useful—even as judged by traditional library collection evaluative criteria—expanding students' conception of information resources and criteria for judgment will necessarily move away from evaluation based on the medium of publication. Librarians will spend smaller proportions of instruction time focused on the dichotomy of scholarly vs. popular sources and instead be challenged to develop instructional approaches that enable students to make contextualized judgments based on the interplay of complex factors as considered from the perspective of an information community (e.g., from the perspective of the discipline, social group, or belief system).

While focusing less on the scholarly vs. popular dichotomous presentation of the information environment, student learning needs will also generate new areas of focus for instruction. Political and social perspectives on information creation, access, use, and dissemination will continue to grow in instructional importance as issues of copyright law, file sharing, and information activism increasingly pervade everyday decision-making of students. Information management education represents an untapped area for librarian prominence in higher education as faculty, graduate students, and undergraduate students all report the challenges of keeping track of information, creating reliable systems for sharing information, and the emotional burdens of the suspicion and fear that one has not located, has lost, or has overlooked information relevant to a task at hand. Academic librarians have begun to work in this area—primarily through the adoption of campus-wide licenses and related instruction programs for tools such as RefWorks—but it remains to be seen whether this work, which is essentially the application of librarian expertise in information organization and management to the information control challenges of individuals and groups will remain tool-focused or if it represents an area of new developments in the scholarship of teaching and learning and instructional content development.

A related issue is whether partnerships will emerge among information literacy programs and scholarly communications initiatives, the latter often encompassing a variety of instructional programs for faculty, graduate students and administrators on various aspects of the information environment. Information literacy librarians have honed expertise in instructional methods and outreach approaches that could benefit scholarly communications librarians in programmatic development. Likewise, connecting with faculty about issues related to scholarly communications could provide an entrée for alerting faculty to the need to educate students through information literacy programs on related topics but as appropriate to student projects and assignments.

## Assessment

The immediate future of information literacy assessment is likely to feature continuous development of both standardized and authentic or performance-based assessment approaches. Standardized approaches such as iSkills from the Educational Testing Service,[5] Project SAILS,[6] and Information Literacy Test from James Madison University[7] have gained momentum and fit with pressures for quantitative evaluation of student learning and institutional productivity.

Authentic and performance-based approaches to information literacy assessment do not necessarily result in easy-to-aggregate findings and so do not have the cross-institutional benchmarking desired by many administrators. The task for academic librarians who find authentic and performance-based approaches to information literacy more meaningful and robust for improving and enhancing teaching and learning will be to interpret those findings into frameworks that can be utilized for programmatic and institutional assessment. If this is not done, the political environment and perceived "objective" nature of standardized testing will become increasingly attractive to library and campus administrators required to provide data for accountability purposes.

## Preparation for the Professional and Ongoing Professional Development

The rapid expansion of instruction into all positions in public services in academic libraries, and even some technical services positions, left academic librarians in great need of professional preparation and development related to teaching responsibilities. Librarians already working in the profession needed additional training for their expanding roles and new librarians often did not have the opportunity to receive such training as part of their professional preparation. In addition, the lack of consensus about and even unwillingness to identify what skills and abilities the teaching role really required left individual librarians and libraries without models to follow or clarity about best practices.

The last ten years have been a time of rapid change related to professional preparation and professional development. An increasing proportion of library and information science programs offer courses related to information literacy and the educational role of librarians as well as integrating these elements into other components of the professional education curriculum. The rise of the Institute for Information Literacy Immersion Program[8] is the high-profile example of the growth in ongoing professional development opportunities for information literacy librarians. The *Proficiencies for Instruction Librarians and Coordinators*[9] promulgated by the Instruction Section of the Association of College and Research Libraries articulated a framework "to help instruction librarians define the skills needed to be excellent teachers in library instruction programs and to foster collaborations necessary to create information literacy programs."

For library and information science programs that have not yet addressed the professional education needs of their students related to teaching it seems inevitable that they will in the coming years. As graduates seek jobs, the message from academic library public services position advertisements is clear—instruction is a core responsibility, preparation is expected, and experience is preferred.

Ongoing professional development opportunities, however, have a more uncertain future. The dominance of information literacy in the sessions at the recent Association of College and Research Libraries conferences have led some to comment on the fatigue generated by a lack of balance in the conference sessions. Many of the sessions appear to present familiar ideas rather than innovative approaches or reflective critiques. Whether the Institute for Information Literacy will have sufficient participation to sustain a second decade of offerings may be dependent on the creation of additional programs beyond the Immersion Program, such as the recent addition of the Intentional Teacher Program, which focuses on renewal of experienced teachers through reflection on practice. An unknown factor is institutional willingness to fund professional development for the development of expertise in instruction rather than basic competency. If institutions see the value of information literacy expertise, then professional development programs that provide advanced training and leadership development will flourish.

## Organizational Structure of Academic Libraries

Instruction is a core service of academic libraries and instructional responsibilities are fully incorporated into the responsibilities of public services librarians; this will remain so for the foreseeable future. Information literacy leadership is less institutionalized and questions remain as to the focus on the "information literacy coordinator" and the status of that position within an organization. Such leadership positions range in responsibility and focus from operational logistics for instruction program management to policy-setting and campus-wide institutional leadership. The role may be held by a front-line public services librarian for whom instruction is the specialty of the position to the articulation of the role as an associate director with the teaching role of the library receiving par emphasis with collections or technical services. The stature of the position appears to be increasing as academic libraries embrace and highlight the educational role of the library and as campuses articulate the importance of the library as a center for student learning on campus. The trend towards explicitly charging a high-level administrator with instructional leadership will continue in the coming years and increasingly focus on integration with campus-wide academic and outreach programs.

The organizational structure of academic libraries is also increasingly recognizing the public engagement role of libraries relative to information literacy. Positions in academic libraries with responsibility for community outreach, partnerships with local elementary and secondary schools, liaison with local public and special libraries, and incorporation of library resources and services for lifelong learning programs reflect a re-engagement with the service mission of institutions of higher education and their role in community development and attainment of social and citizenship skills. Academic libraries have a unique opportunity, particularly with respect to collaboration with elementary and secondary schools, to articulate a developmental approach to information literacy throughout formal education through public engagement activities and appear poised to capitalize on the opportunity in the near future.

## Conclusion

Committing one's predications about the future to writing and submitting them for publication is an unusual experience. Predicting what people will do—because after all the work of information literacy education is fundamentally about people as learners and as teachers, not about information objects per se—is a tricky business. The forces in play today do not dictate a particular future, though they do make certain things more likely than others. For the predications herein that trouble the reader, this chapter presents an opportunity to be moved to action to create an alternative, currently less likely, though perhaps not impossible future. The predications that are perceived as positive and desirable, however, also deserve effort and attention so that they obtain should new factors come into play.

Librarians can create the future. The past gives evidence to this. The present is opportunity. The future awaits.

## Notes

1. American Library Association, *Final Report of the American Library Association Presidential*

*Committee on Information Literacy,* 1989. Available online from http://www.ala.org/ala/acrl/acrl-pubs/whitepapers/presidential.htm. [Accessed 24 August 2007.]

    2. American Library Association, *Information Literacy Competency Standards for Higher Education,* 2000. Available online from http://www.ala.org/ala/acrl/acrlstandards/informationliteracycompetency.htm. [Accessed 24 August 2007.]

    3. American Library Association, *Information Literacy Standards for Science and Engineering/ Technology,* 2006. Available online from http://www.ala.org/ala/acrl/acrlstandards/infolitscitech.htm. [Accessed 24 August 2007.]

    4. American Library Association, *Information Literacy Standards for Anthropology and Sociology Students,* 2007. Available online from http://www.lib.utexas.edu/subject/ss/anssiil/anssil-standards2007.pdf. [Accessed 24 August 2007.]

    5. See http://www.ets.org/iskills/ for more information.

    6. See https://www.projectsails.org/ for more information.

    7. See http://www.jmu.edu/icba/prodserv/instruments_ilt.htm for more information.

    8. See http://www.ala.org/ala/acrl/acrlissues/acrlinfolit/professactivity/iil/immersion/immersionprograms.htm for more information.

    9. *Proficiencies for Instruction Librarians and Coordinators,* 2006, Available online from http://www.ala.org/ala/acrlbucket/is/newsacrl/proficiencies.pdf. [Accessed 24 August 2007.]